CHILD SEXUAL ABUSE

WILEY SERIES
in
CHILD PROTECTION AND POLICY

Series Editor: Christopher Cloke,
NSPCC, 42 Curtain Road,
London EC2A 3NX

This NSPCC/Wiley series explores current issues relating to the prevention of child abuse and the protection of children. The series aims to publish titles that focus on professional practice and policy, and the practical application of research. The books are leading edge and innovative and reflect a multi-disciplinary and inter-agency approach to the prevention of child abuse and the protection of children.

This series is essential reading for all professionals and researchers concerned with the prevention of child abuse and the protection of children. The accessible style will appeal to parents and carers. All books have a policy or practice orientation with referenced information from theory and research.

Published Titles

Bannister	From Hearing to Healing: Working with the Aftermath of Child Sexual Abuse, Second Edition	0-471-98298-9
Butler & Williamson	Children Speak: Child Trauma and Social Work	0-471-97219-3
Cloke & Davies	Participation and Empowerment in Child Protection	0-471-97218-5
Cloke & Nash	Key Issues in Child Protection for Health Visitors and Nurses	0-471-97217-7
Masson & Winn Oakley	Out of Hearing: Representing Children in Care Proceedings	0-471-98642-9
Parton & Wattam	Child Sexual Abuse: Responding to the Experiences of Children	0-471-98334-9
Platt & Shemmings (in association with NISW & PAIN)	Making Enquiries into Alleged Child Abuse and Neglect: Partnership with Families	0-471-97222-3
Wattam	Making a Case in Child Protection	0-471-97225-8
Wattam, Hughes & Blagg	Child Sexual Abuse: Listening, Hearing and Validating the Experiences of Children	0-471-97281-9

Forthcoming Titles

Cloke	Primary Prevention of Child Abuse	0-471-97775-6

Potential authors are invited to submit ideas and proposals for publication in the series to Christopher Cloke, Series Editor.

CHILD SEXUAL ABUSE

Responding to the Experiences of Children

Edited by

Professor Nigel Parton and Professor Corinne Wattam

JOHN WILEY & SONS

Chichester · New York · Weinheim · Brisbane · Singapore · Toronto

Other Wiley Editorial Offices

John Wiley & Sons, Inc., 605 Third Avenue,
New York, NY 10158-0012, USA

WILEY-VCH Verlag GmbH, Pappelallee 3,
D-69469 Weinheim, Germany

Jacaranda Wiley Ltd, 33 Park Road, Milton,
Queensland 4064, Australia

John Wiley & Sons (Asia) Pte Ltd, 2 Clementi Loop #02-01,
Jin Xing Distripark, Singapore 129809

John Wiley & Sons (Canada) Ltd, 22 Worcester Road,
Rexdale, Ontario M9W 1L1, Canada

HV
751
A6
C438

Library of Congress Cataloging-in-Publication Data

Child sexual abuse : responding to the experiences of children /
    edited by Nigel Parton and Corinne Wattam.
        p.   cm. — (Wiley series in child protection and policy)
    Includes bibliographical references and index.
    ISBN 0-471-98334-9 (paper)
    1. Abused children—Services for—Great Britain.   2. Child abuse–
    –Great Britain.   I. Parton, Nigel.   II. Wattam, Corinne.
    III. Series.
    HV751.A6C583   1999
    362.76'8'0941—dc21   99-12585
                                                          CIP

British Library Cataloguing in Publication Data

A catalogue record for this book is available from the British Library

ISBN 0-471-98334-9

Typeset in 10/12pt Palatino by Dorwyn Ltd, Rowlands Castle, Hants
Printed and bound in Great Britain by Biddles Ltd, Guildford and King's Lynn
This book is printed on acid-free paper responsibly manufactured from sustainable forestry, in which at least two trees are planted for each one used for paper production.

CONTENTS

ABOUT THE EDITORS

Nigel Parton is Professor in Child Care and Director of the Centre for Applied Childhood Studies, in the School of Human and Health Sciences, at the University of Huddersfield. A social worker by training, he has been researching and writing about child protection and child welfare for twenty years, his most recent book being (with David Thorpe and Corinne Wattam) (1997) *Child Protection: Risk and the Moral Order* (London, Macmillan) and is also co-editor of the journal *Children and Society*, also published by John Wiley. He is also Patron of MOSAIC (West Yorkshire).

Corinne Wattam is Professor of Child Care at the University of Central Lancashire. She was previously NSPCC Reader in the Centre for Applied Childhood Studies at the University of Huddersfield, and the Coordinator of the Concerted Action on the Prevention of Child Abuse in Europe (CAP-CAE) at Lancaster University. Corinne has practised as a social worker in local authority and voluntary agency field and residential settings. She was also a member of the Pigot Code of Practice Steering Group which drafted the *Memorandum of Good Practice*. Her publications include (with H. Blagg and J. Hughes) *Child Sexual Abuse: Listening, Hearing and Validating the Experiences of Children* (Wiley, 1997), a companion volume to this current book, as well as (with C. Woodward) . . . *And do I abuse my children? No!* in *Childhood Matters: Report of the National Commission of Inquiry into the Prevention of Child Abuse* (HMSO, 1996), and *An Overview of Child Maltreatment Prevention Strategies in Europe* (with CAPCAE) for the EEC.

ABOUT THE CONTRIBUTORS

Mark Anslow is Child Protection Officer, Bradford and Kirklees NSPCC.

Jane Boylan is a Senior Lecturer in Social Work at Staffordshire University. She is co-author of *Promoting Young People's Empowerment* (Representing Children, 1998) and, with Corinne Wattam, *Advocacy and Young People: A Review of the Literature* (The Children's Society, 1998).

Linda Colclough is Project Co-ordinator for MOSAIC (West Yorkshire).

Andrew Cooper is Professor of Social Work at the Tavistock Clinic and the University of East London. In recent years he has developed a particular interest in comparative child protection research, particularly in a European context and his publications include (with Baistow, K., Hetherington, R., Pitts, J. and Spriggs, A.) (1995) *Positive Child Protection: A View from Abroad* (Lyme Regis, Russell House Publishing); (with Hetherington, R. and Katz, I.) (1997) *A Third Way? A European Perspective on the Child Protection/Family Support Debate* (London, NSPCC); and (with Hetherington, R., Smith, P. and Wilford, G.) (1997) *Protecting Children: Messages from Europe* (Lyme Regis, Russell House Publishing).

Marcus Erooga is Area Children's Services Manager for the NSPCC in Lancashire and for a number of years has had experience of practice and management of services relating to sexual abuse and sexual offending. He is a co-editor of *Sexual Offending Against Children: Assessment and Treatment of Male Abusers* (Routledge, 1994); author of *Good Practice in Child Protection: A Guide for the Probation Service* (GMPS, 1997); is co-editor, with Helen Masson, of *The Journal of Sexual Aggression*, and of *Children and Young People who Sexually Abuse: Challenges and Responses* (Routledge, 1999). He is a Visiting Honorary Research Fellow at the Centre for Applied Childhood Studies at the University of Huddersfield.

Donal Fortune is a Research Psychologist at the Department of Behavioural Medicine, Hope Hospital, and Faculty of Medicine, University of Manchester.

Bernard Gallagher is Senior Research Fellow in the Centre for Applied Childhood Studies, at the University of Huddersfield. He has researched extensively in child protection and child care, including among his work studies of organised child sexual abuse; stranger abuse; and the non-prosecution of child abuse cases. The NSPCC (1998) has published his most recent work *Grappling with Smoke—Investigating and Managing Organised Child Sexual Abuse: A Good Practice Guide.*

Rachael Hetherington is Director of the Centre for Comparative Social Work Studies at Brunel University and Editor of *Social Work in Europe.* In recent years she has developed a particular interest in comparative child protection research, particularly in a European context, and her publications include (with Cooper, A., Baistow, K., Pitts, T. and Spriggs, A.) (1995) *Positive Child Protection: A View from Abroad* (Lyme Regis, Russell House Publishing); (with Cooper, A. and Katz, I.) (1997) *A Third Way? A European Perspective on the Child Protection/Family Support Debate* (London, NSPCC); and (with Cooper, A., Smith, P. and Wilford, G.) (1997) *Protecting Children: Messages from Europe* (Lyme Regis, Russell House Publishing).

Bill Jordan is Professor of Social Policy at the University of Huddersfield and Reader in Social Studies at Exeter University. He is the author of some twenty books on social work, social policy and political thought, most recently *The New Politics of Welfare* (Sage, 1998).

Mary MacLeod is Director of Policy, Research and Development at Child-Line. She was a founder member of the Child Abuse Studies Unit at the Polytechnic of North London, and has published on sexual and physical abuse, theorising child abuse, and feminist approaches to work on sexual abuse. Recent work for ChildLine includes studies on child abuse, children living away from home, adults' calls to ChildLine about child protection, family problems, runaway and homeless children, children and racism, boys asking for help, and bullying.

Helen Masson is a Principal Lecturer in Social Work at the University of Huddersfield. Since 1994 she has been researching policy and practice developments in relation to young sexual abusers. As well as being the author of a number of associated articles and co-editor of *Children and Young People who Sexually Abuse: Challenges and Responses* (Routledge, 1999), she is also co-editor (with Marcus Erooga) of *The Journal of Sexual Aggression,* and is a founder member of the Centre for Applied Childhood Studies at the University of Huddersfield.

Nigel Parton is Professor in Child Care and Director of the Centre for Applied Childhood Studies, in the School of Human and Health Sciences, at the University of Huddersfield. A social worker by training, he has been researching and writing about child protection and child welfare for twenty years, his most recent book being (with David Thorpe and Corinne Wattam) (1997) *Child Protection: Risk and the Moral Order* (London, Macmillan) and is also co-editor of the journal *Children and Society*, also published by John Wiley. He is also Patron of MOSAIC (West Yorkshire).

Carole Smith has extensive experience of working in the voluntary and statutory sector. As a team leader and senior manager in local authority social services she has been responsible for a range of services to children and families including adoption and fostering and child protection. Now a Senior Lecturer in Social Work at the University of Manchester, her research interests cover adoption, social work intervention with children and families, socio-legal issues relating to children and children's rights.

Judith Trowell is Consultant Child and Adolescent Psychiatrist at the Tavistock and Portman NHS Trust. She has researched and published widely on the issue of child sexual abuse, as well as other forms of abuse and treatment interventions. She is the author (with M. King) of *Children's Welfare and the Law: The Limits of Legal Interventions*, co-editor (with M. Bower) of *The Emotional Needs of Young Children and their Families* (Routledge, 1995) and author of *Your Three-Year-Old* (Rosendale Press, 1992). She is a member of the President's Interdisciplinary Committee of the Family Division, patron of The Voice of the Child in Care and Chairperson of Young Minds.

Corinne Wattam is Professor of Child Care at the University of Central Lancashire. She was previously NSPCC Reader in the Centre for Applied Childhood Studies at the University of Huddersfield, and the Coordinator of the Concerted Action on the Prevention of Child Abuse in Europe (CAP-CAE) at Lancaster University. Corinne has practised as a social worker in local authority and voluntary agency field and residential settings. She was also a member of the Pigot Code of Practice Steering Group which drafted the *Memorandum of Good Practice*. Her publications include (with H. Blagg and J. Hughes) *Child Sexual Abuse: Listening, Hearing and Validating the Experiences of Children* (Wiley, 1997), a companion volume to this current book, as well as (with C. Woodward) *And do I abuse my children? No!* in *Childhood Matters: Report of the National Commission of Inquiry into the Prevention of Child Abuse* (HMSO, 1996), and *An Overview of Child Maltreatment Prevention Strategies in Europe* (with CAPCAE) for the EEC.

Helen Westcott is a Lecturer in Psychology at The Open University, and was formerly Research Officer with the NSPCC. Helen has researched many aspects of children's testimony, children's experiences of social work intervention, and the abuse of disabled children. She is co-editor (with J. Jones) of *Perspectives on the Memorandum: Policy, Practice and Research on Investigative*

Interviewing (Arena, 1997), and co-author (with M. Cross) of *This Far and No Further: Towards Ending the Abuse of Disabled Children* (Venture Press, 1996).

Karen Woodhead began her career as a solicitor in private practice. She subsequently worked in a local authority legal department specialising in children's cases. Having moved back to private practice ten years ago, Karen is now head of the family department, a member of the Children Panel, and a part-time District Judge. She was one of the first independent chairs of an Area Child Protection Committee and is currently researching legal issues relating to contact in different family proceedings.

Clare Woodward completed a PhD at Lancaster University in the area of child sexual abuse. She has undertaken research for the National Commission of Inquiry into the Prevention of Child Abuse (with Corinne Wattam). She is currently a psychologist in clinical training with the Universities of Coventry and Warwick.

Jan Wyllie is a practising manager of a Children's Society Advocacy Resource for children and young people within the child protection system.

ACKNOWLEDGEMENT

Many thanks to Sue Hanson in the Centre for Applied Childhood Studies at the University of Huddersfield, for bringing the project together and supporting it throughout.

INTRODUCTION: IMPEDIMENTS TO IMPLEMENTING A CHILD-CENTRED APPROACH

Corinne Wattam and Nigel Parton

It is now a decade since *Child Sexual Abuse: Listening, Hearing and Validating the Experiences of Children* (Blagg *et al.*, 1989) appeared. This current volume was originally stimulated by a request for a second edition of the earlier book. After careful review, we concluded that all the chapters remained valid, with the possible exception of the chapter on relevant legislation, which was written before implementation of the Children Act 1989. The Children Act has been one among many changes which have subsequently affected the practice context of the current response to child sexual abuse. Some of the changes are unique to the UK, such as the introduction of the *Memorandum of Good Practice* (Home Office/DoH, 1992); others are international, such as a more general trend towards acknowledging the importance of prevention in child abuse and the introduction of the UN Convention on the Rights of the Child. As a consequence, we considered that a completely new book rather than simply a second edition in the form of an update would be more helpful. Hence this text aims to build on the first and pursue its principle of developing a child-centred approach, but situated in the current child protection context.

Since 1989, awareness of child sexual abuse has continued to grow. The scepticism redolent of public and press reactions to the Cleveland crisis now has the benefit of ten years' hindsight, much of which validates the original claims made by the health and social work professionals (Richardson *et al.*, 1991). More recently, cases such as those concerning Fred West in the UK and DeTreux in Belgium have served to reinforce public outrage and political sensitivity to child sexual abuse at a more European level. The initial recognition of intra-familial abuse has expanded outside the parameters of private family worlds into awareness of wider sexual exploitation. If the 1970s and 1980s marked a period of doubt about the extent of child sexual abuse, the 1990s have validated that awareness and revealed the global market of child sexual exploitation on a scale which could not have been possible prior to the expanding long-haul travel industry and ready access to the Internet. Furthermore, the voices of survivors, many of whom are now adults, have turned attention to institutional abuse (see Gallagher, Chapter 11 this volume). Knowledge of complex abuse reinforces the view that listening to children must be the starting point for any intervention. Had the voices of children been heard prior to their becoming adults, much of what we now know of this form of abuse may have been prevented.

Despite the similarities between what happens to children in households and the web of external exploitation a clear division continues to circumscribe organisational responses. Child protection as a state concern remains in the hands of family-oriented child welfare departments and the extra-familial territory of abuse is carved off as the province of policing and criminal justice professionals. Increasingly, there is a recognition that these boundaries are misleading and mitigate against a concerted effort to tackle the sexual exploitation of children. Those believed responsible can be members of families, joiners of families and participants in the local community establishing and working in children's social groups and thus must inevitably bridge the divide between the family and the outside world in order to gain maximum contact with children. Yet, in the UK at least, most inquiries into child sexual abuse begin with a focus on parental maltreatment or neglect and cases involving alleged and actual perpetrators outside the family are those where children remain least likely to have their needs met (Sharland et al., 1995). This observation, made only three years ago, is closely linked to the notions of 'ideal victim' and relevance (Blagg et al., 1989; Wattam, 1989).

Within child protection there remains a propensity to classify children, and information about them, according to particular frameworks—one that prioritises certain children above others and one that is guided by expectations premised on 'normality' in assessing what might have happened to any particular child (see also Parton et al., 1997). Yet, perhaps more than any other form of significant harm, the sexual exploitation of children turns both of these frameworks around. Any child could be a potential victim; for example, by the broadest definition one UK study found that half of all girls and a quarter of all boys will experience sexual abuse before their eighteenth birthday (Kelly et al., 1991). This brings sexual abuse into the realm of 'normal' childhoods and normal behaviour. However, responses to it assume that it is the exception rather than the rule and that it is an issue which is the preserve of the statutory agencies. The numbers of children reported to social services departments for sexual abuse are a small minority of those who have experience of it. Our child protection system does not safeguard children from sexual abuse: it only attempts to protect those who are made known to the system, the majority of whom fit within the more general profile of child welfare clients—that is, they are economically disadvantaged and often face a number of other difficulties in their home environment. However, as Mary MacLeod (Chapter 8 this volume) demonstrates, children who experience sexual abuse constitute a much more complex picture than is ever made known to statutory agencies.

The observation that the predominant response to child sexual abuse is one which focuses on particular children in particular circumstances points to a first impediment to implementing a child-centred approach. Namely, responses reflect a certain version of childhood, which is brought to the attention of the state when it is obviously contravened.

In the late 1980s a renewed interest emerged in the concept of 'childhood' itself, perhaps best articulated by James and Prout (1997) as a new 'paradigm'. This paradigm argued against the dominant 'conceptual pair' of socialisation and development represented childhood in a particular way: as 'natural, passive, incompetent and incomplete' (James & Prout, 1997, p. x). Kitzinger (1997) applied this approach to child sexual abuse, arguing that viewing children as innocent, ignorant and passive served to make them attractive to abusers, to undermine the legitimacy of their natural responses (artful strategies of avoidance and coping) as deviance and also to maintain 'adult-centric' constructions of childhood. There is also now a recognition that children and childhood can be viewed as conceptually distinct (James *et al.*, 1998). Although membership of the category 'childhood' is constantly changing, childhood constitutes a more permanent social category (Qvortrup *et.al.*, 1994). Developing this theme, Kitzinger argues that sexual violence to children is viewed as the 'the decay of childhood' (Seabrook, 1987) and that 'protectionist' responses are actually about the 'preservation' of childhood.

> 'In this way, childhood is treated rather like a rare animal threatened with extinction. Just as early attempts to preserve endangered species relied on locking up specimens in zoos (rather than intervening against the "man-made" attacks on their environment) so this child protection approach attempts to "preserve childhood" by confining children behind bars.' (Kitzinger, 1997, p. 175)

The 'bars' are a metaphor for the restrictions increasingly imposed on children (and their carers) in the name of protection: restrictions on where to go, with whom, when, how to act, what to say and so forth—restrictions which, Kitzinger claims, children desperately long to escape. Rather than challenging the causes of sexual violence to children, the gaze of a child protection response is on the victim and his or her family.

A response which focuses on individual families has characterised child protection practice since the 'rediscovery' of child abuse in the early 1960s (Parton, 1985). This approach has highlighted, over the last three decades, a tension between the state's duty to protect children and parents' rights to rear children as they see fit (Dingwall *et al.*, 1983). In the 1990s the practical implications of these debates have taken a new turn. Parton (1991) describes the central problem for all neo-liberal states in relation to child protection in the following way;

> 'How can we devise a legal basis for the power to intervene into the private sphere of the family in order to protect children, but in a way which does not undermine the family and convert all families into clients of a sovereign state? Such a question is posed by the demand to ensure that the family is experienced as autonomous and free and the primary sphere for rearing children, while also recognizing that there is a need for intervention in some families where they are seen as failing in this primary task.'

It is in this context that western English-speaking countries, such as the US, UK and Australia, now struggle to 'balance' their services for children. Those in the UK will, by now, be more than familiar with the 'refocusing debate' emanating from the publication of *Child Protection: Messages from Research* by the Department of Health (DOH, 1995). The overriding theme of this overview report was that services should be balanced away from an investigative approach to child abuse and towards a more supportive model of intervention for families. In the US the attempt to move towards a more sensitive, family support framework can also be detected in the growing emphasis on prevention and community development programmes, and in Australia the beginnings of the shift are being seen in 'New Directions', a formal attempt to prevent cases which indicate a need for family support (under the guise of a maltreatment allegation) from being classified as child maltreatment (Thorpe and Bilson, 1998). These shifts are legitimated in two ways. Firstly, there is the claim that actual numbers of all child maltreatment allegations have been rising steadily across the English-speaking world while the level of substantiation has remained relatively constant or even dropped (Besharov, 1986, 1990; Thorpe and Bilson, 1998), with the consequence that too many families are placed under (unacceptable) surveillance. Secondly, this brings with it the difficulty of distributing scarce resources between investigation, validation and support with too much time (and money) wasted on investigations (Besharov, 1990). A central consideration for us, and one that marks a change from ten years ago, has therefore been about the implications for children themselves of the policy changes promoting family support and prevention; that is, away from policing towards meeting need. Family support as a concept applied to child sexual abuse takes a particular turn. It is interpreted less as a primary prevention measure, stopping abuse before it occurs, and more as secondary prevention, supporting non-abusing carers in their struggle to keep their families going after sexual abuse has been discovered (see Colclough *et al.*, Chapter 9 this volume). At that level it is clear that a great deal more could be done in supporting and developing community-based groups which are survivor-focused and/or survivor-led and where community networks are at the centre of children's protection rather than being marginal to a system dominated by professionals and statutory agencies (Smith, 1996; Gray *et al.*, 1997; see also Jordan, Chapter 10 this volume).

However, it is also notable that studies of survivors of child sexual abuse and also work with perpetrators indicate that a more general family support model may prevent future sexual harm to children. Research studies of child sexual abuse survivors find that sexual abuse is accompanied by physical and/or emotional abuse and/or neglect in almost one-third of cases (Wattam & Woodward, 1996; Bifulco and Moran, 1998). The study by Wattam and Woodward (1996), for the National Commission into the Prevention of Child Abuse, contained reports from survivors stating that the sexual abuse, while wrong, could make them feel special and different in otherwise negative environments, and one minority theme was that, although sexual abuse was horrific, emotional abuse could be worse and have a more lasting effect (Wattam and Woodward, 1996).

Thus, more generalised family support approaches may succeed in creating environments which are less open to perpetrators who are likely to target children from families with problems, particularly single female parent families (Gallagher, 1998). Learning from perpetrators, and working with perpetrators, is a further step in prevention, and one which is also not always viewed as compatible with a family support approach. The work of Giaretto (1981) in the US, advocating community treatment programmes which keep offending perpetrators within their families has not been implemented in the UK, although the more family oriented, therapeutic approaches to intra-familial abuse are applied elsewhere in ·Europe (Hetherington *et al.*, 1997; see also Hetherington and Cooper, Chapter 2 this volume).

An integrated multi-agency response, ensuring that work with family members and associates involved in child sexual abuse cases always began from the child's perspective, was advocated by Eileen Craig *et al.*, in the earlier book (Craig *et al.*, 1989). Yet, in practice, responses to perpetrators, children and their carers generally remain separate. Work with perpetrators is not perceived as being central to the child protection response offered by children's welfare departments, but something which is important for other agencies, such as probation, to deal with. As Marcus Erooga and Helen Masson (Chapter 12 this volume) demonstrate, such work needs to be much more central. While it needs to be explicitly multidisciplinary the experiences of and impacts on the child need to be recognised. This is a key area if we are to make progress.

If the first impediment to a child-centred response is the framing of individual children as particular types of victims, the second is the concept of child sexual abuse itself. In relation to sexual abuse, the more intrusive 'policing' investigative child protection response has retained its legitimacy despite the tendency to review children's needs on a less formal, preventative level in relation to other forms of maltreatment. Kilkerr's chapter in the earlier book (Kilkess, 1989), on the development of joint working remains an important piece of history, contributing to our understanding of the increasingly 'forensic gaze' and criminalisation of child sexual abuse (Parton, 1991). The police are involved in joint working such investigations more than in any other form of significant harm, and this is reflected in the nature of cases submitted for prosecutions (Wattam, 1997). It is not customary for families who may have difficulties with child sexual abuse to request voluntary help, counselling and assistance, as it is in some European countries (see Hetherington and Cooper, Chapter 2 this volume). Once such children, and their families, present themselves to protection services questions of investigation, culpability and potential prosecution become the primary consideration, even where the perpetrator is not an immediate family member. This is despite the fact that many children will say that this is not what they want as a first response (Mac-Leod, 1996, and Chapter 8 this volume).

One of the main reasons that children and their families cannot get the support they require is that child sexual abuse is treated as qualitatively different from other forms of abuse. The claim that child abuse is a social construction has been reinforced by the government (DoH, 1995) but is more often applied to physical and emotional abuse and neglect. These forms of maltreatment can be viewed on a 'continuum' ranging from minor (smacking, occasional shouting, sporadic leaving alone and so forth) to severe (murder, constant criticism and rejection, seriously impeded development). This interpretation of social constructionism is premised on relativism: since what is considered to be child abuse varies between time and place, it is not an absolute concept and is, therefore, subject to reinterpretation and 'thresholds' for its definition (DoH, 1995). However, the 'social construction' of child sexual abuse is viewed as different from other forms of abuse. This difference has been described in the following ways (DoH, 1995, p. 19):

— The chronicity and severity of maltreatment is what should authorise intervention. In child sexual abuse 'a relatively minor, one-off event can sometimes be damaging to children and may require a strong response from protection agencies'.

— Generally it is difficult to define child abuse and there are no absolute criteria, however, 'the thresholds which define when sexual abuse has occurred are relatively clear'.
— While context is important in defining other forms of child abuse, 'this rule is less easy to apply in cases of sexual abuse'.
— Child protection work is generally concerned with family problems, whereas sexual abuse more often involves 'outside' perpetrators.

It is difficult to know why sexual abuse should be excluded from the 'continuum' model since the same claims could be made of all other forms of maltreatment. The 'relatively minor' one-off event claim depends on the assumed effects for unqualified seriousness. Yet all other forms of maltreatment could have serious consequences for children even when they are apparently 'minor' one-off events: pushing a child in anger who subsequently runs off across a busy road; a parent verbally insulting a child in front of significant friends; a 5-year-old left alone on one occasion for 15 minutes who finds matches and lights a fire. Furthermore, 'relatively minor' one-off sexual acts do not necessarily have long-lasting effects. Indeed, studies elsewhere in Europe show that what might be considered longer term sexual abuse can result in no lasting effect and there is some concern that we may be so quick to presume negative effects that insufficient attention is paid to learning more about some people's resistance, resilience and capacity to cope in what may, for others, be damaging and debilitating circumstances (Bifulco and Moran, 1998). Furthermore, to state that one-off cases might require a strong protection response is by definition erroneous. That a case is a 'one-off' suggests that the child will not be in need of protection, though may indeed be in need of recovery services. Finally, awareness of the blurred boundary between intra-familial and extra-familial abuse implies that it can no longer be safe for children to see the two as conceptually distinct.

The claim that thresholds are relatively clear in relation to sexual abuse is also misleading. They are only clear if there is a majority consensus on what is sexual abuse. This, therefore, is not a statement about sexual abuse, but a statement about the degree of societal agreement. While it may be that there is a greater consensus about what is sexual abuse, this only indicates that there is a lack of societal agreement on other forms of abuse, not that their thresholds are more relative.

For something to be regarded as relative it must have an agreed meaning in language in the first place. Thus, for example, observations of currency changes between one country and another can lead to the conclusion that money has relative value. It does, however, retain its agreed meaning as money. It does not stop being money because its value changes, though it may become money that is worth nothing. Abuse in that sense is similar, the only difference being that there is less consensus about what constitutes abuse, rather than the high level of consensus about what constitutes money. If certain actions and harms to children are now termed as abuse, they do not cease to be abuse because, in some other time or place, they were not so termed. This merely becomes a matter of competing versions about who has the right, power and authority to make the claims that certain behaviours constitute abuse in the first place. But while it can be a commonplace and quite acceptable matter to state that money has relative value, this is not the case with child sexual abuse—it is, within the majority of the white, western, English-speaking world, quite difficult to state that sexual abuse is relative, or even that it can be viewed on a continuum, as the Department of Health illustrate. This, however, is neither the time nor the place to explore further how this situation has come about. Our intention in this book is to draw attention to the fact that this is the case, and that the tendency towards absolute definitions of child sexual abuse has implications for children and young people who experience sexual acts, behaviours, exploitation, assaults and harms.

One consequence of absolutism in relation to child sexual abuse is the forensic response it almost automatically generates and the fact that many children and young people may not want this response (see MacLeod, Chapter 8 this volume). Such intervention is often justified by the assumption that professional adults know what is in the child's best interests: that bringing sexual abuse out into an open statutory arena, and prosecuting offenders is the only appropriate response, and that this begins the 'healing process'. While, in principle, many could agree with this position, in practice it is difficult to sustain from a child-centred perspective. While very few children approach statutory agencies as a first port of call when experiencing sexual abuse, many do approach friends and helplines. An analysis of children's reports to ChildLine showed that:

> 'One of the greatest impediments to speaking about abuse is that children fear they will not be believed. They are also inhibited by their fear of the consequences, that their families will be broken up, for example, and/or they will be taken away from their parents, and they also fear that decisions will be made over their heads, without their involvement. In many cases, children are very reluctant to tell agencies. They tell us that they are not prepared for the disruption and further fracturing of their lives which may be a consequence of statutory intervention.' (Keep, 1996, p. 39)

It is not just children who feel this way. Large numbers of professionals also fail to report serious abuse to statutory agencies because of similar fears of the consequences even in mandatory reporting systems (Finkelhor, 1984; NCCAN, 1995).

Prosecution of perpetrators of child sexual offences brings a number of difficulties for the child and his or her family, particularly where the child is the main source of evidence (Goodman *et al.*, 1992). But, quite apart from the serious problem of trauma to children in court, there are other more pragmatic issues which mitigate against this approach being child centred. These have to do with the practical workings of the English criminal justice system, many of which have come to light since the admissibility of pre-recorded video evidence and publication of the *Memorandum of Good Practice* (Home Office/DoH, 1992).

The statutory response to child sexual abuse almost always means that if the child is over a certain age (some would have it as young as 3—see, for example, Jones 1987) the child will be considered as a witness for criminal proceedings. The child may never be required to give evidence, but he or she will always be reviewed as a potential candidate. This means that, in practice, very soon after referral contact will be made with the police and consideration will be given to taking a statement (written or video). The referral is effectively a complaint to the police under joint working procedures (Wattam, 1992). Once this happens the constraints imposed by the criminal justice system immediately become relevant and imposing and the only choice left for the child is whether to speak or not, since he or she also becomes a compellable witness. Furthermore, what the child can say, and what others can say to the child, is circumscribed by the rules of evidence and by the anticipation of future defence counsel. This will be the case until the outcome of the prosecution, whether that be dropped, pleaded or trailed. Under the current system this will not change, even with the full implementation of the Pigot report (Home Office, 1989), which many call for. Such changes only tinker within the existing system to make some of it easier for children. The introduction of pre-trial hearings and interlocutors will make the process more sensitive to the needs of children (Home Office, 1998) but will do little to make the child protection response child centred. It does not matter how easy we make it for children to give evidence, the perpetrator and his or her defence can always have available to them the option to refute and undermine it. In itself this is a great principle of our criminal justice system ensuring the rights of the accused, and would seem a minor difficulty to surmount if interviewing practices in court could be improved. In practice, however, the unintended consequences are far more profound.

The refusal of some authorities to offer children therapy until after the trial, despite government and Home Office recommendations that this should happen is one example of the extent of this difficulty (Davies *et al.*, 1994). Children are not offered therapy because it may prejudice evidence— not their version of events, but the capacity of the defence to undermine it through claims of coaching and suggestibility. The fact that children are, as a 'rule of thumb', offered a one-off, no longer than one-hour interview as soon as possible after the complaint is made, is also a consequence of this fear. Changing and amending these rules will only serve to make more children vulnerable to later scepticism and undermining in court. Under the current criminal justice system it is possible, but discouraged and a rare practice, to enable children to 'disclose', seek help from professionals and to later file a complaint when they are ready to do so. Such an approach is inadvisable because the child's evidence would be open to a number of criticisms. Why did the child not come forward sooner? Why is a prosecution being considered now? Who has spoken with the child in ways which might be considered suggestible and leading? Yet taking this route would be more compatible with children's wishes which at present appear to reflect incompatible 'rights': the right to see justice done and the right to retain some control of their information and their future (Keep, 1996).

Many view these unintended consequences as a direct outcome of the adversarial process, proposing that the more inquisitorial European legal systems are better equipped to deal with such difficulties. However, this is not a slight on the practices of defence lawyers who are doing the job they are paid for and who use the resources at their disposal to do it. Such resources are readily obtainable from the wider social environment, otherwise they could not be drawn upon in court: a basic disposition to question children's accounts, a fundamental mistrust of professional practices and, with the advent of 'false memory syndrome' and questionable therapeutic practices in relation to adults, a challenge to the veracity of sexual abuse itself (see Smith and Woodhead, Chapter 1 this volume).

Hence, while we might appear to be discussing a very small area of the protectionist response—the prosecution of offenders—this is a symptom of much wider concerns which have to do with the very nature of professional practices, particularly social work, childhood and child sexual abuse itself. Under the legal systems of other European countries these resources are less available, not because of the inquisitorial style but because of a greater respect for professional accountability and skill (see Hetherington and Cooper, Chapter 2 this volume). The notion, for example, of the 'professional secret' in France and Belgium, where a professional need not inform the authorities about abuse if working with the child to prevent further harm, is one that would be difficult to sustain in western, English-speaking systems. French and Belgian professionals remain accountable if anything should go wrong, and tread a careful and implicitly negotiated line in mandatory reporting systems. However, this enables the professional to keep the child's confidentiality and to work, albeit with therapeutic authority, at the child's pace. Such approaches challenge English ways of thinking and it is important to understand the nature of the challenge. Ultimately, the challenge is less about legality and more about a view of child sexual abuse: that it is not absolute, that it is preventable, that it is possible to work with families and support families in order to bring about therapeutic change and that professionals are competent enough to do it. While the therapeutic models may become a source of further scepticism because of their patriarchal bias towards 'functional' and 'dysfunctional families' (for example, see MacLeod and Saraga, 1988), they are possibly more open to change than a legal system with established, replicated and championed principles which have survived centuries of application and critique.

CHALLENGING THE IMPEDIMENTS TO A CHILD-CENTRED PROCESS

We have identified what we consider to be three fundamental impediments to a child-centred response to child sexual abuse. The first of these is a basic disposition to question children's accounts. Over the last two decades, as a consequence of the historical mistrust of children in the legal process, a large amount of time, money and research attention has been focused on examining the reliability of children as witnesses. The conclusion of this research, so far, is that under certain specified conditions children can be as reliable as adults in giving accounts of their experiences (Spencer and Flin, 1993). Furthermore, there is substantial research evidence that children themselves rarely make false allegations about child sexual abuse, although others may make them on their behalf . Yet the propensity to challenge what children say in relation to sexual assaults perpetrated on them, and to explore the potential for lying, remains part of everyday practice (Wattam, 1997).

> 'The strategy employed by some defence barristers to serve their client's interests involves the discrediting of the child's evidence. Lines of questioning designed to confuse, and asking the same question in different ways to get the child to give a different answer, are adult strategies which children do not understand. Inappropriate language, such as complicated sentences with several negatives or value-laden questions such as "you know it's naughty to lie and you have been lying haven't you?" can confuse and distress a child. Sometimes defence barristers will simply bully the child.' (Keep, 1996)

One fundamental starting point for the appropriation of research into the law is the 'typical case': What can typically be known about children's abilities in relation to talking reliably about events in which they have been involved? This typicality is generated through numbers and replicability. Law can then contrast this to the circumstances of the individual children with whom it has to deal: Would a normal child in these circumstances do X? Unfortunately no amount of research on the typical child will be adequate to challenge the unique circumstances of the individual cases of particular children.

Children's evidence must be produced and offered as a valid account open to cross-examination and its truth value must be a matter of presentation and arbitration. While there are legal rules of evidence which circumscribe questioning and appropriate behaviour in court, these do not wholly cover the issue of truth formation or presentation. For example, a previous study by Atkinson and Drew (1979) proposes that witnesses are approached in ways which build up their credibility, or in ways which are designed to discredit their testimony, which, while structured by the conventions of courtroom practices, depend on considerably more for their interpretative value. The examples they give, through a conversation analysis approach, are the way in which silences can be interpreted depending on the place in the sequence of questioning, the management of accusations, denials and blame and the way in which these can be prospectively managed by both counsel and witnesses, the use of expected response types to infer motive, or culpability (such as where accusations may expectedly precede denials, justifications and the like) and the way in which other activities (such as accusation and blame) are accomplished through accepted questioning techniques. These features exemplify the 'locally managed', rather than procedurally given, aspects of testimony and show how easy it is to undermine adults and children in legal settings without stating overtly that this is what is going on. A similar approach is taken to the meaning of confidentiality for children and their confidantes by Wattam in Chapter 4 of this volume. This chapter reveals the social organisation and rules of confidentiality, which do not necessarily require confidentiality to be stated and can be heavily sanctioned for children and adults alike when transgressed. Yet children's competent requests for confidential hearing are often breached, and must inevitably be so under current procedures. This is a further measure of the priority given to adult competence and versions of reality, over and above that of children.

The difficulty of accepting what children say as a credible version of events and circumstances is exemplified elsewhere in professional practice. In discussing the accounts of two of the children of Fred West brought into care in 1993, Gloucestershire Area Child Protection Committee concluded that:

> 'Adults, including child care professionals, lawyers and doctors, do not believe what children say. The accounts they give are too bizarre or are considered childhood fantasies. The problem is sometimes fuelled by the media who may accuse social workers of being over zealous, removing children from innocent parents because of bizarre child fantasies. Some of the children in this case talked about Heather (their sister) being under the patio. As a potential childhood fantasy this must rate high on anybody's list as not credible, unbelievable.' (Gloucestershire Area Child Protection Committee. Overview report in respect of Charmaine and Heather West by the Bridge Child Care Consultancy, November, 1995)

The problem is further complicated for children with disabilities. In recent years there has been a growing awareness of the abuse of children with disabilities (Marchant and Page, 1997) and a recognition of the problems which such children have with getting others to recognise that they may be sexually abused in the first place, as well as the difficulties of accessing the child protection process.

'Allegations are much less likely when a child has a restricted social understanding, when their access to personal safety information is limited or non-existent, when they have restricted access to the necessary vocabulary or when their account is less likely to be believed or reported . . .' (Marchant and Page, 1997)

A question which must be asked, therefore, is how is it that the assumption that children (and adult survivors) lie or are potentially unreliable remains central and available for exploitation in relation to child sexual abuse? In our view this question bears directly on our earlier observations concerning the social construction of 'childhood'. While childhood continues to be assumed as a period of incompleteness, developmental immaturity and, by definition, containing less than 'adult' knowledge and competence this position will continue. Research evidence on the specific abilities and knowledge of samples of children cannot contravene the 'adult-centricism' of our society. For example, recent research on sexuality and intimacy in relation to children in normal families reveals a large range of variation and evidence of behaviours: 77% of children have bathed with their parents, 67% have been seen masturbating by their parents; over a third had drawn genitalia and just under a third had witnessed sexual intercourse on films or TV (Smith and Grocke, 1995). These findings cut across assumptions about 'innocence' and unknowing children, vulnerable victims shielded from the sexual mores of adults.

Ironically, it is those who abuse children who are most accepting of a notion of childhood sexuality: their (adult) construction of it, not the child's. Rather than acknowledge children's own sexuality and sexual knowledge as a positive component, the only societal acknowledgement and agreement comes in response to its exploitation by putting children 'behind the bars' of non-sexuality. If it can be exploited it shouldn't be there. Yet, could it not be possible to acknowledge, nurture and develop these dimensions of children and young people in a positive and non exploitative fashion. Adult survivors call for greater, appropriate sexual awareness raising in children well before they reach puberty. This is because for many their abuse began before they were 10 (Wattam and Woodward, 1996). Kitzinger (1997) reinforces the need for the discussion of power with children as a preventive measure. She notes that many education programmes manage to avoid 'sex' and 'power' in their content, further substantiating their taboo status.

'A radical, deconstructionist approach to preventive work with children would focus not on "giving" children a "sense" of power and telling them their "rights" but, instead, on supporting them to recognise and name their own oppression. Rather than encouraging adults to be nicer to children by simply negotiating with them or "involving" them in decision making, a radical approach would explore ways of openly discussing power with children and would encourage us to consider how we, as adults, manipulate children in order to obfuscate our own power.' (Kitzinger, 1997, p. 183)

In order to start directly from the concerns of children this book is structured by the accounts of child sexual abuse given by survivors to the National Commission of Inquiry into the Prevention of Child Abuse (Wattam and Woodward, 1996). Each of the survivors' accounts was unique; but quite unexpectedly, given that they were not asked to write to any brief, many of the accounts could be characterised by certain themes which are reflected in the titles of the chapters. A key underpinning principle that emerged from the study was a need to respect children:

> 'All people responsible for children, including parents, should be trained to respect children's minds and bodies. How many children hate PE? All mine did and loads of their friends. Simple, everyday activities children can't enjoy because they are herded en masse, shoved into large classes. There needs to be more individual attention everywhere just for a start. It's not impossible. There's loads of dedication to the principle of respect for children. Just the wrong people so often in the wrong jobs.' (A survivor cited in Wattam and Woodward, 1996, p. 122).

The observation that children can be 'herded en masse' offers a clear insight into the implicit categorisations of childhood available within our contemporary social environment. Children are available for grouping routinely, whereas adults are grouped for special purposes. Children are rarely 'singled out' unless something goes wrong (or exceptionally right). Respect is a difficult concept to apply to a group and is more customarily attached to individuals. To ask people to respect children is actually to request that people respect childhood. A child-centred approach would require respect for children as individual people, not childhood as it is socially defined.

Empowering individual children is a reflection of respect. It is a concept that is addressed in the chapter on advocacy (Wyllie and Boylan, Chapter 3 this volume), which touches on the dangers of token representation of children's views as opposed to using advocacy as an empowering strategy. Just as Jeannie Well's pointed out in the first book (Wells, 1989) taking a child's perspective and advocating from it can be quite uncomfortable for professionals, who can be undermined just as children are. In adopting child-centred practices professionals should know that they will be challenging dominant ideologies about childhood and thus joining the 'radical' approach to which Kitzinger refers. This can be uncomfortable and is, ultimately, a political choice, one that is far removed from the toy-filled, brightly painted, innocent and protected from 'real'-world environment that is no more and no less than an advocacy of majority white visions of nostalgia (Jenks, 1996).

Following from this, child-centred approaches must address other structural imbalances which children encounter, concerning gender, ethnicity, culture, class and disability. Dutt and Phillips (1996) criticise the Department of Health (DoH, 1995) for failing to address race adequately, failing to collate the findings from individual studies (even though limited) in the summary document and, as a consequence, losing an important opportunity. They draw attention to the findings of Farmer and Owen (1995) that many black children did not have access to services because of the lack of appropriate resources, and those of Thoburn *et al.* (1995) who identified the over-representation of children of mixed race parentage in referral processes. Dutt and Phillips challenge the stereotypical assumptions made, for example by Gibbons *et al.* (1995) who conclude that physical abuse was a particular concern in relation to black families and that there are 'cultural differences in childbearing'. They maintain that such statements cannot be made on the basis of data on referral rates to social services, not the incidence of physical abuse in particular communities. Such research reveals the continued focus on physical abuse and the reticence in addressing the sexual abuse of black children which was identified and explored by Stubbs in the earlier book (Stubbs, 1989). It is with regret that we endorse the finding that:

> 'A consistent message from research for practitioners from the research (that is all the relevant research and not just messages) is that what is required in assessing families is less generalisation about "patterns of child-rearing" and more understanding that racism is a factor in all black families lives, that it will distort assessments and judgements about how they care for their children, and that it is a variable in the whole child protection dynamic.' (Dutt and Phillips, 1996, p. 172)

In this book we do not, as we did in the last, have a separate chapter on child-centred approaches for black children. As Dutt and Phillips point out, if ethnicity only appears in research and publications which refer to black children, this colludes with the idea that to be white is normal, and to be black is to be defined as different from white norms. The central aim of this book is to promote a child-centred approach to child sexual abuse responses. In this task we have embarked on a tremendous struggle to find ways of redefining children more generally, as something other than different from adults. This does not mean, however, that the particular plight of black children who experience sexual abuse can be ignored or marginalised. There are many issues which black children and white children will share in relation to sexual abuse, but child-centred responses cannot avoid the difficulties that racism presents and these must be taken into account.

What we are arguing is that while the ten years since the publication of the last book have witnessed an increased public debate and awareness of child sexual abuse, we cannot assume that policy and practice have become more child centred. Far from it. In many respects the position of children and young people generally means that their social position has become more marginal and that is particularly the case among certain social groups. It is not simply that children should become more included and central but that in relation to the issues and practices which concern us here the whole nature of the way we view and constitute policies and practices has to be fundamentally re-thought. This is not to say that there are easy answers, but that the basis and criteria by which the questions are posed in the first place takes on a different form when we are serious about being child centred.

REFERENCES

Atkinson, J.M. and Drew, P. (1979) *Order in Court: The Organisation of Verbal Interaction in Judicial Settings*. London, Macmillan.

Besharov, D. (1986) Unfounded allegations—a new child abuse problem. *The Public Interest*, Spring: 18–33.

Besharov, D. (1990) Gaining control over child abuse reports. *Public Welfare*, **48**: 34–9.

Bifulco, A. and Moran, P. (1998) *Wednesday's Child: Research into Women's Experience of Neglect and Abuse in Childhood and Adult Depression*. London, Routledge.

Blagg, H., Hughes, J. and Wattam, C. (1989) *Child Sexual Abuse: Listening, Hearing and Validating the Experiences of Children*. Chichester, Wiley.

Craig, E., Erooga, M., Morrison, T. and Shearer, E. (1989) Making sense of sexual abuse: charting the shifting sands, in Blagg, H., Hughes, J. and Wattam, C. (eds) *Child Sexual Abuse: Listening, Hearing and Validating the Experiences of Children*. Chichester, Wiley.

Davies, G., Wilson, C., Mitchell, R. and Milsom, J. (1994) *Videotaping Children's Evidence: An Evaluation*. London, HMSO.

DoH (1995) *Child Protection: Messages from Research*. London, HMSO.

Dingwall, R., Eekelaar, J. and Murray, T. (1983) *The Protection of Children: State Intervention and Family Life*. Oxford, Basil Blackwell.

Dutt, R. and Phillips, M. (1996) Race, culture and the prevention of child abuse, in *Childhood Matters: The Report of the National Commission of Inquiry into the Prevention of Child Abuse*, Vol. 2, Background Papers. London, HMSO.

Farmer, E. and Owen, M. (1995) *Child Protection Practice: Private Risks and Public Remedies: Decision Making, Intervention and Outcome in Child Protection Work*. London, HMSO.

Finkelhor, D. (1984) *Child Sexual Abuse: New Theory and Research*. New York, Free Press.

Gallagher, B. (1998) *Grappling with Smoke: Investigating and Managing Organised Child Sexual Abuse: A Good Practice Guide*. London, NSPCC.

Giaretto, H. (1981) A comprehensive child sexual abuse treatment program, in Mrazek, P. and Kempe, C. (eds) *Sexually Abused Children and Their Families*. New York, Pergamon Press.

Gibbons, J., Conroy, S. and Bell, C. (1995) *Operating the Child Protection System: A Study of Child Protection Practices in English Local Authorities*. London, HMSO.

Goodman, G.S., Pyle, L., Jones, D.P.H., Port, L. and Prado, L. (1992) *Testifying in Court: Emotional Effects of Criminal Court Testimony on Child Sexual Victims*. Monographs of the Society for Research in Child Development, USA.

Gray, S., Higgs, M. and Pringle, K. (1997) User-centred responses to child sexual abuse: the way forward. *Child and Family Social Work*, 2(1): 49–57.

Hetherington, R., Cooper, A., Smith, P. and Wilford, G. (1997) *Protecting Children: Messages from Europe*. Lyme Regis, Russell House.

Home Office (1989) *Report of the Advisory Group on Video Evidence*. London HMSO.

Home Office (1998) *Speaking up for Justice*. Report of the Interdepartmental Working Group on the Treatment of Vulnerable or Intimidated Witnesses in the Criminal Justice System. London, The Stationery Office.

Home Office DoH (1992) *Memorandum of Good Practice on Video Recorded Interviews with Child Witnesses for Criminal Proceedings*. London, HMSO.

James, A., Jenks, C. and Prout, A. (1998) *Theorising Childhood*. Cambridge, Polity Press.

James, A. and Prout, A. (1997) *Constructing and Reconstructing Childhood*, 2nd edn. London, Falmer Press.

Jenks, C. (1996) *Childhood*. London, Routledge.

Jones, D.P.H. (1987) The evidence of a three-year-old child. *Criminal Law Review*, pp. 677–81.

Keep, G. (1996) *Going to Court: Child Witnesses in their own Words*. London, ChildLine.

Kelly, L., Regan, L. and Burton, S. (1991) *An Exploratory Study of the Prevalence of Sexual Abuse in a Sample of 16–21 Year Olds*. Child and Woman Abuse Studies Unit, University of North London.

Kilkerr, A. (1989) A police response: devising a code of practice, in Blagg, H., Hughes, J. and Wattam, C. (eds) *Child Sexual Abuse: Listening, Hearing and Validating the Experiences of Children*. Chichester, Wiley.

Kitzinger, J. (1997) Who are you kidding? Children, power and the struggle against sexual abuse, in James, A. and Prout, A. (eds) *Constructing and Reconstructing Childhood*. London, Falmer Press.

MacLeod, M. and Saraga, E. (1988) Challenging the orthodox: towards a feminist theory and practice. *Feminist Review*, 28: 15–55.

MacLeod, M. (1996) *Talking with Children about Child Abuse: ChildLine's First Ten Years*. London, ChildLine.

Marchant, R. and Page, M. (1997) *Bridging the Gap: Child Protection Work with Children with Multiple Disabilities*. London, NSPCC.

NCCAN (1995) *Study of National Incidence and Prevalence of Child Abuse and Neglect*. National Centre for Child Abuse and Neglect, Washington DC, US Department of Health and Human Services.

Parton, N. (1985) *The Politics of Child Abuse*. London, Macmillan.

Parton, N. (1991) *Governing the Family: Child Care, Child Protection and the State*. London, Macmillan.

Parton, N., Thorpe, D. and Wattam, C. (1997) *Child Protection: Risk and the Moral Order*. London, Macmillan.

Qvortrup, J., Bardy, M., Sgritta, G. and Wintersberger, H. (eds) (1994) *Childhood Matters: Social Theory, Practice and Politics*. Aldershot, Avebury.

Richardson, S., Bacon, H. and Cashman, H. (1991) *Child Sexual Abuse, Whose Problem? Reflections from Cleveland*, Birmingham, Ventura Press.

Seabrook, J. (1987) The decay of childhood. *New Statesman*, 10 July: 14–15.

Sharland, E., Jones, D., Aldgate, J., Seal, H. and Croucher, M. (1995) *Professional Intervention in Child Sexual Abuse*. London, HMSO.

Smith, G. (1996) Reassessing protectiveness, in Batty, D. and Cullen, D. (eds) *Child Protection: The Therapeutic Option*. London, British Agencies for Adoption and Fostering.

Spencer, J. and Flin, R. (1993) *The Evidence of Children: The Law and the Psychology*, 2nd edition. London, Blackstone.

Smith, M. and Grocke, M. (1995) *Normal Family Sexuality and Sexual Knowledge in Children*. Royal College of Psychiatrists, Gorkill Press.

Stubbs, P. (1989) Developing anti-racist practice: problems and possibilities, in Blagg, H., Hughes, J., and Wattam, C. (eds) *Child Sexual Abuse: Listening, Hearing and Validating the Experiences of Children*. Chichester, Wiley.

Thoburn, J., Lewis, A. and Shemmings, D. (1995) *Paternalism or Partnership? Family Involvement in the Child Protection Process*. London, HMSO.

Thorpe, D. and Bilson, A. (1998) From protection to concern: child protection careers without apologies. *Children and Society*, **12**(5): 373–386.

Wattam, C. (1989) Investigating child sexual abuse: a matter of relevance, in Blagg, H., Hughes, J. and Wattam, C. (eds) *Child Sexual Abuse: Listening, Hearing and Validating the Experiences of Children*. Chichester, Wiley.

Wattam, C. (1992) *Making a Case in Child Protection*. London, Wiley.

Wattam, C. (1997) Is the criminalization of child harm and injury in the interests of children? *Children and Society*, **11**: 97–107.

Wattam, C. and Woodward, C. (1996) And do I abuse my children? . . . No, in *Childhood Matters: The Report of the National Commission of Inquiry into the Prevention of Child Abuse. Vol. 2: Background Papers*. London, The Stationery Office.

Wells, J. (1989) Powerplays: Considerations in communicating with children, in Blagg, H., Hughes, J. and Wattam, C. (eds) *Child Sexual Abuse: Listening, Hearing and Validating the Experiences of Children*. Chichester, Wiley.

1

JUSTICE FOR CHILDREN

Carole Smith and Karen Woodhead

It is evident that any discussion about justice and, more particularly, justice for children who have been sexually abused, is fraught with difficulty. It is problematic for three central reasons. First, there is arguably a good deal of confusion about how we understand both the concept and operation of justice itself: where are the parameters of justice and what must be done, how must it be done, and what must be achieved to demonstrate its effective accomplishment? Second: what is the relationship between justice for children and their needs, interests and welfare? There is widespread concern, for example, that the criminal justice system, geared as it is to the adult world of legalistic arrangements for deciding upon guilt or innocence, is emotionally harmful to children who enter its domain. It is also argued that for those sexually abused children who endure the distress and confusion of giving testimony, and for those many more who are never heard, the criminal justice system actually fails to deliver justice (see, for example, Plotnikoff and Woolfson, 1995; Westcott, 1995; Mitchell, 1997; Westcott and Jones, 1997). Additionally, it is contended, even family proceedings under the Children Act 1989, with their emphasis on children's welfare and an inquisitorial rather than adversarial process, cannot but revert to a narrowly defined contest between interested adults and their respective lawyers. A crucial concern with identifying 'significant harm' in the context of rights and responsibilities, must necessarily neglect the subtleties and complexities of children's socio-emotional experience and fail to engage adequately with their broad-ranging therapeutic and welfare needs (Audit Commission, 1994; DoH, 1995a; Parton, 1997). It is thus suggested that children's welfare becomes invisible as the law and its operations inevitably focus upon adult conceptions of justice, which concentrate upon the right to a fair contest, proof of facts (on the balance of probability) and the apportionment of responsibility (King and Trowell, 1992; King and Piper, 1995). Third, in any discussion about children's rights and welfare it is impossible to avoid a long-running debate about how children's perceived vulnerability and their relative immaturity may be accommodated while, at the same time, according them those rights which are routinely enjoyed by adults (see Veerman, 1992; Franklin, 1995; Franklin & Franklin, 1996; Fox-Harding, 1997; Smith, 1997a for a detailed discussion of this area). Such accommodation usually takes the form of adult discretion in allowing children to exercise their rights, conditional upon an assessment of their age and understanding. In commenting upon the child's right to justice in the context of the criminal justice system, Westcott and Jones (1997, p. 172) suggest that:

> 'What *is* apparent is the need for more open and honest debate about what 'justice for children' is actually taken to mean by the different actors involved in child protection and criminal justice.' (Original emphasis)

This is a view with which we must agree, given the complexities of attending to children's rights and best interests to which we have briefly referred. We would argue, however, that justice in a limited legalistic sense is informed by substance, process and outcome. Substantive justice depends upon a respect for legal rights as these are identified in statute law and evolved through common law. The administration of justice requires that its process is experienced as enabling appropriate participation and fair treatment. This, in its turn, necessitates an understanding of the process, an appreciation of the individual's role within it, the opportunity to exercise choice insofar as this does not conflict with the public interest and the ability to have an effective voice in 'getting justice done'. Achieving a just outcome requires, at its most basic, that wrongdoing is acknowledged, that the wrongdoers are identified and made to face the consequences of their actions and that reparation is made to society and to the person who has suffered harm. These characteristics of justice are equally relevant whether individuals are caught up in the procedural machinery of child protection enquiries (DoH 1991a), legal intervention in family proceedings under the Children Act 1989, or the criminal justice system.

For children, however, achieving justice is a particularly equivocal business which cannot but reflect the ambiguous and contradictory ways in which childhood is understood and children are treated in different situations. Where children are the subjects of professional and judicial activity which is primarily concerned with their welfare needs, it is arguable that their rights are eroded by presumptions about their lack of cognitive, emotional and experiential competence to make decisions in their own best interests (see, for example, Freeman, 1992a; Dickenson and Jones, 1995; Lyon and Parton, 1995; Roche, 1996; Smith, 1997a). Adults, having achieved maturity, are prone to think that they have a better understanding of children's best interests than children themselves. However, when children as victims of sexual abuse encounter the criminal justice system, the relationship between rights and welfare is argued in rather different ways. It is suggested, first, that the criminal justice system does not differentiate *sufficiently* between children and adults in terms of enabling children to participate effectively in achieving justice. Second, because children's immaturity relative to adults is *not* adequately recognised and accommodated, justice will be frustrated. Third, in failing to respond to the particular vulnerability of sexually abused children, the criminal justice system may cause distress and confusion and, at its worst, perpetuate a sense of continuing abuse. The arguments and dilemmas may be summarised thus:

> 'From police and social services staff, trained and embedded in child protection experience and values, protecting children was seen as an essential and irreducible priority. For those in the criminal justice system, it was an important element within a broader picture. The higher priorities lay elsewhere. The aim in care proceedings must be to *"protect the interests of children"*; in criminal proceeding that aim must be to *"respect their interests and protect the interest of defendants"*.' (DoH 1995b, 2.4; original emphasis)

Recent policy, legislation and case law have at least acknowledged the issue of justice for children. The question which now demands attention is: how far have such developments achieved an effective response to children's rights and welfare needs in such a way that children themselves might experience justice as being done? The following discussion will refer to children, while recognising that *particular* groups of children are likely to encounter additional difficulties in achieving justice, as will some especially vulnerable adults.

THE CHILD'S RIGHT TO BE HEARD

The United Nations Convention on the Rights of the Child

The UN Convention on the Rights of the Child, to which the UK became a signatory in December 1991, had by June 1996 attracted ratification by 174 countries, representing 'a level of commitment unprecedented in the history of the UN' (CRO, 1995, p. 12). The significance of the Convention is that, following ratification by 20 States, it assumes the status of international law for the signatories concerned (see CRDU, 1994; Childright, 1995; CRO, 1995; Jenkins, 1995 for detailed discussion of the Convention and its implementation in the UK). A wide range of rights are enunciated by the Convention, but for our purposes the most significant are the right to protection from all forms of physical or mental violence, exploitation and abuse (Article 19); the imperative that in all actions concerning children by any State agency, including social welfare institutions, courts, administrative or legislative bodies, the child's best interests shall be a primary consideration (Article 3); and the child's right to be heard (Articles 9(2) and 12). Clearly, listening to children must be accompanied by a willingness to hear and to respond, if children are to experience justice as we have described it. Article 12 of the Convention states:

1. States Parties shall assure to the child who is capable of forming his or her own views the right to express those views freely in all matters affecting the child, the view of the child being given due weight in accordance with the age and maturity of the child.
2. For this purpose, the child shall in particular be provided the opportunity to be heard in any judicial and administrative proceedings affecting the child, either directly, or through a representative or an appropriate body, in a manner consistent with the rules of national law.

More recently, Article 1.2 of the European Convention on the Exercise of Children's Rights has reinforced the message that a child's right to be heard necessitates information and participation in legal proceedings:

> 'The object of the present convention is, in the interests of children, to protect their rights, to grant them procedural rights and to facilitate the exercise of these rights by ensuring that children are, themselves or through other persons or bodies, informed and allowed to participate in proceedings affecting them before a judicial authority.' (Representing Children, 1995, p. 10)

Such rights should not be understood simply as formal imperatives which require compliance. Essentially they reflect an awareness of children as thinking, experiencing subjects who are capable of forming a view about their own best interests (Veerman, 1992; Freeman, 1993). Sir Thomas Bingham, speaking in the English Court of Appeal,[1]* makes a similar point about the Children Act 1989. He asserts that the purposes of the Act are not solely legislative, but are intended to convey a policy declaration about the attitudes which should direct courts and other agencies in dealing with children, including an emphasis on enabling children's views to be communicated and explained through independent representation.

The Children Act 1989: Enabling Children to be Heard?

The Children Act 1989 was hailed as a 'Charter for Children' (DoH, 1993, p. 3) and, together with the Children (Scotland) Act 1995, has generally been

---

* Cases are listed on p. 33.

interpreted as a vehicle for children's empowerment (Bainham, 1990; Hodgeson, 1990; Freeman, 1992b; Hough, 1995). The Children Act 1989, for example, requires local authorities to ascertain the wishes and feelings of children whom they are 'looking after', or proposing to look after, and to give them 'due consideration' having regard to the child's age and understanding, (ss. 22(4) and (5)). Similarly, in considering whether to make, vary or discharge an order under s. 8 or Part IV (care and supervision) of the Act, a court must have regard to the ascertainable wishes and feelings of the child as one element of the 'welfare checklist' under s. 1. Children may initiate legal action by seeking the discharge of an emergency protection order (s. 45(8)(a)), applying for a contact order in care proceedings (s. 34(2)), requesting that a care order should be discharged (s. 39(1)) and applying for leave to make a section 8 application in relation to where they should live and with whom they should have contact (s. 10(2)(b)).

For many children who are subject to legal proceedings under the Act, the UN Convention's insistence that their views should be represented in court will be met by the provision of a *guardian ad litem*. Independent representation of children by *guardians ad litem* has been available since 1984 as a result of Regulations made under the Children Act 1975. However, the Children Act 1989 introduces a *presumption* that a guardian will be appointed unless the court is satisfied that it is not necessary to do so in order to safeguard the child's interests (s. 41). The *guardian ad litem's* role is enhanced in a wide range of specified proceedings (s. 41(6)) and that person is charged with playing a proactive role in advising the courts on case management and other relevant matters (DoH 1991b, 1992). Indeed, the *guardian ad litem* has such an influential role that if a court departs from a guardian's recommendations it must clearly express the reasons for doing so.[2] Additionally, where a guardian and child disagree about the latter's best interests and the child is considered to be capable of instructing a solicitor, the child may give instructions direct and the guardian may seek separate legal representation. Rule 9 of the Family Proceedings Rules 1991 governs arrangements for a child to begin or defend proceedings, or to be joined as a party in existing proceedings, without a *guardian ad litem* or 'next friend', and applies to those situations where a child wishes to remove a *guardian ad litem* who has already been appointed (see Hamilton, 1995, for a fuller explanation of these procedures).

/ In family proceedings it is accepted that a court requires as much information about the child and his or her circumstances as possible, in order to make a judgement based on the paramountcy of the child's welfare. Justice for children in this context may therefore require that their story is told for them where they are unable to tell it themselves. We should note two developments which enable the court to gain as complete a picture as possible about the child and the issues which have attracted legal intervention. First, the severely limited admissibility of hearsay evidence in criminal proceedings is completely abrogated in civil proceedings relating to the upbringing, maintenance or welfare of children (Children Act, s. 96 and Children (Admissibility of Hearsay Evidence) Order 1993). This means that a court may hear evidence about something which was said, documented or taped outside of the court and which is reported by a witness who has knowledge of such information, rather than the person who was directly responsible for the statement or other recording. Second, recent case law has clarified the circumstances in which usually privileged information may or must be disclosed to parties in family proceedings. Thus, it is now well established that when the court grants leave for documents to be disclosed to an expert, it also has power to direct that the resulting report must be disclosed to the court and all the parties.[3] Further clarification is now available about when it is acceptable for a *guardian ad litem,* a social worker or the court to pass on information, most usually to the police, which has been disclosed by a parent and which bears upon the issue of 'significant harm' and the child's welfare.[4] The issue of disclosure is complicated but further clarification can be gleaned from McEwan (1995), Brasse, (1996) and the Children Act Advisory Committee (1997).

THE CRIMINAL JUSTICE SYSTEM

Children who have been abused may be the only source of evidence against an alleged perpetrator. This is likely to be particularly so in situations involving sexual abuse where secrecy and power are central to the abusive regime (Wells, 1989; Wattam, 1991; National Commission of Inquiry into the Prevention of Child Abuse, 1996; Wade and Westcott, 1997). Concern was beginning to surface in the 1980s about the appropriateness of arrangements for hearing children's evidence in criminal proceedings, both with regard to children's effectiveness as credible witnesses and the emotional consequences of their involvement in the criminal justice system (Spencer, 1987; Lawrence, 1988). A limited response to these concerns can be found in the Criminal Justice Act 1988 which allows children to give their evidence via a live television link to the courtroom and administrative measures designed to achieve speedy progress for child abuse cases (Mitchell, 1997).

The Pigot Committee Report (Pigot, 1989) provided the opportunity for changes in policy and legislation through a series of recommendations which sought to accommodate both the requirements of the criminal justice system and the interests of child witnesses. The Committee supported the use of videotaped interviews with children, conducted jointly by a police officer and social worker and made as soon as possible following an allegation of abuse, which could then be used in court as the child's evidence in chief. | It further recommended that, in criminal proceedings, cross-examination of child witnesses should also be videotaped, thus protecting a child from any contact with the court and its 'criminal environment'. Initial interviews with children would have the dual purpose of investigating allegations and recording evidence. Currently, then, there exist a number of measures which are designed to improve the adequacy of children's evidence and to protect them from those potentially distressing requirements of the criminal justice system which are routinely imposed upon adults. The Criminal Justice Act 1991 extends the use of the live television link for children up to 17 years old who are appearing as witnesses in cases of sexual assault. Following the Pigot Committee's recommendations, it allows initial statements to be videotaped and, with the trial judge's permission, introduced in Crown and Youth courts as the child's evidence in chief. The *Memorandum of Good Practice* (Home Office DoH, 1992) provides guidance for those conducting videotaped interviews with the aim of ensuring sensitive investigation and evidential acceptability. In cases of alleged sexual or violent offences which involve child witnesses, the Director of Public Prosecutions can issue a notice of transfer which directs the case to the Crown Court for trial without first requiring committal proceedings in the magistrates' court (s. 32A CJA 1988 as amended by CJA 1991). This provision thus avoids the possibility of a child having to face cross-examination in two sets of proceedings and should also have the effect of expediting trial. Additionally, courts are required to: 'have regard to the desirability of avoiding prejudice to the welfare of any relevant child witness that may be occasioned by unnecessary delay in bringing the case to trial' (CJA 1991, Schedule 5(7))

This provision, of course, echoes the no-delay principle in s. 1(2) of the Children Act 1989. Prior to recent legislation, case law had established the convention that younger children were generally incompetent to give evidence in criminal proceedings. Children considered too young to take the oath were therefore subjected to a 'competency test', during which a judge attempted to determine a child's understanding of the truth. Not only did this leave the assessment of a child's competence at the mercy of judicial discretion, but it necessarily raised a doubt about the child's veracity. The Criminal Justice Act 1991 has changed all that. Now, children under 14 years old give unsworn evidence and all children are *presumed* to be competent witnesses unless they are proved to be otherwise, (s. 52, CJA 1991). In recent cases[5] where a defendant has appealed on the basis that very young children are incompetent, the courts have found that age alone is not sufficient proof of incompetence. The test in *R v. Hampshire* [1996] QB 1 has been followed in determining that a child is capable of giving intelligible testimony if he or she is able to understand questions and to answer them in a manner which is coherent and comprehensible (Childright, 1998). A child's right to give testimony is now comparable to that of an adult, a position which is further emphasised by the Criminal Justice and Public Order Act 1994. (The Children's Legal Centre (CLC, 1992, 1994) has produced excellent guides on law and practice in relation to child sexual abuse and the criminal justice system.)

THE LEGAL FRAMEWORK: JUSTICE FOR CHILDREN?

Recent legislation and case law arguably demonstrate a laudable intention to promote justice for children. Legislative implementation, however, has attracted considerable criticism and demands for more radical reform. Concern has been expressed for a number of reasons, some of which relate to administrative and organisational shortcomings and some of which arise from the inherently adversarial nature of the justice system. All in all, it is contended that the legal framework continues to frustrate the UN Convention's imperative that children should have an effective opportunity to be heard and fails to recognise adequately their welfare needs.

Delay

Despite reference to minimising delay in both the Children Act 1989 and the Criminal Justice Act 1991, this continues to be a source of concern. The Children Act Advisory Committee (1994/95) notes that the average disposal time for public law Children Act cases has persistently increased since implementation of the Act. In her investigation, Dame Margaret Booth (Booth, 1996) identifies a number of significant factors which contribute to delay, including lack of adequate resources, poor administration, lax procedures for transferring cases from the family proceedings court, listing problems, lengthy hearings, the instruction of experts and, most fundamentally, the lack of firm case management in which magistrates, clerks, *guardians ad litem* and the judiciary all play a crucial role. The criminal justice system has attracted similar attention. Davies *et al.* (1995) identified an improvement over Davies and Noon's (1991) findings regarding the time taken from committal to trial. The Crown Prosecution Service Inspectorate (CPSI, 1998) similarly points to a general improvement in the progress of child witness cases. However, although a 'fast track' procedure exists for police and the Crown Prosecution Service to identify and expedite child witness cases, this is not uniformly established. In its recent study, the Crown Prosecution Service Inspectorate (CPSI, 1998) found that the police identified only 57.88% of child witness cases which could benefit from special arrangements, compared to 66% in Plotnikoff and Woolfson's (1995) research. It is argued with some force that, for children particularly, the passage of time exacerbates uncertainty and anxiety and adversely affects the detail and quality of their evidence when it is finally heard (Flin *et al.*, 1993). Westcott and Jones (1997) have launched a trenchant attack on the lack of urgency in tackling delay, suggesting that this represents 'yet another damning indictment of policy and practice in this area' (p. 173).

Supporting Children

Cumulative research suggests that children often experience child protection investigations as confusing, distressing and disempowering, whether such intervention is conducted under the protective mantle of the Children Act 1989 or is integral to the functioning of the criminal justice system (Roberts *et al.*, 1993; Farmer, 1993; Roberts and Taylor, 1993; Farmer and Owen, 1995; Butler and Williamson, 1994; Wade and Westcott, 1997). In specified proceedings under the Children Act, *guardians ad litem* can provide support, guidance and advocacy throughout the legal process. Plotnikoff and Woolfson (1995) suggest that child witnesses might benefit from similar arrangements in criminal courts. However, this much admired system of independent representation is itself in danger of erosion as a consequence of growing curbs on legal aid (Cooper, 1997; Timms, 1998). The criminal justice system presents particular difficulties for children which could be ameliorated by appropriate support. Even at the initial stage of an investigative interview, evidential requirements cannot but cause a degree of discomfort and difficulty for children who are struggling to convey the substance and detail of their abusive experience. Clearly an interviewer can do much to support children in this situation, but Davies *et al.* (1995) identified a tendency to rush children into questioning without allowing them time to tell their story in a 'free narrative' form, to ask closed questions and to finish the interview without properly addressing the child's understanding of its purpose and what to expect next. Advantage may be taken of the *Memorandum's* (Home Office DoH, 1992) recommendation that a supportive adult can accompany a distressed or very young child during the initial interview(s). It is also recognised that a child giving evidence via a television link should receive appropriate support. Unfortunately, however, a practice direction from the Deputy Chief Justice (1991) states that the child's supporter should ordinarily be a court usher. Only in exceptional circumstances will judicial discretion allow the presence of an alternative supporter and it is clear that practice varies enormously between Crown Courts (CPSI, 1998).

As might be expected, children generally have only a limited understanding of the criminal justice system (Aldridge, 1997). Provision of information, familiarisation with the legal process and physical environment of the court,

and the emotional support which is available from a consistent adult supporter, have been partially met by NSPCC and Victim Support initiatives (CLC,
1992; Mitchell, 1997; Aldridge, 1997). Unlike the *guardian ad litem* arrangements in family proceedings, support for child witnesses depends on individual initiatives, resulting in patchy implementation and in some children
receiving no help at all (Plotnikoff and Woolfson, 1995; Davies *et al.*, 1995).

DELIVERING JUSTICE

It is frequently argued that a child's ability to give a coherent account of his or
her views or experiences is impeded by obstacles which are embedded in the
Anglo-American system for delivering justice. This system is characterised by
a contest between opposing parties in which procedural and evidential rules
are designed to ensure 'fair play' and to establish the truth of the matter in
question according to the relevant burden of proof. Critics assert that this
adversarial approach misses the subtleties and complexities of children's
needs and undermines their participation in the process of accomplishing
justice. The criminal justice system has attracted much critical comment in this
context. Frequently heated criticism points to a lack of regard for the welfare
needs of child witnesses who are caught up in the adult-centred administration of criminal justice. Thus, there appears to be widespread confusion and
local difficulty about arranging therapy for sexually abused children who may
subsequently give evidence in a criminal trial. Withholding therapy antici-
pates, and attempts to pre-empt, a claim by the defence that the child's evidence has been 'contaminated' and cannot constitute a reliable account. The
Crown Prosecution Service, however, has made it clear that there is *no* pro-
hibition on responding to a child's need for therapeutic help, provided that
the local CPS is informed and prosecuting counsel is aware of the arrangements (see CPSI, 1998, 7.25 and 7.26). Social workers and others who are
concerned about the need for therapeutic intervention pending a criminal trial
may thus refer to clear policy if local difficulties arise.

Concern has been expressed that any deviation from guidance in the
Memorandum of Good Practice may prompt the defence to request a ruling of
inadmissibility in respect of videotaped evidence. The introduction of the
Memorandum makes it clear that lack of strict compliance is not an automatic
ground for inadmissibility, and judicial discretion in this matter is governed
by the interests of justice. Further clarification is provided in *G v. Director of
Public Prosecutions*[6] where the prosecution's intention to introduce videotaped interviews with two young children was challenged by the defence.
While the court found that the *Memorandum* should be followed, videotaped
interviews would not be excluded only because of a failure to comply with
the guidance.

It has been noted, with some outrage, that defence barristers attempt to discredit a child's evidence by intimidation, accusations of falsehood and aggressive questioning (Westcott, 1995). The use of language and questions which are inappropriate to a child's age and understanding has also fuelled criticism of the police, defence barristers and the judiciary. Commentators assert that this adversarial approach to child witnesses is oppressive and reminiscent of the power differential inherent in their experiences of abuse. While we appreciate the protective intentions behind this critique, there is evidence to suggest that the case may be overstated. Davies *et al.* (1995) observed 150 children giving evidence in criminal proceedings. Although half of the defence barristers were judged to be unsupportive of child witnesses compared to none of the prosecution barristers, and 17% of the former used age-inappropriate language, only 34% of children were rated as being 'very unhappy' during cross-examination. Despite the discomfort felt by some children, the vast majority were judged to have given effective testimony throughout their evidence insofar as they spoke clearly and gave a detailed, consistent account. Although these findings do not obviate the importance of improving practice, it appears that most children are able to give an effective account and suffer discomfort, rather than serious trauma, while they are giving evidence.

Defence lawyers may attempt to use a further avenue for discrediting the evidence of child witnesses and thus frustrating their right to be heard. This involves making a case for the disclosure of files which are held by Social Services in anticipation of identifying information which will cast doubt upon a child's truthfulness and reliability. While recognising that the judiciary must have discretion to order disclosure in the interests of justice, the courts have stamped firmly upon defence counsels' attempts to go on 'fishing expeditions' for discrediting information. As Beldam LJ asserted in the Court of Appeal[7]:

> 'These cases make it clear that it is not proper to issue a witness summons for disclosure of a document or documents, still less for the whole contents of a file or files for the speculative purposes that material may come to light which could discredit a complainant. In the present case there is no evidence that the appellants ever considered whether there were reasonable grounds for the application.' (p. 49)

As will be evident, many critics of the criminal justice system focus upon an apparent conflict between the welfare needs of sexually abused children and the requirements of justice within an adversarial system. They point to a failure to implement the Pigot Committee's recommendation (Pigot, 1989) that cross-examination of child witnesses should also be videotaped, thus removing the need for a child to attend court and clearing away any contention that subsequent therapy may 'contaminate' a child's evidence.

Combined with an entrenched reliance upon *oral* evidence, this failure places children at the mercy of adversarial practices and exposes them to hostile cross-examination by the defence. This situation may be compared with the emphasis on children's welfare found in proceedings under the Children Act 1989. In Re P,[8] which concerned care proceedings following allegations of sexual abuse, the judge refused to order that a child of 12 years old should give oral evidence and be cross-examined. Her judgement was upheld by the Court of Appeal:

> 'Nevertheless, courts are increasingly aware of the further grave damage which can be done to a child who has been sexually abused, or indeed a child who has not been sexually abused but for some reason has spoken of being sexually abused (and such a child may well also have been damaged), if she or he is subjected to the trauma of questioning by a stranger whose task is to attack her or his truthfulness in this supremely sensitive area. I would expect that in most cases where the child, whether or not a family member, is of N's age or younger, the court would favour the absence of oral evidence even though the concomitant were to be the weakening, or sometimes perhaps the fatal weakening, of the evidence against the adult.' (p. 454)

This welfarist approach has been transposed to criminal proceedings by way of suggesting that a child's welfare must be paramount even if this means that a suspected abuser avoids prosecution (Hoyal, 1995). However, it must be acknowledged that a concentration upon protecting vulnerable children may, despite its virtuous intentions, *also* frustrate their right to be heard. As we have noted, children's rights to privacy under Article 16 of the UN Convention and their rights to express their views and to intervene in s. 8 applications, may all be undermined by adults' unwillingness to concede children's strengths and ability to make decisions in their own best interests (CRDU 1994; Lyon and Parton, 1995; Davies *et al.*, 1996; Smith, 1997a). While much concern is expressed about child witnesses having to attend a criminal court, equivalent concern has been voiced about excluding children from family proceedings courts (CAAC, 1994/95, 1997). There is some uncertainty in individual cases about whether care proceedings should be heard in advance of criminal proceedings against the child's parent(s). The Court of Appeal has made it clear, however, that children's welfare should be prioritised and that care proceedings should be completed as quickly as possible unless particular circumstances warrant waiting for the conclusion of a criminal trial.[9]

CONCLUSION: MAKING SENSE OF IT ALL

Piecemeal tinkering with our current arrangements for delivering justice is insufficient for those who argue that an adversarial system must necessarily compromise an effective response to children's needs, both in family and criminal proceedings. They point to the advantages of a completely different model most usually practised in Europe. Thus King and Piper (1995) comment favourably upon the French and other European legal frameworks for working with and supporting families and children. The essentially inquisitorial rather than adversarial approach to justice allows a broad-ranging and flexible quest for relevant information; the supportive, ongoing and reviewing role of specialist children's judges transforms 'legal intervention' into a *process* of enquiry and response rather than a once-and-for-all contest between opposing parties; the continuity and oversight provided by children's judges ensures ongoing and responsive familiarity with families such that intervention can be rapid, flexible and developmental; children's welfare is the subject of continuous judicial review in contrast to episodic and heavy-handed intervention (see also Cooper *et al.*, 1995; Hetherington *et al.*, 1997). In the context of the criminal justice system, Spencer (1997) similarly identifies the inquisitorial characteristics of European models. He refers to arrangements in France and Holland for records of pre-trial police and judicial interviews with witnesses and defendants to be maintained in a dossier which is admissible as evidence. Whether a child witness has to face the defendant or give evidence during a criminal trial is a matter for judicial discretion and, in any event, aggressive cross-examination is avoided by the convention that witnesses are questioned by the judge and not by prosecution or defence lawyers. Spencer also cites Norway, Israel, New Zealand and Australia as allowing child witnesses in sexual abuse cases to give the whole of their evidence prior to trial. He concludes:

> 'In the broadest terms, it looks as if the inquisitorial and the accusatorial (adversarial) systems are converging on one aspect of the law relating to children's evidence. This is the necessity of providing for at least some child witnesses, something on the lines of the Pigot scheme, under which all the child's evidence is taken ahead of trial, the defence are given at that stage a chance to put their questions, and the child thereafter takes no further part in the proceedings.' (p. 103)

It is important to note three points about the current passion for seeking solutions in alternative models of justice. First, we have to concede that there is not a perfect solution. Reviews of European family justice systems acknowledge their strengths and weaknesses (Cooper *et al.*, 1995; Hetherington *et al.* 1997). The desirability of ongoing judicial involvement and review in child care cases has already gone through the mill of exhaustive debate in this country (Review of Child Care Law, 1985; Brasse, 1995a, 1995b; Hayes, 1996; Smith 1997b, 1997c). Similarly, it is worth considering whether an adversarial system of criminal justice does, overall, protect the interests of individuals such that anyone anticipating involvement, as witness or defendant, would want justice to be administered in this way (Spencer, 1997). Second, we think there is evidence from legislation and case law, governing both family and criminal proceedings, which indicates a responsiveness to children's welfare needs. But, and this is a big but, crucial to this accommodation must be the implementation of the Pigot Committee's recommendation (Pigot, 1989) that *the whole* of a child's evidence should be given before trial. Such an arrangement would, at a stroke, obviate many existing difficulties such as the delay between an allegation of abuse and trial, the patchy availability of support over a long period, the length of time child witnesses have to wait in court before giving evidence, and all the anxiety and uncertainty which is associated with the process of delivering justice as it is currently managed (National Commission of Inquiry into the Prevention of Child Abuse, 1996; Utting, 1997, Mitchell, 1997). Similarly, an adversarial system can accommodate initiatives that are designed to support child witnesses and to help them give effective evidence, and also incorporate closer team work between the prosecution service, police and welfare professionals. Children's Advocacy Centres in the United States exemplify how this might be achieved (Siddall, 1997; Hughes, 1997).

Our third point concerns a crucial aspect of enabling children to be heard, which depends less on looking to alternative systems for administering justice and more on examining how adults can listen to children. In the midst of critical attention to deficiencies in the criminal justice system few commentators pay attention to engaging with children's own wishes about what they want to happen. An interest in *researching* children's experiences of professional intervention tends to concentrate on their welfare needs, rather than focus upon their rights and how children might be empowered to exercise them. For example, there appears to be little discussion about enabling children to choose between the alternatives for giving their evidence, via video-recorded evidence in chief, live-link television arrangements, or in the courtroom (CLC 1992; CPSI, 1998) or of the importance of gaining children's consent to videotaped interviews (Home Office/DoH, 1992, para. 2.29; O'Neill, 1997). Similarly, the Crown Prosecution Service Inspectorate (CPSI, 1998) comments critically upon the failure of police to provide the CPS with information about the wishes of the child, family or carer which should inform decisions about prosecution (paras 7.18 and 7.19). Adequate explanations, appropriate information, facilitating understanding and enabling children to participate effectively in the process of administering justice depends not only on systems but on adults who intervene in children's lives. Tunnel vision, which sees only vulnerable children and their need for protection, may obscure this obvious point in both family and criminal interventions.

There has clearly been much activity aimed at improving justice for children. It may be the case that our adversarial system of justice cannot 'stretch' sufficiently to satisfy its critics. However, we think there is some way to go before we can reach this conclusion. In the meantime, ten years after the Cleveland crisis, it is apparent that much of the debate about justice for sexually abused children still resonates with the child, not as a person but as an 'object of concern' (Butler-Sloss, 1988). This will continue to be a barrier to justice no matter whether an adversarial or inquisitorial system governs family and criminal proceedings. Children are unlikely to be heard while adults are arguing vociferously above their heads about how best to protect their welfare.

CASES

1. *Re S (A Minor)* (Independent Representation) [1993] 2 FLR 440 CA.
2. *S v. Oxfordshire County Council* [1993] 1 FLR 452 FD.
3. *Oxfordshire County Council v. M* [1994] 1 FLR 175 CA.
4. *Cleveland County Council v. F* [1995] 2 All ER 236 FD; *Oxfordshire County Council v. P* [1995] 2 All ER 225 FD; *Re EC* (Disclosure of Material) [1996] 2 FLR 725.
5. *R v. Hampshire* [1996] QB1; *Director of Public Prosecutions v. M* [1997] 2 FLR 804.
6. *G v. Director of Public Prosecutions* [1997] 2 FLR 810.
7. *Re a Solicitor* (Wasted Costs Order) [1996] 1 FLR 40.
8. *Re P* (Witness Summons) [1997] 2 FLR 447; see also, *R v. Highbury Corner Magistrates Court* ex parte D [1997] 1FLR 683 DC, where it was found that a magistrate acted prematurely in refusing to issue a witness summons for a 9-year-old boy to give evidence in assault proceedings. The balancing act in deciding whether harm to the defendant should be outweighed by a child's interests should be performed by the trial court when the issue arises for determination.
9. *Re TB (minors)* (Care Proceedings: Criminal Trial) [1996] 1FCR 101CA.

REFERENCES

Aldridge, J. (1997) Next steps after the *Memorandum:* preparing children for court, in Westcott, H. and Jones, J. (eds) *Perspectives on the Memorandum.* Aldershot, Arena, pp. 125–140.

Audit Commission (1994) *Seen But Not Heard: Co-ordinating Community Child Health and Social Services for Children in Need.* London, HMSO.

Bainham, A. (1990) The Children Act 1989: adolescents' and children's rights. *Family Law Journal,* 20: 311–314.

Booth, M. (1996) *Avoiding Delay in Children Act Cases.* London, Lord Chancellor's Department.

Brasse, G. (1995a) After the care order: into forbidden territory, Part I. *Family Law,* January: 31–33.

Brasse, G. (1995b) After the care order: into forbidden territory, Part II. *Family Law,* February: 75–77.

Brasse, G. (1996) The confidentiality of a child's instructions. *Family Law,* December: 733–735.

Butler, I. and Williamson, H. (1994) *Children Speak Out: Children, Trauma and Social Work.* London, Longman.

Butler-Sloss, E. (1988) *Report of the Inquiry into Child Abuse in Cleveland 1987*. London, HMSO.

Children Act Advisory Committee (1994/95) *Annual Report*. London, Lord Chancellor's Department.

Children Act Advisory Committee (1997) *Final Report*. London, Lord Chancellor's Department.

Childright (1995) *UN Committee Criticises UK Rights of Child Report, No. 114*. March: 3–5.

Childright (1998) *Legal Monitor*, January/February, No. 143: 21.

CLC (1992) *A Guide to the Law: Child Sexual Abuse*. London, Children's Legal Centre.

CLC (1994) *Supporting the Child Witness, Information Sheet No. 169*. London, Children's Legal Centre.

CPSI (1998) *The Inspectorate's Report on Cases Involving Child Witnesses*. London, Crown Prosecution Service Inspectorate.

CRDU (1994) *UK Agenda for Children*. London, Children's Rights Development Unit.

CRO (1995) *Making the Convention Work for Children*. London, Children's Rights Office.

Cooper, A., Hetherington, R., Baistow, K., Pitts, J. and Spriggs, A. (1995) *Positive Child Protection: A View from Abroad*. Lyme Regis, Russell House.

Cooper S (1997) Whither children's representation? *Childright*, November, No. 141: 17–18.

Davies, G.H. and Noon, E. (1991) *An Evaluation of the Live Link for Child Witnesses*. London, Home Office.

Davies, G., Wilson, C., Mitchell, R. and Milsom, J. (1995) *Videotaping Children's Evidence: An Evaluation*. London, Home Office.

Davies, M. *et al.* (1996) Partnership from the child's perspective, in Platt, D. and Shemmings, D. (eds) *Making Enquiries into Alleged Child Abuse and Neglect*. Brighton, Pennant, pp. 99–114.

Deputy Chief Justice (1991) *Live TV Link Cases. Persons to Accompany the Child in the Video Room: Guidelines*. 21 October.

Dickenson, D. and Jones, D. (1995) True wishes: the philosophy and developmental psychology of children's informed consent. *Philosophy, Psychiatry and Psychology*, 2(4): 287–303.

DoH, (1991a) *Working Together under the Children Act 1989*. London, HMSO.

DoH, (1991b) *The Children Act 1989. Guidance and Regulations*, Vol. 7. *Guardians ad Litem and other Court-Related Issues*. London, HMSO.

DoH, (1992) *Manual of Practice Guidance for Guardians ad Litem and Reporting Officers*. London, HMSO.

DoH, (1993) *Children Act Report*. London, HMSO.

DoH, (1995a) *Child Protection: Messages from Research*. London, HMSO.

DoH, (1995b) *The Child, the Court and the Video*. London, Social Services Inspectorate.

Farmer, E. (1993) The impact of child protection interventions: the experiences of parents and children, in Waterhouse, L. (ed.) *Child Abuse and Child Abusers: Protection and Prevention*. London, Jessica Kingsley.

Farmer, E. and Owen, M. (1995) *Child Protection Practice: Private Risks and Public Remedies*. London, HMSO.

Flin, R., Bull, R., Boon, J. and Knox, A. (1993) Child witnesses in Scottish criminal trials. *International Review of Victimology*, 2: 319–339.

Fox-Harding, L. (1997) *Perspectives in Child Care Policy*. London, Longman.

Franklin, B. (1995) *The Handbook of Children's Rights*. London, Routledge.

Franklin, A. and Franklin, B. (1996) Growing pains: the developing children's rights movement in the UK, in Pilcher, J. and Wagg, S. (eds) *Thatcher's Children*. London, Falmer Press, pp. 94–113.

Freeman, M. (1992a) Removing rights from adolescents. *Adoption and Fostering*, 17(1): 14–20.

Freeman, M. (1992b) In the child's best interests? Reading the Children Act critically. *Current Legal Problems*, 45(1): 173–211.

Freeman, M. (1993) Laws, conventions and rights. *Children and Society*, 7(1): 37–48.

Hamilton, I.M. (1995) Representation of children in private law proceedings under the Children Act 1989. *Representing Children*, 8(3): 32–37.

Hayes, M. (1996) The proper role of the courts in child care cases. *Child and Family Law Quarterly*, 8(3): 201–215.

Hetherington, R., Cooper, A., Smith, P. and Wilford, G. (1997) *Protecting Children: Message from Europe*. Lyme Regis, Russell House.

Hill, M. and Tisdall, K. (1997) *Children and Society*. London, Longman.

Hodgeson, D. (1990) Power to the child. *Social Work Today*, 12 July.

Home Office/DoH (1992) *Memorandum of Good Practice on Video Recorded Interviews with Child Witnesses for Criminal Proceedings*. London, HMSO.

Hough, J. (1995) Why isn't it the Children's Act, in Dalrymple, J. and Hough, J. (eds) *Having a Voice: An Exploration of Children's Rights and Advocacy*. Birmingham, Venture Press, pp. 53–74.

Hoyal, J. (1995) In practice: the child, the Court and the video. *Family Law*, March: 84–85.

Hughes, S. (1997) Management of child sexual abuse: learning effective American strategies. *Childright*, September, No. 139: 10.

Jenkins, P. (1995) Advocacy and the 1989 UN Convention on the Rights of the Child, in Dalrymple, J. and Hough, J. (eds) *Having a Voice: An Exploration of Children's Rights and Advocacy*. Birmingham, Venture Press, pp. 31–52.

King, M. and Piper, C. (1995) *How the Law Thinks about Children*. Aldershot, Arena.

King, M. and Trowell, J. (1992) *Children's Welfare and the Law: The Limits of Legal Intervention*. London, Sage.

Lawrence, K. (1988) Let the child be heard. *Police Review*, 20 May: 1074–1075.

Lyon, C. and Parton, N. (1995) Children's rights and the Children Act, in Franklin, B. (ed.) *The Handbook of Children's Rights*. London, Routledge, pp. 40–55.

McEwan, J. (1995) Privilege and the Children Act 1989: confusion compounded? *Child and Family Law Quarterly*, 7(4).

Mitchell, E. (1997) Children as witnesses in the Crown Court, in John, M. (ed.) *A Charge Against Society: The Child's Right to Protection*. London, Jessica Kingsley, pp. 126–134.

National Commission of Inquiry into the Prevention of Child Abuse (1996) *Childhood Matters, Vol. 1*. London, The Stationery Office.

O'Neill, T. (1997) The Memorandum and the guardian ad litem, in Westcott, H. and Jones, J. (eds) *Perspectives on the Memorandum*. Aldershot, Arena, pp. 39–50.

Parton, N. (1997) Child protection and family support: current debates and future prospects, in Parton, N. (ed.) *Child Protection and Family Support*. London, Routledge, pp. 1–24.

Pigot, T. (1989) *Report of the Advisory Group on Video Evidence*. London, Home Office.

Plotnikoff, J. and Woolfson, R. (1995) *Prosecuting Child Abuse: An Evaluation of the Government's Speedy Progress Policy*. London, Blackstone.

Representing Children (1995) *European Convention on the Exercise of Children's Rights and Explanatory Report*, 8(4): 19–29.

Review of Child Care Law (1985) *Report to Ministers of an Interdepartmental Working Party*. London, HMSO.

Roberts, R., Taylor, C., Dempster, H., Bonnar, S. and Smith, C. (1993) *Sexually Abused Children and their Families*. Edinburgh, Child and Family Trust.

Roberts, R. and Taylor, C. (1993) Sexually abused children and young people speak out, in Waterhouse, L. (ed.) *Child Abuse and Child Abusers: Protection and Prevention*. London, Jessica Kingsley.

Roche, J. (1996) Children's rights: a lawyer's view, in John, M. (ed.) *Children in Our Charge: The Child's Right to Resources*. London, Jessica Kingsley, pp. 23–38.

Siddall, R. (1997) Damage limitation. *Community Care*, 23–29 October: 24–26.

Smith, C. (1997a) Children's rights: judicial ambivalence and social resistance. *International Journal of Law, Policy and the Family*, **11**: 103–109.

Smith, C. (1997b) Judicial power and local authority discretion: the contested frontier. *Child and Family Law Quarterly*, **9**(3): 243–257.

Smith, C. (1997c) Mutual respect or mutual distrust: social workers and the courts in child care decisions. *The Liverpool Law Review*, **xix**(2): 159–179.

Spencer, J.R. (1987) Child witnesses and video technology. *Journal of Criminal Law*, **51**: 444.

Spencer J.R. (1997) The Memorandum: an international perspective, in Westcott, H. and Jones, J. (eds) *Perspectives on the Memorandum*. Aldershot, Arena, pp. 95–108.

Utting, W. (1997) *People Like Us: The Report of the Review of the Safeguards for Children Living Away from Home*. London, The Stationery Office.

Veerman, P. (1992) *The Rights of the Child and the Changing Image of Childhood*. London, Martinus Nijhoff.

Wade, A. and Westcott, H. (1997) No easy answers: children's perspectives on investigative interviews, in Westcott, H. and Jones, J. (eds) *Perspectives on the Memorandum*. Aldershot, Arena, pp. 51–66.

Wattam, C. (1991) *Truth and Belief in the Disclosure Process*. London, NSPCC.

Wattam, C. (1992) *Making a Case in Child Protection*. London, Longman.

Wells, J. (1989) Power plays: considerations in communicating with children, in Wattam, C. *et al.* (eds) *Child Sexual Abuse*. London, Longman, pp. 44–58.

Westcott, H.L. (1995) Children's experiences of being examined and cross examined: the opportunity to be heard? *Expert Evidence*, **4**: 13–19.

Westcott, H. and Jones, J. (1997) The Memorandum: considering a conundrum, in Westcott H and Jones, J. (eds) *Perspectives on the Memorandum*. Aldershot, Arena, pp. 167–179.

2

NEGOTIATION

Andrew Cooper and Rachael Hetherington

A Ukrainian psychologist once told us the following story: A young woman of 17 who was said to be suffering with depression was referred to him. After a few sessions she revealed that her father had been sexually abusing her for many years. She was still living at home, unable to afford a place of her own, and so the situation continued. The psychologist suggested that she go to the police, and offered to support her in seeking to prosecute her father. The woman said this was impossible, since her father was a rich and powerful man with connections to the courts, which were thoroughly corrupt. The psychologist felt agonised and could not accept this situation. He contacted an old friend in another city who had Mafia connections, and soon afterwards a gang of three men confronted the father in a lift, shoved an iron bar up his trouser leg and ordered him to pay a large sum of money into a particular bank account. A week later the woman had bought a flat and moved into it.

We relate this story, which we have no reason to disbelieve, because we think that the underlying logic of child abuse, and the child protection work it presents, is everywhere much the same. If the resolution effected in the lift does not, on the face of it, appear to be the outcome of negotiation, we will nevertheless argue that there is no inherent contradiction between the principles of compulsion and negotiation. Rather, the capacity of a child protection system to manage the tension between the two is a crucial test of how well it can serve children in the long run. In this chapter we examine the nature of the systemic framework within which official responses to child sexual abuse occur in England and Wales. We look to the child protection systems of other European countries, as a means of developing our understanding of how child protection systems work. We are not proposing the introduction of foreign models as solutions to difficulties at home, but we do think there are difficulties at home. In the context of exploring other models of child protection, it is important to recognise that the English model represents just *one* possible means of handling these dilemmas; there are others, and these provide us with a means to see our own attempted solutions and difficulties in a new light.

It was the terrible paralysis which afflicted English child protection work in the wake of the Cleveland affair, which first prompted us to look across the channel at other ways of doing things. The sudden explosion of popular awareness and controversy about sexual abuse and its detection constituted something more than just another episode in the unfolding history of 'child abuse' in this country. The idea that large numbers of children were suffering—and by extension had always suffered—sexual violation and intrusion within their families, struck at the very heart of our idea of ourselves as a civilised people.

SECRETS AND LIES

The uncovering of sexual abuse reveals how it is both similar to, but different from, other patterns of mistreatment we label 'child abuse'. In our view the key differentiating factor is the interaction of secrecy and power which pervades relationships in which children are being sexually abused, whether by adults or other children. Starting from this recognition, it quickly becomes apparent that 'listening to children' who are experiencing inappropriate sexual relationships is fraught with complexities, and this has radical implications for how we might think about designing our system of institutional responses. This leads directly to our first proposition, which is that in the significant majority of cases in which children are being abused by someone within their family or close circle of relations and contacts, they want two things: (1) they want the abuse to cease, and (2) they want their link with the family members concerned to be maintained in the longer term. If this is correct, it has, in its turn, important consequences for the structuring of our formal responses, both in facilitating 'disclosure' and in working with family systems in the period following disclosure.

Sexually abusing families or networks are closed systems, and the closure is a function of power relations which work to keep children silent. Secrets and lies dominate communication in these systems, and while there is no doubt that power and responsibility lies with abusers, we sometimes overlook the reciprocity of fear at the heart of the relationship between abuser and abused; there is nothing which abusers fear more than children breaking their silence, hence the regime of psychic distortion and fear they inculcate. A key question, then, is whether 'child protection' work serves to help unlock such closed communicative systems and guide them in the direction of more openness, or to reinforce the dynamics of closure. Unless we believe that working for a single, clean and permanent break in the relationship between abused child and abuser is a desirable and viable aim, which is only rarely the case, then *time* must be a critical dimension in our thinking. When we intervene in favour of the welfare of children we must remember that we cannot ever control the development, behaviour or wishes of individuals or human systems with complete certainty. Facilitating more 'openness' in the functioning of abusive systems—that is, creating the systemic and psychic space in which protection, therapy, confrontation, reparation, renegotiation of relationships can occur—involves living with new uncertainties, new choices and fresh dilemmas for everyone involved. Intervening decisively at the earliest opportunity to protect children from further sexual abuse may be necessary and right in some circumstances, but it is normally only the beginning of a process. Part of the failure of English child protection work is that it has increasingly come to be seen as an end. Why has this happened?

IMPASSE

At the root of all child protection work there is a tripartite relationship involving children who are harmed or suffering, carers who are either causing or adjudged to be failing to prevent harm or suffering, and responsible professionals whose mandate is to intervene in favour of ameliorating the circumstances of the children. There are really only three possible modalities through which relationships in this tripartite system can proceed: through voluntary co-operation between professionals and carers; through the exercise of some degree of compulsion by professionals; or through impasse. Impasse is not a state of 'no relationship' but a particular state *of* relationships. To the extent that the structure of the formal system of child protection allows impasse to occur, or does not provide satisfactory means to attempt resolution in cases of impasse, it will tend to reinforce the dynamics of abusive relationships which are themselves a particular variety of impasse. In England and Wales, although particular cases may be worked successfully and specific local institutional arrangements sometimes succeed in opening up the necessary systemic space for creative work to occur, the tendency of the system is towards impasse.

- A situation arises in which sexual abuse may be known about, but no one in authority is capable of exercising this authority in the service of either organising assured protection or releasing children to begin to speak. This comes about where parents or carers are unco-operative with professionals who suspect sexual abuse or are unwilling to allow professionals unrestricted access to the children, and where sufficient evidence in the form required by the courts is unavailable.

- This situation may evolve very rapidly in the history of intervention, partly because intervention is initiated on the assumption of the need to gather evidence for a potential prosecution. Perpetrators' anxieties, guilt, and fear of exposure are reinforced; children's anxieties, guilt and fear of reprisal are equally reinforced. Confidentiality is not offered to any party, and a situation in which psychological resistance to change already predominates, rapidly evolves into one where resistance to authority and fear of the damaging consequences of disclosure predominate.
- In such situations, a relationship of defensive antagonism is likely to develop immediately between the 'intervening' professionals and the parents or carers (one or more of whom we are assuming to be a 'perpetrator'). The possibility of engaging the latter in a programme of work, aimed towards the cessation of abuse and better protection for children, is likely to be defeated before it has started. *In the service of fulfilling what we take to be the usual wishes of children—that the abuse should cease and that contact with parents should be maintained—we leave ourselves no space in which exploration or negotiation within a framework established by those in authority is possible.*

The implicit assumption in the above, that it is in principle possible to establish such a 'space', entails a further presupposition—that there may be some part of the abuser, some wish in him or her, that he or she stops abusing and becomes engaged in the process of renegotiating the damaged adult–child relationships which they have instigated. This is what is almost invariably and inevitably precluded by the dominant procedural and legal imperatives of English and Welsh child protection.

AUTHORITY, CONFIDENTIALITY AND NEGOTIATION

The lesson we have learned from studying other European systems is that child protection work does not have to proceed in this way. What, then, are the fundamental requirements of a child protection practice and system which might enable more children to be better protected, and allow a process of negotiative intervention or engagement which would maximise the preservation of family ties according to the wishes of children? We propose that they are four-fold:

- The legitimation within the system of professionals who carry sufficient socially legitimated *authority* to intervene in families and networks where there is abuse, within a framework where legal compulsion is ultimately possible.
- The development of *negotiative spaces* open to families and professionals on the basis of a reciprocal understanding (explicit or implicit) that the

law *could* be used if progress towards objectives defined by the professionals are not achieved. Such space depends both on the structuring of the system, and on the confidence of the professionals in their own authority.

- The operation, within this framework, of a principle of conditional confidentiality. This does not mean confidentiality which is confined to the individual professional–child/adult relationship, but confidentiality within the joint professional/family system which says that *on condition that progress towards the necessary objectives are achieved, protection from prosecution or referral to the judicial domain can continue.* These are the principles which have guided the work of the Confidential Doctor Centre in Belgium, and which underpin the objective of creating 'confidence in the service' as a consequence of the assurance of 'conditional confidentiality' (Adriaenssens *et al.*, 1998).

- The commitment to the overarching principle that *no more compulsion is used at any one time than is necessary to secure the primary objectives of the intervention.*

ALTERNATIVE APPROACHES

The following three case examples demonstrate how child protection systems using these approaches can respond to abusive situations. The examples have been described in more detail elsewhere (Cooper *et al.*, 1997; Hetherington, 1996).

A Flemish case: the social worker, who was based in a Confidential Doctor Centre, was contacted by a social worker in the benefits office, asking for help on behalf of a young single woman aged 19, one of a large family, who was worried about her younger siblings. This young woman agreed to speak to the social worker only on the basis of anonymity. She was afraid that her younger sister, Sylvie, was being sexually abused by their father. She herself had been abused by her father, and thought that her elder sisters had also been abused by him. She agreed to arrange that Sylvie should visit her after school and stay the night and she persuaded her to meet with the social worker. The social worker met Sylvie, who confirmed that she was being abused by her father. All this was done without the parents' knowledge. The social worker obtained Sylvie's agreement to interview the parents. Without this agreement the social worker would not at that point have contacted the parents. She would have continued to work with Sylvie to persuade her that it was necessary for the parents to be contacted and that it could be done safely. Emergency action was possible, to provide a safe place for the child, but was held in reserve. The social worker contacted the parents and asked them to come and see her. Both parents came, and the father tried to minimise what had been happening, denying that there had been abuse, saying that 'it was just tickling'. The social worker would not accept this; if that was all that had been going on, she would not be taking it so seriously. The social worker, with the support of her colleagues in a multidisciplinary team, continued to work with the family. Sylvie and her siblings stayed at home, and the work involved the whole family. At one family meeting, the father accepted that his behaviour towards the children did constitute sexual abuse, and this then became part of the continuing work with the family. (Cooper *et al.*, 1997)

A German case: the social worker, who worked for the local authority children and young people's service, was telephoned by a young mother with whom she was working. The young woman was accompanied by her husband's younger sister, Maria, age 14. Maria agreed to speak to the social worker on the telephone; she was upset and in tears, and afraid to go home. After some discussion, she agreed to remain at her sister-in-law's flat and see the social worker. She told the social worker about physical abuse over a long period and sexual abuse involving herself and other children outside the family. Maria was very afraid of her father, and did not want anyone to approach him because she was afraid he would kill her. The social worker was able to persuade Maria to let her take action. With Maria's agreement, she rang the police and asked them, without giving any names, whether they thought they would be able to take immediate police action against the father on the information that Maria had given so far. The police confirmed that this would be possible and, on that basis, Maria agreed to go with the social worker to the police and make a statement. She also agreed that the social worker should contact her mother. The social worker told Maria's mother what was happening, and suggested that Maria's father should be told that Maria was at the youth office being questioned about shoplifting. Maria gave a full account to the police of the abuse, and her account was confirmed by the other children who she named as having also been abused. Maria's father was arrested, charged and convicted. Specialist help and counselling for Maria and her mother were arranged by the social worker. (Cooper *et al.*, 1997)

A French case: a social worker, based in a non-governmental organisation working under contract with the local authority, was asked to work with a family well known to the social services department. There were many problems in the Laville family, centred around the neglect of the children and the father's alcoholism. There were also some unsubstantiated anxieties that the children might be being sexually abused. Services, such as support from a family aide, improved things, but improvements were always only temporary. The social services department, with the reluctant agreement of the parents, set up a formal contract of work between the family and the social worker. The initial agreement was for three months, later extended to six months. The social worker worked with the children (two girls of 14 and 6 and a boy of 10) and with the parents. Her primary aim was to gain their trust. She worked with the children around hygiene and acceptable behaviour, in quite practical ways, helping them to clean out their bedrooms, arranging for them to go on weekend breaks with a local group. She also worked with the parents. There was some improvement in the standards of care within the family, but the behaviour of the elder children continued to cause concern. The contract was extended for another six months, and plans were made for the eldest daughter to go to a residential establishment where she would be able to gain a sought-after qualification in the hotel and catering trade. Shortly after this, Mr Laville asked see the social worker on his own. He said that, when he was drunk, he had been making improper sexual approaches to his eldest children. He agreed that the social worker could talk to his wife and the children about this. The social worker did so, but mother and children all denied that there was any problem. The arrangements for the eldest child to attend the training school went ahead, and the social worker continued to work with the family. All this work took place on the basis of a voluntary agreement between the parents and the local authority. Mr Laville and the social worker *both* knew that the social worker could at any point have asked for a referral to the Judge for Children. She often considered it, but decided, with the support of her team, that it was more effective to work on the basis of the voluntary contract and the trust that she had established with the family. (Hetherington, 1996)

Reactions

When these cases are presented to English social workers, they are at first shocked. These three cases present very different situations (apart from some superficial similarities of age and family structure in the first two), but English social workers who have heard these cases in a variety of training contexts, have responded to all of them by saying that they could not possibly have worked in the ways described. English child protection procedures would have required different action, and there would have been problems in the first two cases over seeing the child without the parents' knowledge. It all felt too risky, both for the child and for the social worker. In the first and third cases, by not referring the case into the legal arena, the social worker was felt to condone the abuse. The power given to the child in the first two cases was not acceptable, some social workers were shocked at the construction of a subterfuge with the mother in the second case, and some social workers were shocked that nothing was done to remove the younger children from risk in the third case.

However, after further consideration, English social workers begin to wonder what might have happened in this country. Their conclusion has usually (though not always) been that in all three cases they would probably have been powerless. In the first two cases, it was likely that they would have been unable to engage with the family effectively in any way. The requirements of procedures and the need to work in partnership with parents would have made it very difficult to establish the initial basis of trust with the child that could make any further progress possible. They were both impressed and shocked by the importance attached by the Flemish and German social workers to getting the agreement of the child to the action that should be taken. If Maria had not agreed to go to the police, the German social worker would not have done so. She would have gone on trying to persuade Maria and, under German law, the social worker has the right to interview a child without her parents' knowledge if it is in the child's interests (Kinder und Jugendhilfegesetz (KJHG) 1990, para. 8, s. 3). The Flemish and German social workers were both confident that in time they would have succeeded, and considered that it was right to allow this time, even though they were well aware that the abuse would be continuing. They were also clear that there might come a point at which they would decide to act without the child's agreement.

The conclusion that the English social workers often reached was that, while the alternatives they were hearing about seemed in our terms too risky, the reality in this country would be that we ran different risks. The risk in our system is that the procedures will frighten off the children and parents who need help, and that we will never be able to establish with either child or perpetrator the bridgehead of trust that might make change possible.

THE CHILD'S EXPERIENCE

Within the English child protection context, the child's wish for the abuse to cease, and her wish for the family to be maintained present us with contradictory messages. How can we respond to both? It is important to recognise that the contradiction may not be as apparent to the child as it is to us. Our reading of the child's wishes is coloured by the assumptions that the child may not be making. We assume that abusers will normally continue to abuse; that children are at risk of further abuse if they remain with abusers; that abusers can only rarely, even with treatment, stop abusing or 'repent' of their behaviour; that abusers who do not 'repent' should be punished because this is important in restoring the self-esteem of their victims. These assumptions make it very difficult to do anything except intervene directly to distance the child from the abuser. The abuse may stop, but the family will be severely disrupted. As a dependent and powerless family member, one of the child's interests in maintaining the family unit is likely to be a fear of the disintegration of such support as the family offers. The changes that are likely to follow from an allegation of sexual abuse within the family are dramatic and far reaching. They cover every aspect of life, social, emotional and economic. A system that responds swiftly and punitively to the revelation of child sexual abuse thus makes it difficult and dangerous for a child to disclose abuse or for a perpetrator to admit to it.

The formal administrative (i.e. non-statutory) structures in the child protection system of England and Wales have developed in response to a series of crises, and have been dominated by inquiry reports (Parton, 1991). The reports are conflicted over 'not doing enough' (for example, the Beckford inquiry report) and 'doing too much' (the Cleveland inquiry report), but all agree on the importance of better communication, co-operation and information sharing. The premise is, that if all information were shared and were available to the decision makers, tragedies could be avoided. The procedures, therefore, mount a very direct challenge to the secrecy inherently involved in child sexual abuse; they throw down a gauntlet, escalating fear and anxiety within the entire family system and thereby undercutting the potential for a problem-solving approach. There is an imperative to share information within the professional network, which can become the driving force. The child's view of her interest, at that point in time or in the longer term, may be heard, but may not be regarded. Working with the child to help her to think about different courses of action is unlikely to be possible.

The English child protection conference, the structure within which information sharing is institutionalised, to a considerable extent mimics the legal process. There is an emphasis on the uncovering of the 'truth' and the presentation of evidence. The decision whether a child is 'at risk' is based on the same criteria as may be used at a future stage in the court. A decision has to be reached, and it is in the same binary form as a legal decision, yes or no. It has to be remembered that, in the eyes of parents, the child protection conference is very powerful. In some respects it has greater powers than the law, because, collectively, the members control a considerable range of resources. The child protection conference has developed skills in sharing and collating information, and uses this information to decide on a plan to protect the child, but it cannot easily take account of a child's wishes, particularly if the child's primary desire at this point is not to disrupt the family. It is difficult for a child protection conference to take no action and wait.

ALTERNATIVE PRINCIPLES: TIME, SPACE AND CHANGE

What structures might make it more possible for children to disclose abuse and perpetrators to admit to it? How can this be enabled? Current information suggests that our existing structures are not effective in bringing perpetrators to justice. For example, recent Home Office figures show a steep fall since 1992/93 in prosecutions of men for unlawful sexual intercourse with girls under 13 (*Guardian*, 1998). While there may be a range of explanations for this decline, it suggests that our present procedures are not leading to any increase in the successful prosecution of perpetrators. This does not, of course, necessarily mean that children are not protected from abuse and, indeed, decisions not to prosecute may be based on an assessment of the 'best interest of the child'. But it suggests that any arguments for current procedures on the basis that they enhance the likelihood of successful prosecution are on shaky ground.

How *relevant* is the notion of punishing the perpetrator in child protection work? If we discard it, what does this change? It reduces the standard of evidence required to the rather lower level required by the Child and Family Court. It reduces (though it does not remove) the pressure on the perpetrator to deny. It still leaves us with the dilemma that is presented by our knowledge and our assumptions about the nature of child sexual abusers.

Our formal response to child sexual abuse is that change is impossible—or too unlikely to be seriously considered. A number of factors contribute to this response. One is the information from research which suggests that the treatment of sexual offenders has a very low rate of success; another is that we know that specialist treatment resources are very limited. There is also the more pervasive anxiety that intervention, whether with the abuser or with the family system, does not effect change and can only monitor. (We have lived in an ethos of non-intervention for nearly two decades, and the ideology is powerful.) But change is what abused children are asking for. One aspect of that change is for abuse to stop, but to stop within the context of other changes taking place within their world; only very rarely are they asking for a complete new world. To be able to respond to the child's wishes—for abuse to cease and the family links to be maintained—we need to be able to envisage the possibility of change within some part of the family system that will create a 'good-enough' situation for the child. We therefore need a system that will encourage change and allow time for that change to take place.

A number of European systems of child protection have built into the system a means by which negotiation between the family and the state can be developed. This gives recognition to the fact that, although there is conflict and although compulsion may ultimately be necessary, negotiation should precede legal compulsion and can replace it. In some countries this negotiation can take place within a legal framework. Thus the French Judge for Children has, in the first place, to try to get the agreement of parents to any plan he makes for the child. The parents know that he can enforce his plan if they do not agree, but they also know that he has to make a real attempt to get their agreement. They can appeal against an order on the grounds that a proper attempt to obtain their agreement was not made and that an alternative and suitable order to which they would have agreed was not offered. A very different structure in Flanders also creates opportunities for negotiation (Pieck, 1995). There the importance of the voluntary engagement of the family structures the system. It is formally labelled as 'mediative', although it would not fit a strict definition of mediation (Roberts, 1997). Both the Service for Special Youth Assistance, the main social service for children and families, and the Confidential Doctor Centres, work only on a voluntary basis. Before a case can be referred into the legal system by these services, or any other service, the family has first to be invited to attend the Mediation Committee. This Committee consists of three lay members, and their brief is to try to arrive at a solution to that is agreed by the parents, the child and the social worker, and is acceptable to the Committee. If there is no agreement, the case is either dropped or referred to the court.

An important aspect of both these systems is that the family—both parents and children—can ask to be heard if they consider that the help or service they are being offered is inappropriate or inadequate. They can also choose to approach the Judge or the Mediation Committee if there is conflict between parents and child, without defining themselves as abusing or neglectful parents.

SOCIAL WORK AND SOCIAL WORK AUTHORITY IN THE NON-STATUTORY SPHERE

How do these organisational differences affect the position of the social worker? In spite of great similarities between social workers in different countries in the way they view their work, the theories they use and the values that inform their decision making, there are important differences in their roles which flow from the interaction between different parts of the system. The most influential part of the system, which has most impact on the role of social workers, is the law. The nature of the legal system (that part of it that is involved with child protection) and the role and responsibility of the judge (or equivalent) have a profound effect on the way in which social workers carry out their tasks, and on the way in which those tasks are defined. In England, the discourse of the law dominates in the legal sphere of child protection, and it has come also to dominate the social work sphere (King and Piper, 1994). Where the discourse of welfare dominates the legal sphere it is possible for social workers to work within the same framework as the law without abandoning the welfare and social problem orientation of their discipline. The law and social work cannot work in different discourses; one or the other has to dominate. In France, and in many other European countries, the dominant discourse of child protection is welfare. In the grounds for judicial intervention, primacy is given to the safeguarding of the child's ability to progress and develop from childhood to adult membership of society. The languages of the French Civil Code and of the German Children and Youth Act (KJHG 1990) are about development and upbringing. In the Flemish community of Belgium, children with 'a problematic up-bringing situation' are legitimately the concern of the Service for Special Youth Assistance. Compared to these, the English grounds for intervention are 'event' focused. The language is about evidence and harm. In comparison with other European countries, English social workers in children and families teams are preoccupied with the law and with procedures (Cooper *et al.*, 1995; Hetherington *et al.*, 1997). Their role is circumscribed by the need to respond to the requirements of a legal discourse.

The requirements and the processes of the law thus reflect back on the activities in the non-statutory sphere that precedes legal intervention. Two aspects of the English legal system for children particularly affect work in the non-statutory sphere. The first is the adversarial system. This has the effect of increasing the potential for conflict between social worker and family, because, as the name implies, it is premised on the assumption that there will be two parties set up as adversaries to each other. It is difficult to make a case for an order under this system without making a very clear statement that a parent has failed and is 'guilty' of failure. The second is the need for evidence of harm. The imperative to approach interventions in terms of proving that a parent has harmed their child undermines the authority of the social worker by shifting the emphasis of the intervention from understanding the child's suffering to collecting information about what has happened. Operating within a legal discourse tends to reduce the authority of the social worker.

Just as the English legal system determines the nature of the system which precedes its interventions, so do others. The French administrative child protection system (the equivalent of our non-statutory system) foreshadows entry to their legal system. It is built on the establishment of trust between worker and family, and gives considerable flexibility for the worker in deciding whether or when to refer. Referral to the judge happens much more frequently than in England, and the basis of referral is different. It may be as much about the need for the extra authority and weight of judicial intervention in bringing home to the family the seriousness of the situation and the need for effective co-operation, as about the risks of the situation. The wider grounds for referral increase the authority of the social worker because his or her judgement is clearly important.

In the Flemish community of Belgium, the Mediation Committee is the gateway to compulsion, and tries to prevent it. As in France, the workers have the authority that derives from the power of referral, in this case to the Mediation Committee, when the grounds for referral are widely drawn. The emphasis on working in the voluntary sphere also gives the workers the implicit support of the community and the authority to take greater risks and work more extensively through negotiation than would be possible in England. This is not without complications; professionals in Flanders are bound by a contradiction, being required by law both to preserve confidentiality (the professional secret) and to report suspicion of abuse to the public prosecutor. Workers in the Confidential Doctor Centres ignore the latter, and the authorities turn a blind eye, because to date the society believes these services work and thus continues to legitimate their practices.

The space for negotiation is therefore greater in both these countries than in England. Their systems demonstrate ways of working to protect children that can more effectively hear the child's view, while still providing protection in a way that takes account of the child's wishes. We think that the key to the operation of these systems lies with the combination of legitimated authority to intervene easily when faced with an impasse, which allows both early intervention and the possibility of staying 'down tariff' in the system as opposed to escalation of the degree of compulsion because there is no way out of the impasse created by non-co-operation. What this arrangement creates is a *space for negotiation* between professionals, parents or carers, and children, which depends on the possibility of exercising formal or legal authority, but where this has not yet happened.

SEMI-COMPULSION

The domain of semi-compulsion can be conceived of as a spectrum. Someone castigating their neighbour for ill-treating his children and threatening to contact social services is functioning at one end of this spectrum; a family with children under an interim order but attending a family centre for intensive assessment prior to a final hearing, is very near the other end of the spectrum; a family with children on the Child Protection Register, a family being investigated under Section 47 of the Children Act, or a family with a long-term relationship with a local authority social worker who acts as a guiding parental figure (if anything like this still exists) are all placed at different points on this spectrum. Impasse between the key parties involved may occur within any of these contexts, or there may be a continued willingness to continue arguing, talking, exploring and problem solving. The presence or absence of explicit legal or procedural controls is not in our view the main, or even a particularly important, determinant of whether the former or the latter is happening. Even the most 'voluntary' of contacts between professionals and parents with children believed to be at risk of harm occurs in circumstances where all parties involved know that law and statutory intervention exist or are possible; all social conduct within the civil domain occurs *in the shadow of the law* and the shadow is cast over each and every one of us. This may be understood from a psychological standpoint, in terms of whether and how 'law' is experienced as internal or external to the individual (Cooper, 1998), or from a sociological perspective in terms of the knowledgeability of social actors concerning the conditions of their own action (Giddens, 1984). Either way, the point is neither as complex nor as controversial as it may at first sight appear—citizens generally well understand the basic principles of acceptable and unacceptable behaviour enshrined in statute.

Thus all child protection professionals know that even in severe cases of child abuse it is occasionally possible to engage those responsible without resort to compulsion, and that much less severe cases may escalate dramatically towards compulsion when there is hostility and resistance to professional help for the children involved. Our argument in this chapter is that, first, some systems of protection tend to support the possibility of engagement with minimal compulsion better than others; and, second, that some more than others continue to provide ways of sustaining negotiative space even when such escalation does occur. Recently a similar argument has been advanced by Danya Glaser and Vivien Prior (1997) in their paper 'Is the term "child protection" applicable to emotional abuse?'. The authors argue (p. 326) that:

> 'The implications of emotional abuse for the child's development are as serious as in other forms of abuse and neglect . . . However, since emotional abuse is integral to the relationship between the primary carer(s) and the child, the child cannot, immediately and in the short term, be protected from likely further abuse unless constantly supervised, which is not feasible, or removed from the relationship.'

The only other possibility, and the one advocated by Glaser and Prior in many circumstances, is a process of 'assessment and time-limited trial of intervention for change . . . *prior* to the initiation of formal child protection procedures . . . Viewed in this way, child protection in emotional abuse is a process of working *towards* protection' (1997, p. 326). Although they do not use the term, such a model exemplifies the use of semi-compulsion and a negotiative space for intervention; importantly, the conditional character of the intervention (a trial), and its dependence on time (to test whether change can occur) embody two of the key principles for which we have already argued in this chapter. This way of conceptualising protection for children locates it firmly *within* the domain of family support, showing that the two cannot be clearly and simply distinguished from each other. Our case examples are intended to illustrate that this is no less true when we are dealing with child sexual abuse.

THE THIRD POSITION

Since the publication of *Child Protection: Messages from Research* (DOH, 1995) the prevailing tendency to see child protection and family support in binary (either/or) rather than non-binary (both/and) terms, has continued a familiar trend towards polarisation in our conceptualisations of child welfare and protection in England. We propose that this tendency is linked to the systemic difficulty in providing and sustaining negotiative spaces in child abuse work. Non-binary principles of thought and practice are inherently more uncertain, but also inherently more creative, than binary ones; from the interchange between any two practices or principles, a third may arise to make matters more complex. Equally, a third party or position may be required in order to allow the two principles, practices or people, to begin to manage interchange in the first place. The joining or intermingling of the two domains or objectives of protection and support entails being prepared to take risks in work with families, to be neither only 'with' them, nor only 'against' them, but potentially both; this in itself requires the capacity for an 'independent' professional stance with respect to the interests of the child *and* the carers. It also requires the worker to be ready to relinquish this stance if, for example, decisive intervention to protect a child suddenly becomes necessary when it previously was not.

The everyday logic of this rather abstract set of formulations is well illustrated in the work of the Avon NSPCC Child and Family Centre team (Essex *et al.*, 1996). The team have described their work with families where child sexual and/or physical abuse is known to be occurring. Often there is a dispute between the local authority SSD and the parent(s) or carer(s) about 'responsibility' for the abuse, and in cases of sexual abuse, whether it has occurred at all. There is an impasse.

> 'The nature and degree of the dispute regarding responsibility for abuse also merits careful consideration, it is usually unclear at the beginning of therapy as to whether the disagreement is due more to a negative encounter with the child protection system or a fixed response indicative of absolute resistance to change. The denial may be a true psychological defence mechanism or an understandable reluctance to admit responsibility because of fear of prosecution, family break-up, social stigma and job loss. . . . Alleged abusers often want to find a way of admitting responsibility, without laying themselves open to the above penalties.' (Essex *et al.*, 1996, pp. 193–194).

An initial phase of work may focus on the construction of a family safety policy. Subsequently the method involves the co-construction with the family of a similar or 'hypothetical' family in which abuse has been confirmed, and the exploration of the feelings and predicaments of members of the hypothetical family by the real one while in role as the former.

> 'The result (in role) is often that non-abusing carers are able to express their feelings openly and ask the most difficult questions of the alleged abuser. Alleged abusers in turn are better able to understand the impact of abuse on all family members, and are given an opportunity to apologise, at least in the hypothetical.' (1996, p. 198)

There are several points to be made about the Avon team's work; in the first place, the service itself occupies a third position with respect to the parties who have reached impasse (the SSD and the carers), creating the possibility of a resumption of dialogue, exploration and, as the team put it, 'resolution'; while attendance is voluntary 'the family is usually under some pressure to attend. This can include the threat of care proceedings . . . ' (1996, p. 194). Thus the resumption of positive engagement occurs in the context of what we have termed 'semi-compulsion'. Finally, the use of the method of 'hypotheticals' is a way of creating a 'third position', enabling that which is unspeakable between family members to become speakable through the use of a symbolic arena *about which* two people can communicate.

Writing about family mediation, Marion Roberts (1997, p. 93) says:

> 'Firstly, a simple bi-lateral process is obviously transformed into one involving a third party. Secondly, the very presence of this third party imposes the rudiments of a framework upon the encounter.'

There can be negotiation without mediation, but as Cormick (1991) stresses, there can be no mediation in the absence of negotiation. Mediation, which depends upon the introduction of a third party, is designed to enable negotiation where impasse has been reached. We are not proposing that 'mediation' as a practice offers a solution to the problems of child protection practice in cases of sexual abuse. However, we are struck by the power of the principle surrounding the presence or absence of a 'third position' to help us understand the way in which closed family systems in which sexual abuse is occurring, *require a response from child protection services capable of avoiding a repetition of these closures, by avoiding impasse between those who fear intervention and those who are offering it. This can only be achieved by creating and sustaining what we have called negotiative spaces, both inside and outside the framework of the law.*

THE STRUCTURE OF CHILD PROTECTION SYSTEMS

Figure 2.1 represents our view of the fundamental principles and processes which any modern child protection system must embody, if it is to fulfil the aims outlined above.

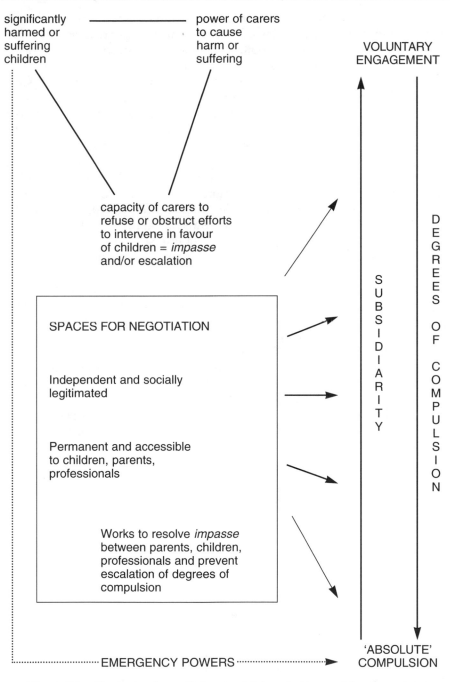

Figure 2.1 The logic of negotiation in child protection and family support

The conflict between the power of abusing carers over children, and their capacity to resist the intervention of professionals or other helpers, is fundamental to all societies which accept any degree of state responsibility for the welfare of children. How this basic contradiction is handled is very differently elaborated even within the small geographical area of north-west Europe. All systems we have studied provide for emergency access to judicial protection. But between the top and the bottom of the diagram different nations exhibit a huge range of cultural, political and historical variance. We propose that two rational principles can inform the way in which this area is structured. Firstly, that interventions should be as close to the family as possible, and as voluntary as possible. This is the way that 'subsidiarity' in this context is defined, and it is important to note that it is not about non-intervention, but about the level at which intervention takes place. Secondly, that we recognise the reality of semi-compulsion, so that negotiative spaces can be established wherein optimal protection is achieved with maximum attention to children's desires for the maintenance of their ties to significant adults.

Giving primacy to the interests of children is not compatible with our normal way of delivering the state response to criminal activity. But we tend to forget that, in cases of sexual abuse, children usually hold power, because they can decide whether or not to disclose abuse and whether to retract a disclosure. Children need time, and need help to traverse a painful process of exploration in order to decide whether and how to exercise this power, if at all. If we give the child more opportunity and time to make decisions, and if we recognise the power that the child effectively already has to choose whether criminal proceedings should take place, we do not decriminalise sexual abuse, but we may enable the process to give primacy to the interest of the child.

REFERENCES

Adriaenssens, P., Smeyers, L., Ivens, C. and Vanbeckevoort, B. (1998) *In Vertrouen Genomen*. Tielt, Publ. Lannoo.

Cooper, A. (1998) With justice in mind: complexity, child welfare and the law, in King, M. (ed.) *Moral Agendas for Children's Welfare*. London, Routledge.

Cooper, A., Baistow, K., Hetherington, R., Pitts, J. and Spriggs, A. (1995) *Positive Child Protection: A View from Abroad*. Lyme Regis, Russell House.

Cooper, A., Hetherington, R. and Katz, I. (1997) *A Third Way? A European Perspective on the Child Protection/Family Support Debate*. London, NSPCC.

Cormick, G.W. (1981) Environmental mediation in the US: experience and future directions, I. Unpublished paper presented to the American Association for the Advancement of Science Annual Meeting, Toronto, Canada.

DoH (1995) *Child Protection: Messages from Research*. London, HMSO.

Essex, S., Gumbleton, J. and Luger, C. (1996) Resolutions: working with families where responsibility for abuse is denied. *Child Abuse Review*, **5**, 191–201.

Guardian (1998) Surprise fall in unlawful sex cases. *The Guardian* 25.6.98, p. 9.

Giddens, A. (1984) *The Constitution of Society*. Cambridge, Polity Press.

Glaser, D. and Prior, V. (1997) Is the term 'child protection' applicable to emotional abuse? *Child Abuse Review*, **6**: 315–329.

Hetherington, R. (1996) Prevention and *éducation* in work with children and families, in Batty, D. and Cullen, D. (1996) *Child Protection: The Therapeutic Option*. London, BAAF.

Hetherington, R., Cooper, A., Smith, P. and Wilford, G. (1997) *Protecting Children: Messages from Europe*. Lyme Regis, Russell House.

Hooper, C.-A. (1992) *Mothers Surviving Sexual Abuse*. London, Routledge.

King, M. and Piper, C. (1994) *How the Law Thinks About Children*. Aldershot, Gower.

Pieck, A. (1995) *Special Youth Assistance in Flanders*. Lier, Ministry of the Flemish Community.

Parton, N. (1991) *Governing the Family: Child Care, Child Protection and the State*. London, Macmillan.

Roberts, M. (1997) *Mediation in Family Disputes*. Aldershot, Arena.

3

ADVOCACY AND CHILD PROTECTION

Jane Boylan and Jan Wyllie

This chapter considers the role of advocacy in promoting young people's involvement in the child protection process. While children are undoubtedly involved at present, it is generally as subjects of intervention and concern. The notion of participation, extended to parents with the principle of partnership under the Children Act 1989, has not been formally applied to children who legitimate intervention and who experience the consequences of protection practices first hand. A key opportunity to involve children and young people was recently missed when the government published *Child Protection: Messages from Research* (DoH, 1995) in which no study took, as its main subject matter or starting point, the consultation of children and young people about their experiences of the child protection system, their needs, perceptions and views. This omission reflects a general attitude within formal child protection systems, that decision making and services are directed towards the protection of children on their behalf. Using the available research and literature, and the views of young people involved with a Children's Society Advocacy Project, we propose that advocacy is a method by which this biased approach to child protection may be challenged.

Advocacy is understood by different people in different ways but is generally associated with concepts of justice, autonomy, rights and conflict. In this sense it has been described as a 'politically controversial, professionally daring and conceptually divergent practice modality within several applied professions' (Weber and McCall, 1978.)

A recurring theme in advocacy literature and practice is the link with empowerment, reflecting the origins of advocacy in users of social welfare who sought to challenge what they considered to be oppressive policies and practices which did not reflect their needs and wishes. This challenge has taken the form of both individual and collective action (Melton, 1987; Boylan and Boylan, 1998). The process of empowerment and the identification of disempowering elements in services is recognised as a first step in improving the quality of help and support (Dalrymple, 1993).

Historically, social workers have been regarded as advocates for their clients and parents for their children. The limitations of this are now recognised (Wattam and Barford, 1991) and more recently have been subject to serious challenge and criticism in the light of disclosures of abusive and negative caring practices in substitute care (Utting, 1997). An example of advocacy used to address this issue is the use of collective advocacy—a form of advocacy which involves groups of individuals coming together to draw attention to a particular set of issues (Brandon, 1995). The perspective offered by young people is uniquely experiential and begins to illustrate the potentially radical challenge that advocacy presents to policy and practice. This challenge is reflected in Sir William Utting's report (Utting, 1997). In focusing on the growing awareness of widespread sexual, physical and emotional abuse in children's homes, the report supports the development of a children's rights service, and for children wishing to use the complaints and representations procedures with the support of an advocate. One conclusion is that local authorities 'need to be committed to life becoming less comfortable for them—in the interests of the children they are looking after' (Utting, 1997, para. 10.10).

Organisations such as Voices from Care support young people wishing to set up advocacy groups. The aim is to develop an empowering relationship rather than foster dependency using the skills of the young people themselves. This process is reflected on by Jenkins (1995) who refers to a continuum from passive to active advocacy. The former involves an advocate speaking on the child's behalf, whereas in active advocacy the child does the speaking, either individually or collectively. There is, however, a danger that advocacy 'for' young people, rather than 'by' young people, will serve to perpetuate rather than challenge children's dependent status on adults. Traditionally advocacy, as applied to children and young people, has been on the passive end of the continuum. For example, Melton (1987, pp. 357–358) describes the role of the child advocate as an

'endeavour to raise the status of children and increase the responsiveness and accountability of institutions affecting them. Advocacy consists of social action on behalf of children whether to increase their self determination or to enhance the social, educational, and medical resources to which they are entitled.'

Recent years have seen a proliferation of advocacy services for young people. Over thirty Children's Rights Officers are now employed in the UK, and the National Youth Advocacy Service was launched in 1998. The majority of these services offer support and representation to young people but have a tendency to fall at the 'passive' end of the continuum, advocating *for* rather than promoting advocacy *by* them. This is less a criticism and more an acknowledgement of the context in which advocacy for children and young people has emerged. This wider social context reflects a particular construction of childhood which makes it difficult for active advocacy to progress. The constitution of modern childhood provides a host of expectations and limitations which impact on the position of children and young people. Assumptions have been made about the capacity of children to engage in decision making and their ability to exercise rights responsibly, particularly on the basis that, as adults, they may regret decisions they make as children and also on the basis that rights engender responsibility which children are unable, unwilling or morally prevented from taking. The perception of children as social actors rather than passive recipients brings with it a challenge to dominant and deeply entrenched views and assumptions about children's capacity to make reasoned and informed choices (Boylan and Boylan, 1998).

The prevailing construction of childhood which underpins such arguments against rights continues despite ratification of the UN Convention. This concept of childhood is crucial to the way in which all children are understood, interpreted and responded to, including those who have experienced significant harm (see Introduction) and is indicative of the power which adults have to define how children should and will be. While all children and young people are subject to adult power relations, in the context of child sexual abuse this power has the added dimension of being used for the gratification of the adult perpetrator. This lack of power of children *vis-à-vis* adults has been recognised across a range of perspectives on child sexual abuse as a vital factor in the sexual exploitation of children (Finkelhor, 1986). Not least for this reason, power relations between adults and children who have experienced sexual abuse must be open to challenge. Yet, as Kitzinger (1997) points out, power and empowerment are not the central concerns of intervention, which is more often focused on investigation and can often lead to the child not being heard and being manipulated as an object of evidence (Wattam, 1992).

Alongside the power of dominant constructions of childhood, this exclusion from the child protection system as an active participant may also be related to debates about family autonomy and the status of children within the family. While there is increased awareness of sexual and physical violence towards children within families there remains a reluctance to sanction state interference in parents' relationships with their children. The case of *Sutton London Borough Council v. Davis* [1994] Fam 241 demonstrates the paternalistic nature of existing case law. Parents with parental responsibility are not prohibited from administering 'reasonable' chastisement to their child or from instructing another to do so on their behalf. Children remain firmly the subject of adult discipline and punishment with (adult) discretion, over and above, and reinforced by, the legislation within which adults are themselves restrained.

Views of childhood and respect for family autonomy are reflected in the way in which children's views have been predominantly sought through an adult informant: the parent, carer or professional. Invariably a judgement is made about the reliability and validity of what the child has to say and, significantly in relation to child sexual abuse, the adult has the power to enforce that decision. The extent to which this is institutionalised within our legal system is demonstrated by the requirements of the *Memorandum of Good Practice on Interviewing Children for Criminal Proceedings.* (Home Office/ DoH, 1992). This guidance encourages interviewers to allow children to speak and give their account of events in their own words, but in application it is dominated by the rules of evidence and psychological research which are founded on adult frameworks and developmental views of childhood which represent children *a priori* as incompetent and immature (to be tested for ways in which they are not) and measurable in relation to adult competence.

Historical analysis lends further evidence to the way in which constructions of childhood can vary, and challenges assumptions about the parameters of contemporary childhood. It is now generally recognised that the constitution of childhood is both culturally and historically relative (Stone, 1977; Flekkoy and Hevener, 1997; James and Prout, 1997). Therborn (1995) provides a comparative and cross-cultural analysis of legislative frameworks and intervention strategies in relation to childhood. She finds a more progressive, less paternalistic approach to children and young people's rights in Scandinavian countries which is reflected in law, policy and practice. Therborn (1995, p. 109) concludes that: 'The less a legal system contains early modern patriarchy and/or the more it has of explicitly egalitarian ground rules, the more room there is for child-friendly legal thought.'

The responses and practices of social welfare organisations to young people accessing the child protection process (or choosing not to) have evolved from, and are underpinned by, socially constructed beliefs about the nature of childhood. Advocacy poses a challenge to these dominant modes of understanding children and the value base which underpins them. An awareness of this process is of direct relevance to those involved in promoting children's rights to participation and caution should be taken with regard to promoting particular versions of childhood. Despite the progress towards children's rights, an increasing body of literature reflects a system that leaves many young people feeling not listened to, not taken seriously and not respected (Butler and Williamson, 1994; Wattam and Woodward, 1996; Boylan and Boylan, 1998).

THE EVOLUTION OF THE CHILD ADVOCACY MOVEMENT

Both the 1924 and 1948 Declarations on the Rights of the Child had strong paternalistic and developmental themes, with an emphasis on the right to protection. By the time the 1959 Declaration was formulated principles of provision and 'best interests' appeared. It was not until the 1989 Declaration that specific reference was made to the rights of children and young people to have their views heard and considered, expressed in Article 12 in the following way:

> 'State Parties shall assure to the child who is capable of forming his or her own views the right to express those views freely in all matters affecting the child, the views being given due weight in accordance with the age and maturity of the child.' (UN Convention on the Rights of the Child)

The focus of attention onto children's rights was no doubt spearheaded by a number of events and developments which raised the profile of children's rights in the UK and internationally, such as the International Year of the Child in 1979. In the UK the establishment of the Children's Legal Centre and its journal *Childright*, together with the emergence of the pioneering National Association of Young People in Care, led the way for subsequent organisations. A more recent development is 'Article 12', an organisation run for and by young people to ensure full adoption of the UN Convention on the Rights of the Child by the UK government.

Comparable initiatives can be identified in Europe, Australia, America and Canada. Each demonstrates the cultural context involved and divergent understandings of the meaning of advocacy. In the United States, for example, a range of advocacy services exist, including a network of government-funded child and family advocacy centres. The aim of these centres has been to streamline the investigation and prosecution of child sexual abuse cases (Reichard, 1993). There is a strong emphasis on minimising the trauma of the investigation process for the child. A multidisciplinary approach is adopted whereby the child and carer are interviewed at the Child Advocacy Center. The emphasis appears to be on obtaining evidence for prosecution in the least traumatic way, rather than a needs-led assessment with the child which may or may not involve the prosecution of the alleged perpetrator. The interpretation of advocacy as directly linked to the legal process in the USA is also evident in the system of Court Appointed Special Advocates (CASA) which has operated since 1974. This service aims to provide a reliable, approachable and personal channel for the children who have been abused to voice their concerns to the court (Leung, 1996). The role is underpinned by a best interests perspective and recognises that the views of the advocate may not be shared by the child or carer. The CASA represents and supports the child but will work with the non-abusing parent/carer and their family. Duquette (1990) identifies the advocate's role in this context as having five key tasks:

- fact finder
- legal representative
- case monitor
- information and resource broker
- mediator.

Children whose cases do not come before the court do not have access to a CASA. Studies undertaken to examine the effectiveness of the CASA conclude that these trained volunteer advocates are as effective as specially trained attorneys in terms of assessing children's needs and advocating in their interests (Leung, 1996). There is no indication, however, of the extent to which children themselves participated in the evaluative process. Finally, a third example of the American approach is the National Association of Child Advocates, whose primary activity is the 'defense of state budgets for children's projects'. The organisation campaigns and lobbies administrative officials on behalf of children and young people and has rather philanthropic connotations. It is not clear how young people are themselves involved. It remains the case that the USA is one of only two countries in the world which have not ratified the UN Convention and it is thus unlikely that this beneficent and legalistic approach to advocacy will alter in the short term.

Elsewhere in the world advocacy is more closely linked to children's rights and empowerment. The appointment of Malfrid Flekkoy as the world's first Children's Ombudsman in Norway in 1981 was a significant event in raising the international profile of child rights, giving official recognition and legitimacy to child advocacy (Flekkoy, 1991). There followed the appointment of Children's Rights Commissioners in New Zealand and Sweden and the Australian Children's Interests Bureau in 1989. Calls for a Commissioner for Children have now been made in the UK (National Commission of Inquiry into the Prevention of Child Abuse, 1996). In Canada a range of child advocacy services emerged, including Canada's National Youth in Care Network (NYICN), established in 1986. This organisation is run for and by young people who have experience of social welfare agencies, with the principal aim of empowerment though peer advocacy. A key objective is stated as the need to facilitate an empowering and constructive dialogue between young people in care and adult service providers in which young people are taken seriously.

While the UK government has ratified the UN Convention there is still a long way to go before children are accorded the rights it specifies. It is also the case that these rights cannot be taken on an individual one-by-one basis, as if ticking off which have been complied with and which need further work. The UN is clear that the convention should be interpreted in its entirety and that it has to be implemented as a whole.

CHILD PROTECTION AND ADVOCACY: THE CHILD'S EXPERIENCE

Working Together states that 'the involvement of children and young people in child protection conferences will not be effective unless they are fully involved from the onset in all stages of the child protection process' (DoH, 1991).

Despite this guidance, researchers describe the experience of young people who have been subject to a child protection investigation as marginalised in decisions affecting them (Spencer, 1994; Barford, 1993). Young people with disabilities are similarly marginalised, and some are arguably more vulnerable to not having their views heard or acted upon (NSPCC/DOH, 1997). Notwithstanding the special requirements for assisted communication for some disabled children, there is the wider problem of prejudice in relation to disability and abuse which allows people to deny that children with disabilities are as vulnerable as all children to the sexual attention and gratification of adults (Westcott and Cross, 1996). There are also particular issues to do with differential placement and the lack of services which parallel those offered to children who do not have disabilities. Below, we give the example of Susan, who was separated from her family and her non-disabled siblings, who were placed in foster care. Black and other ethnic minority children are similarly marginalised by institutional racism (Dutt and Phillips, 1996). The overlay of dominant modes of understanding childhood, with constructions of disability and race, present a challenge to the child protection system. It is our belief that advocates have a central role to play in enhancing the participation of all children and young people who become involved in the child protection process, thus avoiding such marginalisation and stereotyping.

The priority of child protection intervention has not been the child's experience but rather the collection by adults of evidence and information which is then used to determine whether the experience was abusive or not (Wattam, 1992; DoH, 1995). The child's ability to determine what actions and behaviours are unacceptable, harmful and significant has largely been ignored, although some research has been undertaken to explore the child's perception of significant harm (Brandon, 1996). The child's involvement in assessments of risk, planning and decision-making forums such as child protection case conferences and reviews, does not have a good track record.

The Children's Society, influenced by research findings about young people's experiences of the child protection process and experiences of witnessing the impact of the child protection system on children and their families, established an independent advocacy project. The project aimed to provide an advice and representation service which gave a voice to the child and enhance his or her participation in child protection. Since the service began young people have found that advocacy has meant many things. In their own words it has:

'encouraged me to spell out my wishes and concerns'
'helped me discover and demand my rights'
'played a part in my return from foster care'
'helped me get home sooner rather than later'
'helped speed up legal action on my behalf'.

In addition advocacy has incorporated contact issues, privacy of telephone contact while being looked after, attendance and participation at case conferences and review meetings. For example, Susan was removed from home when she was 14 following allegations of sexual abuse by her older brother, who left home immediately. She was placed in residential care provision for children with learning difficulties, while her three siblings were found placements with foster carers. Throughout the 14-month separation and subsequent court proceedings Susan asked to go home. The removal appeared to affect her interactions with family, friends and school. After making contact with the advocacy project Susan began attending meetings where decisions about her placement were made. She also re-established contact with her family in settings other than social service establishments which had not been the case for the previous 11 months. Similarly, John, aged 12, was placed in foster care following allegations of sexual abuse. He was placed with foster carers a considerable distance away from his family home. After contacting the advocacy project he described feelings of not being listened to, and not being consulted about what he wanted or what he thought was important. As a consequence, John was not happy in the foster home and contemplated running away. With the support of the advocate, John participated in planning for his return home. During this process John did not run away as he had been contemplating.

A key message from these and other young people's experience was the extent to which their participation was seen to be determined by (i) the efforts of good social work practice and (ii) the involvement of an advocate. Young people, their families, advocates and social workers can work together to achieve positive outcomes for children. The cases of Susan and John demonstrate that this can be helpful from the early stages of intervention. One difficulty facing our project has been that children were well into the child protection system before they were made aware of the existence of the advocacy project. This highlights a danger of advocacy being interpreted only as representation in the formal part of the child protection process, somewhat akin to the interpretation of advocacy described in the USA.

However, the formal decision-making apparatus of child protection is inevitably important to children. We have found that it is not uncommon for children to be excluded from case conferences and reviews, for all or part of the meeting. Yet it is also our experience that children and young people have been eager to communicate their feelings and wishes in these decision-making forums, and also in core group meetings. Within our service, most have elected to present their views by way of a report prepared in advance with the advocate. The reports produced address a range of issues, spanning the welfare continuum. With the permission of the young person concerned we present an example of such a report. As always, names and identifying details have been altered.

An Example of Advocacy within Child Protection

Kylie has been subject to a Care Order since she was 6. She is now nearly 16. During the last ten years she has been in and out of residential and foster care. The most recent period of substitute care has lasted for six months so far. Her name is also on the child protection register.

Kylie wanted advocacy in the lead-up to her forthcoming child protection review meeting. She had been given a leaflet about the advocacy project by her social worker and asked us to contact her. The advocate met with Kylie twice before her review meeting. The first time was taken as an opportunity for introduction, to explain about the advocacy project and the role an advocate might play and to start Kylie talking about the things in which she was interested. The second session was more focused on child protection issues, with both Kylie and the advocate sharing information on their knowledge and understanding of the child protection system. Kylie was encouraged to review her position in relation to the child protection process and consider what she felt was working for her and what was not. She raised matters important to her that she would want taken to the meeting and recorded them herself.

Kylie's Report to her Review Child Protection Case Conference

To come off the child protection register:

I'm old enough to make my own decisions.

If I know I'm in danger, I'm old enough to know and do something about it.

Strange why I'm on two lists at the same time—child protection and care order.

To go home:

If I had a choice I would like to go back home, but if I can't I am happy here with Mr and Mrs Jones.

My Mum was a little unstable at first when social services first took Anne, Tom and me away from Mum, but since she has proven to be stable by the doctor at the hospital and has said 'she has proven no signs to be an alcoholic' and she is stable so there is no reason why I and Anne and Tom shouldn't go back home. The only problem is my mum is moving. She can't move until she has paid off the £800 arrears to the council, which is for the damage she did not do.

And I would like to contact with Anne and Tom on weekends without supervision.

If I stay in foster care with Mr and Mrs Jones I would like to have overnight stays at my mother's on the weekend. This was agreed by the social worker before I came into care.

Following the Case Conference

Kylie had worked hard on preparing her report for the meeting and wanted her points about contact or consideration of return home from foster care to be addressed. They were not. The reason for not addressing her report, given to Kylie by the professionals involved in the conference, was that it was not the appropriate forum. As a consequence she said that she

> 'Didn't feel listened to at the child protection meeting—or at least I wasn't understood. Felt like nothing was going to go my way, felt like they were ganging up on me, felt over-powered. It would have been better if they would have given me answers to my questions.'

Although Kylie's comments to the advocate following the meeting were very negative, she did nonetheless feel that without the advocate she would not have even raised the issues at the meeting, and she felt more involved for having attended. Her views were also fully recorded in the minutes of the meeting and in the ensuing briefing which children and young people now receive. With the dissatisfaction of that meeting, the advocate continued to pursue issues with Kylie. Another meeting was arranged between Kylie, the advocate and the social worker. Kylie felt that this meeting was a much more comfortable forum, both in terms of hearing the young person more fully and the social worker giving more complete explanations, for example, with regard to procedures for overnight stays. Kylie's need for more independence was acknowledged, as was her desire to accept more responsibility. Following that meeting Kylie was more positive. She stated that 'the meeting was good 'cause some things have changed—I'm glad you (the advocate) organised it'.

Since seeking advocacy support for her review meeting, Kylie has been in contact with the project again to explore the revocation of her Care Order. She wants to live in her present placement under the auspices of supported lodgings rather than foster care. In this way she would be more independent and less restricted by foster care restraints. Kylie views both her Care Order and social services involvement in her life primarily as a form of surveillance. The point she made in her case conference report, that it was strange that she was on two lists at the same time, reinforced that feeling. She felt that it was 'not good' being on the child protection register; 'They really keep a close watch on me and want to know where I'm going all the time—social services are really on my case.' From a child protection perspective this is recast as monitoring children to ensure they are safe, and is part of the duty of social services. However, problems arise and these have been noted elsewhere (see, for example, Farmer and Owen, 1995) when the interpretation is that this is the main and primary focus of child protection. For Kylie, the important things for her, and in relation to her protection, were expressed in her report: having the responsibility to take some risks for herself ('If I know I'm in danger, I'm old enough to know and do something about it').

Kylie's case not only demonstrates some difficulties in the child protection system, it also indicates the limits of the advocacy process within it. At the present time, the advocacy project provides a way of starting to offer children the opportunity for dialogue. There is, however, still an adult frame of reference deeply embedded within it, in terms of writing reports, the way in which the advocate directs the debate prior to the writing of the report, and the kind of language used. Even this limited initiative faces obstacles within a system which appears either not to understand or not to recognise the principle of empowerment with young people. We anticipate that this early beginning will form part of an evolutionary process which may eventually allow advocacy to occur. The issues from Kylie's case were taken up in a meeting of Independent Chairs, Child Protection Co-ordinator, Principal Officers and Team Leaders and practice was changed to bring about improvements for the participation of other children and young people.

It is important that advocacy is viewed as process and dialogue. One worry we have is that it becomes proceduralised. For example, we do not want it to become an expectation that young people will produce reports for meetings; this should only happen if it is appropriate for the individual concerned. Our work shows that children can and should be able to make significant contributions to the formal child protection process, if they want to. Conference and formal meeting forums need to be reformulated to accommodate children and young people, and more radical change is required in relation to planning and decision making generally so that children can be involved, not as victims, but as participants from the outset. The restrictions and ideologies surrounding advocacy by children and young people are demonstrated in the issues we currently face in our project:

- A reliance on social services to inform children and young people of advocacy services. Social workers may be against advocacy and against greater involvement and participation of young people in the child protection process.
- Some practitioners genuinely do not have the time to explain advocacy (even with a leaflet provided) and empower young people to seek help.
- We still find that practitioners use parents as a referral route. Social workers are still saying, for example, 'I asked Mum and no, they don't want advocacy'. We have to ask, 'Have the young people been asked, are they saying no?'
- Respecting young people's rights to confidentiality. The project requested a leaflet to be used systematically to inform children/young people of advocacy and not to give their names and addresses if they did not want to do so. This leads into issues about which rights take precedence. Should children's right to be heard whenever decisions are being made about them take precedence over, for example, rights to privacy and the right to be consulted and make a choice?

The experience of the project indicates that starting to incorporate advocacy into the child protection process as a whole involves the following:

1. Meeting and working alongside a child or young person at a venue of his or her choice.
2. Exploring the situation from the child's perspective and proceeding if and as he or she wishes to do so.
3. Listening to what the young person has to say and clarifying as necessary.
4. Providing access to information to enable the child/young person to make informed choices and maximise participation
5. Supporting the child/young person in decision making forums and representing him or her when requested.
6. Supporting the child/young person through the complaints and representation procedures.
7. Maximising the child/young person's capacity to communicate his or her wishes and feelings in the most appropriate way. This may include letters, tapes, drawings or any other medium selected by the child/young person.

THE WAY FORWARD

If children and young people are to participate positively in conferences, reviews and the child protection process more generally, their agendas have to form part of the process from the beginning, given that the child has often played little or no part in the decision to enter the child protection system in the first place (MacLeod, 1996).

A recurring theme in the feedback from children and young people to the project was the benefit of having time to build up confidence and communicate their feelings, together with a marked awareness of who holds the power within the process. Clearly, the advocate has a role in ensuring that the young person's views are heard in a meaningful, rather than a tokenistic way. An evaluation of our project in 1996 noted that:

> 'All the enquiries from families themselves (rather than from agencies) called on the need for help dealing with the facts, feelings and effects which arise from involvement in the child protection process.' (Newport Advocacy Project, 1996)

The advocacy role is therefore very much one of challenging the way in which the child protection system operates. Advocacy is, and has been described as, a potential force for change as well as for the empowerment of children and young people (Boylan and Wattam, 1998). It challenges previously held assumptions about childhood and the denial of child rights to autonomy and self-determination. Significantly, advocacy challenges the responses and practices of some social welfare organisations to children and young people. It demands, as survivors writing to the National Commission of Inquiry into the Prevention of Child Abuse (1996) similarly demanded, a position of respect for children as people and citizens.

The current child protection process appears to fail some young people and requires modification which is informed by young people themselves, on whose behalf it is authorised. Our current system has evolved within a paternalistic and protectionist tradition. However, young people's rights to participation and protection are compatible concepts and they will enrich adult knowledge and understanding. Advocacy provides an opportunity for children and young people to be listened to and to inform child protection. To begin with, however, adults need to accept that participation is a right and not a privilege.

REFERENCES

Barford, R. (1993) *Children's Views of Child Protection Social Work*. Social Work Monographs, University of East Anglia.

Boylan, J. (1997) *A Chance to be Heard: Listening to Children in Reviews*. Wrexham, Prospects.

Boylan, J. and Boylan, P. (1998) Promoting young people's empowerment. *Representing Children*, **11**(1): 42–49.

Boylan, J. and Wattam, C. (1998) *Advocacy and Child Protection: A Review of the Literature*. A Report for the Children's Society.

Brandon, D. (1995) *Power to People with Disabilities*. Birmingham, Venture Press.

Brandon, M. (1996) Conference presentation, Dartington Social Research Unit.

Butler, I. and Williamson, (1994) *Children Speak: Children, Trauma and Social Work*. London, Wiley.

Dalrymple, J. (1993) Advice, advocacy and representation for children. *Childright*, **9**: 1–13.

DoH (1991) *Working Together under the Children Act 1989*. London, HMSO.

DoH (1995) *Child Protection: Messages from Research*. London, HMSO.

Duquette, D. (1990) *Advocating for Children in Child Protection Proceedings*. Lexington.

Dutt, R. and Phillips, M. (1996) Race, culture and the prevention child abuse, race equality unit, in *Childhood Matters: Report of the National Commission of Inquiry into the Prevention of Child Abuse, Vol. 2: Background Papers*. London, The Stationery Office.

Farmer, E. and Owen, M. (1995) *Child Protection Practice: Private Risks and Public Remedies*. London, The Stationery Office.

Flekkoy, M.G. (1991) *A Voice for Children: Speaking Out as their Ombudsman*. London, Jessica Kingsley.

Flekkoy, M.G. and Kaufman, N.II. (1997) *Rights and Responsibilities in Family and Society*. London, Jessica Kingsley.

Finkelhor, D. (1986) *Sourcebook of Child Sexual Abuse*. London, Sage.

James, A. and Prout, A. (1997) *Constructing and Reconstructing Childhood*, 2nd edition. London, Falmer Press.

Jenkins, P. (1995) Advocacy and the 1989 UN Convention on the rights of the child, in Dalrymple, J. and Hough, P. (eds) *Having a Voice: An Exploration of Children's Rights and Advocacy*. Birmingham, Venture Press.

Kitzinger, J. (1997) Who are you kidding? Children, power and the struggle against sexual abuse, in James, A. and Prout, A. (eds) *Constructing and Reconstructing Childhood*, 2nd edition. London, Falmer Press.

Lansdown, G. (1998) Children's rights and the law. *Representing Children*, **10**(4): 213–223.

Leung, P. (1996) Is the court-appointed special advocate programme effective? A longitudinal analysis of time involvement and case outcomes. *Journal of Child Welfare*, **75**, May–June: 269–285.

Melton, G. (1987) Children, politics and morality: the ethics of child advocacy. *Journal of Clinical Psychology*, 16(4): 357–367

MacLeod, M. (1996) *Talking with Children about Child Abuse: ChildLine's First Ten Years*. London, ChildLine.

National Commission of Inquiry into the Prevention of Child Abuse (1996) *Childhood Matters*. London, The Stationery Office.

NSPCC/DoH (1997) *Turning Points: A Resource Pack for Communicating with Children*. London, NSPCC.

Parton, N. (1991) *Governing the Family: Child Care, Child Protection and the State*. London, Macmillan.

Reichard, R. (1993) Dysfunctional families in dysfunctional systems? Why child advocacy centres may not be enough. *Journal of Child Sexual Abuse*, **2** (4): 103–109.

Spencer, J. (1994) Evidence in child abuse cases. *Cambridge Journal of Child Law*, **6**(4).

Stone, L. (1977) *The Family, Sex and Marriage in England 1500–1800*. London, Weidenfeld & Nicolson.

Therborn, G. (1995) The rights of children since the constitution of modern childhood: a comparative study of Western Nations, in Moreno, L. (Ed.) *Social Exchange and Welfare Development*. Madrid, C.S.I.C., pp. 67–121.

Thorburn, J., Lewis, A. and Shemmings, D. (1995) *Paternalism or Partnership: Family Involvement in Child Protection*. London, HMSO.

Utting, W. (1997) *People Like Us: The Report of the Review of the Safeguards for Children Living Away from Home*. Department of Health and the Welsh Office, London, The Stationery Office

Wattam, C. and Barford, R. (1991) Children's participation in decision making. *Practice*, **5**(2).

Wattam, C. (1992) *Making a Case in Child Protection*. London, Wiley.

Wattam, C. and Denman, G. (1996) *An Evaluation Report of the Newport Advocacy Project*. London, The Children's Society.

Wattam, C. and Woodward, C. (1996), And do I abuse my children? . . . No!— Learning about prevention from people who have experienced child abuse, in *Childhood Matters: Report of the National Commission of Inquiry into the Prevention of Child Abuse*. Vol. 2: Background Papers. London, The Stationery Office.

Weber, G.H. and McCall, G.J. (eds) (1978) *Social Scientists as Advocates: Views from the Applied Professions*. Beverly Hills, Sage.

Westcott, H. and Cross, M. (1996) *This Far and No Further: Towards Ending the Abuse of Disabled Children*. Birmingham, Venture Press.

Westcott, H. and Jones, J. (eds) (1997) *Perspectives on the Memorandum*. London, Arena.

Young, I. and King, P. (1989) The child as client. *Childright*, **62**: 6–7.

4

CONFIDENTIALITY AND THE SOCIAL ORGANISATION OF TELLING

Corinne Wattam

Confidentiality is a concept which has long been recognised in child protection work, both officially in the form of government guidance and professionally as a principle of social work practice. While principles and guidance underpin intervention and influence it in particular ways, the concept of confidentiality as one which can have meaning to children and young people caught up in child protection processes has received less attention. On the basis of previous research with children (Butler and Williamson, 1994), children who have experienced abuse (MacLeod, 1996), and adults who relate their experiences of abuse as children (Wattam and Woodward, 1996), it is apparent that children value confidentiality and require a response which respects *their* confidentiality (rather than that of other professionals).

The way in which confidentiality is treated in a procedural fashion (DHSS, 1988; DoH, 1991) reflects its framing as an adult, professional concern of some importance. Practitioners are guided by the general principle that 'disclosure of confidential information may be made either with consent (express or implied) or where disclosure is justified in the public interest' (DoH, 1998). The breach of confidentiality is justified by the best interests, or welfare, of the child. Thus, if a child gives information in confidence and his or her welfare is thought to be prejudiced, a professional is validated to ignore the child's request for confidentiality. Most children who approach adults for support in relation to child abuse experiences are likely to be, or to have been, in situations which prejudice their welfare. It is often when they are still in those situations that their welfare is most in danger, and paradox-ically it is also those cases in which confidentiality may be most sincerely requested. Thus, it is possible that *the child's confidentiality will be broken at the point at which it is most acutely felt to be needed* by the child. As I have argued elsewhere (Wattam, 1996) this probably constitutes one reason for so few children reporting themselves to agencies which cannot offer confidentiality, and helps to explain why so many take advantage of confidential services such as ChildLine. Indeed, a conclusion of an analysis of ten years' of calls to ChildLine was that:

> 'Social services departments should be able to offer *confidential* discussions to children and parents about their circumstances so that they can be encouraged to come for help and support early.' (MacLeod, 1996, p. 89; my emphasis)

What MacLeod is referring to here is not confidential in terms of exchange of information with other professionals, but confidential discussions with the child. This concept of confidentiality is a difficult one for practitioners in the context of: increased accountability (what if something should go wrong and it was known that the child was talking to a social worker?); risk (what if the situation gets worse?); and clinical literature which supports the importance of speaking out and breaking the silence for therapeutic reasons (this child may not know it but he or she would feel better if the secret was out). These arguments should, however, be contrasted with the knowledge that children tend not to report child abuse (Finkelhor, 1984; Waldby, 1985; Nash and West, 1986; Wattam and Woodward, 1996) and therefore manage their own risks daily, with which they may welcome help. In addition, the child/young person may find speaking to others the first step to recovery, but it is a very tentative first step and one which is likely to be retracted (Sorenson and Snow, 1991) if it is not handled with care—that is, with respect for the child as a person *with* whom information can be exchanged, rather than as an object of concern *about* whom information may be exchanged. This notion of the child as a person puts the child in the same category as an adult (all persons). It is for this reason that I have chosen to look at what con-fidentiality means in everyday life, rather than as a recommendation in guidance. What are held in common understandings about confidentiality that people trade on in their everyday affairs, and therefore that children and young people can expect, use, and anticipate they might count on too?

CONFIDENTIALITY AND REPORTING

Reasons given for not reporting, by those who have experienced abuse, centre on fear (of blame and of not being believed) (Nash and West, 1986;

Finkelhor, 1979; Waldby, 1985; Wattam and Woodward, 1996). Reasons given for not reporting by parents included the preference for parents to try to handle the situation themselves and feeling it was no one else's business (Finkelhor, 1984). In the same study, the variable that most differentiated reported and non-reported cases was the relationship of the perpetrator to the child. Where the perpetrator was a relative, none was reported, whereas acquaintances were reported in 23% of cases and strangers in 73%. With regard to adults involved in a professional capacity (teachers, doctors, nurses, day care staff, etc.) there is some indication that they are also reticent about the positive value of reporting (Besharov, 1990; Finkelhor, 1984; James *et al.*, 1978; Sedlak, A.J. and Broadhurst, 1996). The literature suggests that professionals may be distrustful of the investigation and doubtful of its effectiveness and that reporting seems to present a compromise to confidentiality.

From this research it can be concluded that:

- a major reason given by adults and children who experience abuse for not reporting is fear, or anticipation of disbelief, shame and stigma;
- it is more likely that strangers will be reported than relatives, and more likely that these will be juveniles;
- professionals themselves do not always report and one reason for this is a compromise to confidentiality.

Thus, reporting in the research literature is closely linked to issues of fear, what can be handled privately, relationship (who can be more easily told about) and confidentiality.

THE SOCIAL ORGANISATION OF TELLING

Despite the clear statements concerning the difficulties surrounding the reporting of sexual assault it is still widely accepted that children should report at the first opportunity, and that if their complaint is recent (after the assault) it has more validity in a court of law. Stating that children are afraid or shameful, that they may not report relatives, and that professionals are compromised by confidentiality can appear remedial. For example, it is often thought that the confidentiality problems of professionals such as doctors and teachers can be remedied by training or clearer guidelines, or that the fear and misgivings of victims can be remedied after the success of intervention has been established. However, I want to propose that there are socially organised rules attached to the exchange of information—a social organisation to the telling about social problems, which help us to better understand these impediments to telling. Understanding these rules may help to facilitate children and young people to come forward, rather than proposing that we deal with the repercussions of breaking the rules (which can be anticipated by all who know them) after the event. Below I consider an interview with a teacher to illustrate the way in which guidance, guidelines, procedures and the like must be applied in the context of these socially organised rules. The interview demonstrates the impetus to follow the rule in the *context* of such guidelines rather than the guidelines determining action. It also shows how guidance cannot, in itself, remedy the difficulties produced by breaking the rules. In doing so it can be seen how the socially organised rules associated with confidentiality impose powerful constraints on adults and thus equivalent constraints on children which, if ignored, have serious consequences. When these consequences are ignored adults and children are left to deal with them and, in general, there is little acknowledgement of what those consequences are for children, or of help provided to assist children to deal with them. Part of the reason for this may be that it is not accepted that these rules are as important for children as they are for adults, that adults know better than children and that children do not know what is in their best interests.

Very few children report themselves to a statutory agency, with reports tending to come from adults personally or professionally involved with them (DoH, 1995). One group of people who are directed to act on information about possible harm or injury to a child in a professional capacity are teachers. The text I present here is extracted from an interview with a teacher who provides an account of his discussions with a pupil who approached him. As a professional group, teachers have a clear set of procedures to follow in the event of disclosure of sexual assault by a child, but, as for any other organisational group, procedures, however clearly written, require some degree of interpretation, especially when making decisions about when to enact them, and with respect to whom.

The respondent is in a particular organisational role, that of a senior teacher in a large secondary school, who has some organisational responsibility for pastoral care. What is being presented in the teacher's account are his organisationally and socially accountable actions. Bittner's work on organisations (Bittner, 1969) reveals that what the analyst of a members' talk might explicate is 'the organization-incumbents discourse'. The term 'discourse' here refers to the interactional vehicles members mobilise in order to arrive at the disposition of their work—in this case, a teacher who finds out about a case of child sexual assault. Thus the respondent gives an account of his organisationally relevant actions and reports on the actions of (relevant) others: the head, his assistant, the child, his wife and his colleagues. In doing so the teacher is revealing something of the accountable 'rules' of the discourse in which he is situated. Confidentiality turned out to be very much a feature of that discourse.

The Interview

1. *She never openly said 'I have been sexually abused', but that she had a problem with her father*
   and

2. *I said something to the effect 'what's the problem?'*
   and

3. *looked at her*
   and

4. *she sort of looked up as if to say 'don't ask stupid questions if I've said that I mean it'*
   and

5. *I said 'Oh God'*
   and

6. *—er—something to the effect 'would you be prepared to—er—have my assistant in and then you can tell her?' 'No, I'll deny everything'*
   and

7. *she really closed up. 'No, I'm telling you and you said this was in confidence.' I said 'All right, all right, I'll respect confidentiality'*
   —er—but

8. *it was becoming increasingly more difficult for me to respect confidentiality, I couldn't, I had to tell the Head*
   'cos

9. *he ultimately carries the can for whatever goes on in his school. I was getting now rather to the point where I wanted my assistant to be involved*
   'cos

10. *she's a good professional teacher, she's a mother—er—I wanted her involved. The girl said 'No, if you tell her I'll deny everything'*
    so

11. *I said 'Well, what you've said is quite serious'*
    and

12. *I said 'When does this happen?' or something like that*
    and

13. *she told me a date*
    and

14. *I said—er—it's very serious you know. I thought for God's sake if you make an accusation like this you'd better be right*
    and

15. *yet in my heart of hearts I knew that she was right*
    because

16. *everything so far had said this girl's got a big problem—um—*
    and

17. *she said her sister had had the same problem, her elder sister, so we finished this particular interview*
    and

18. *I said you know 'D'you want to come back tomorrow, whenever?' 'Yeah.' I then went*
    and

19. *told the Head. He said 'Oh what we've got to do now is involve your assistant. We've got to get her to open up to her. I think you've gone as far as you can with her'*
    and

20. *I said to him 'I can't. I'm finding it difficult to live with the confidentiality. Here is a problem that I can't really take any further'—um—I told my wife. My wife is—er—well she was a teacher—um*
    and

21. *she all the time kept saying you know 'Watch what you're doing, be careful, make sure' or something. We trod very carefully on this one.'*[1]

IDENTIFYING CONFIDENTIALITY 'RULES'

Clearly, from this (and other similar interview data), one conclusion can be drawn: some things can be said to some people and not others and there are rules guiding what may be said, to whom and how[2]. To get closer to these 'rules' a distinction can be made between descriptions of how things were said, and the content of what was reported to have been said.

The first observation I want to make is about a comment which comes in item 1, 'she never openly said'. There is a first reference to something being said but not said 'openly'. This, at least, suggests that the 'what' of confidential information—the actual information to be treated as confidential—does not have to be stated to invoke confidentiality. This provides a means of accountability for the teacher. If the child was reported to have said the 'what' in detail, as in 'I have been sexually abused', a responsibility would have been placed on the teacher to pass this information on—whether or not it had been given to him in confidence. Thus, not 'openly' stating words worked to provide for the accountability of the teacher. How could he tell anyone else when there wasn't any*thing* to tell? Yet the content of the discussion, as reported by the teacher, shows that both he and the child knew something of what they were talking about. In item 7 the child is reported to have said that she is telling something, 'I'm telling you', and later in item 10, 'I'll deny everything'.

Other descriptions of how information was given include 'something to the effect', 'as if to say', 'she closed up' and 'something like that'. All of these descriptions denote that the actual, accountable, 'what' of what is being talked about is not given. If these were not the actual things said, and the actual 'what' was not said, there can be no sanction for either retaining or breaking confidentiality. This use of (a rule of) confidentiality demonstrates the competent use of a rule: if the content of information given in confidence is given explicitly, in detail, outside of the initial giving of it there will be sanctions. The teacher is demonstrating his competence through his account. I want to propose that the child is also demonstrating her competence in presenting the information as she did, and that other children will do the same. Learning about confidentiality requires learning about such rules. Requesting confidentiality demonstrates competence in their application.

This initial description of not openly stating sexual abuse, but others knowing that is what is being talked about, is referred to in the clinical literature (Summit, 1983). For example, Sorenson and Snow (1991) suggest that certain patterns emerged in disclosure, including a 'tentative' stage where it is suggested that children test out the response they may get by tentatively suggesting something might be wrong—such as in the case above 'having problems with her father'. Watson (1987) analyses the use of 'pro-terms' (I, we, you, my, etc.) and highlights their use in relation to talk about problems. He proposes that, among other things, they give meaning to expressions of the term 'problem', particularly when used in relation to certain categories.

> 'Combinatorial references such as "your father", particularly when closely accompanied by references such as ". . . got his problem", can do highly delicate and extremely compressed interactional work concerning the discussion of a problem. . . . It may also be said, however, that uses of personal and (perhaps particularly possessive pronouns may be said to constitute the multi-faceted relationship of a "possessable" such as "a problem" to a category such as "father". Unlike a category such as "kleptomaniac", a category such as "father" does not, at least in any routine or immediately observable way, involve "category-bound" or "built-in" personal problems.' (Watson, 1987, pp. 279–280)[3]

Thus a lot of work can be going on, without it having to be explicitly, and in detail, explained. The meaning is produced by the way in which the talk is articulated. This knowledge of how information can be transacted, without the meaning of words having to be explained, is one which presents clear difficulties to practitioners. Through the conversational 'rules' attached to confidentiality, known and shared, practitioners know that something has probably happened to a child. How information is transacted is equally important to *what* information is transacted in establishing validity. Thus practitioners (as in the case above) can believe something has happened to a child but cannot know it in a factual sense (in the kind of way that might be required for legal or para-legal purposes, for example).

Bellman (1981) makes a similar point in relation to 'secrets'. In her attempt to move towards a sociology of secrecy she states that,

> 'secrets cannot be characterized either by the contents of the concealed messages or by the consequences and outcomes that follow their exposure. Rather, they are understood by the way information actually gets withheld, restricted, intentionally altered, and exposed. The practice of secrecy involves a do-not-talk-it proscription that is contradicted by the fact that secrecy is constituted by the very procedures by which secrets get communicated. This I called the paradox of secrecy.' (Bellman, 1981, p. 21)

This is one reason why the practical task of deciding whether a case is a case is so difficult. While secrets and confidences may not be the same thing (Hughes & Wattam, 1989), the case example above does demonstrate that the property of understanding by and through the way information actually gets withheld, restricted, intentionally altered, and exposed provides a connection between the two. This property provides an element of ambiguity which does not sit well with defined legal actions and interventions, yet it is one which is so shared in common that workers will base interventions upon it. This is why such recommendations following the Cleveland inquiry of 'listening to the child' are difficult to apply in practice—as the above shows, it is a case of listening to what is *not said*, and *how* it is said, as much as what is.

A second 'rule' is that confidential talk must be marked as such. One action in treating information 'in confidence' exemplified in the above extract is to state the status of the talk as 'in confidence'. For example, 'you said this was in confidence' (item 7) or 'I'll respect confidentiality' (item 8). A commonplace feature of confidential talk is that it can be prefaced by remarks such as 'This is a secret . . .', 'Don't tell anyone but . . .', 'OK, I'll tell you, but in confidence'. Such remarks, it can be noted, are on occasions offered by a putative recipient of a secret or confidence and are offered in contexts, such as professional encounters where, it might be supposed, confidentiality could be taken for granted. Why preface seemingly self-evidentially confidential topics in this way? It is true that there are activities which have an in-built motive for concealment from others, but, as Bellman (1981) points out, virtually any kind of information can be made into a secret. The operative word here is 'made' since one of the acts performed by this kind of preface is to make a request that the information to follow is of a special status in terms of its availability to others.

Conversation analysts have identified a number of speech acts which serve as 'pre's' to talk which is to follow sequentially to the 'pre'. 'Invitations', 'requests' are, for example, regularly but not invariably prefaced by utterances identified as 'pre-invitations' or 'pre-requests'. Briefly, the work such 'pre's' do is 'hold off' a possible rejection on the invitation or the request being explicitly put. So, a 'pre-invitation' of the order 'Doing any-thing tonight?' gives a hearer a chance to make a move in response indicat-ing that the invitation not be put, one such as, 'Yes, I've got an evening class', so saving face on both sides.

Thus, phrases such as 'This is in confidence' serve as preparatories; actions that tell the listener the kind of information or the kind of action that is to, or might, follow. It tells the listener about the status of the talk and the action that talk accomplishes and, at the same time, makes a request that what is to be told as a confidence will be treated as such and not passed on to 'just anyone'. The framing of information as confidential talk gives information about infor-mation and does so by making confidences and secrets visible. The nominated recipient of the confidence can decline the request in advance of receiving the information, so declining too the obligation incurred on accepting the confi-dence. This is characteristic of the 'guidance' line: I cannot promise to keep what you tell me in confidence if I consider it is not in your best interests to do so. This declines the request. In declining it the option is then presented to the child not to put the information. In this way practitioners place the respon-sibility of passing on the information back on the child. The teacher, however, accepted and the obligations and social force of treating information in confi-dence becomes clear. For example, the teacher states twice that he found it 'difficult' to respect, or live with, the confidentiality he had accepted. This difficulty had to be practically resolved and the account given of looking for resolution shows something of its social organisation.

There are official and institutional 'pre's' which act as a means of enforcing the restriction of information sharing, such as the signing of the Official Se-crets Act. One way of understanding the fundamental import of what might at first appear to be commonplace observations such as that some information needs to be prefaced, and understood as, 'in confidence' is to examine what happens when such rules are breached. In an official capacity, there are quite clearly personal and professionally damaging sanctions for such breaches. There are a host of organisationally relevant reasons for guarding official, institutional or organisational secrets, and thus clearly reasons for sanction. In a book on the topic (Wattam, 1992) I showed, for practitioners' practical purposes, the informal 'rules' which, in part, ordered evidence in cases of offences against children. Prior to publication I sought the permission of the CPS to reproduce the materials obtained from their files. These were pre-sented to explicate rules in relation to practical reasoning about children, the nature of offences, the qualities of evidence and so forth. The headquarters branch of the CPS objected to these citations because the documents were subject to 'Public Interest Immunity'· The reason was given, as follows:

'It is essential for the proper enforcement of the criminal law and in particular for the proper fulfilment by the Crown Prosecution Service and the Police of their respective statutory and other duties, that correspondence or other communication between them (or those acting on their behalf) should be able to be made *fully, frankly and in confidence and without fear that such correspondence, enquiries and communications be used for purposes* other than the enforcement of criminal law. As can be seen from the quotes you have used, such advice, or communications may well involve the formation of personal judgements by officers as to the appropriate course to be taken on the reliability of witnesses'. (My emphasis)

The reasons for objecting to the public disclosure of the documents were given as the need to protect full and frank communication, and this was stated as 'essential'. Thus, it may be supposed that breaching the rules effectively makes the job impossible. This is a serious position for any organisation to be in, and, predictably, the sanctions are heavily legal for transgression. The point that part of an organisation's work can *only* be done by exercising the rules of confidentiality, not as a matter of politeness or moral prescription, but as a matter fundamental to the work indicates, once again, the importance (and power) tied to it. Paradoxically, the defining of information as restricted, 'in confidence', also opens it up to a fuller and franker telling than information otherwise offered. The paradox of secrecy may be not just that secrets get told, but that prefacing the information performs the function of lifting other boundaries, thus inviting and enabling more to be told than would be in routine conversation. We might speculate that the pre 'in confidence' effectively licenses the telling of anything, and therefore other rules to do with relevance must start to operate to bound what is told. This is indicated in the letter above by stating what police officers and others consider relevant in talking about witness credibility. When the boundaries are achieved in this way they operate to bring in matters which would not in themselves be considered hard evidence (i.e. matters of proclaimed official relevance), such as the 'personal judgements' referred to above.

In an earlier paper (see Hughes and Wattam, 1989) it was suggested that members orient to the fact that talk is massively reportable, and that what 'pre-confidences' do is request a suspension of that understanding for *this* information. However, what actually gets reported in interaction between people is circumscribed by other rules, and also by what is known, and known to be known, in common—what is taken for granted as shared knowledge and therefore need not be stated (Garfinkel, 1992). The pre, 'in confidence', suggests that what is about to be heard is not 'shared knowledge' and therefore may require full (for practical purposes) explanation, that other types of knowledge might not. There are other situations in which 'full explanations' are given and which are also marked by their difference from routine day-to-day ordinary conversation, e.g. teaching, telling a joke, reporting in a newspaper. In routine conversations where people customarily give 'full and frank' detail on every topic, this is generally viewed as a negative trait, such as 'gossiping' and being 'nosey' or 'being a bore'. In relation to children, stating that talk is in confidence might make it possible to express a whole range of context-dependent information which otherwise would not be made available.

Thus, in terms of the social organisation of confidentiality, the following 'rules' have been identified;

1. Information may be given 'in confidence' but this must be stated in some way.
2. The 'what' of the information does not have to be stated.
3. The treating of information confidentially is a request which can be declined, and declining makes it possible that the information may not be presented.
4. There are sanctions for breaching confidentiality which depend for their impact and import on who is imposing them and which can be serious, burdensome, and consequential.
5. Information can be shared, where it might not otherwise have been, and where it is not public knowledge; that is, to provide for 'full and frank' information sharing which would otherwise *not* be possible.

These 'rules' are known and shared by adults and children alike, once children understand the meaning of confidentiality. When children request confidentiality they are demonstrating this (cultural) competence.

USING THE 'RULES': THE SOCIAL ORDER OF TELLING

To return to the interview narrative, item 8 reveals difficulties in retaining confidence and clarifies the reason for this; that the respondent has an information obligation which conflicts with the interpretation of confidentiality so far. That is, someone else ('the head') has an entitlement to know, and further that he wanted his 'assistant' to be involved (item 9)—thus acknowledging that speaking 'in confidence' acts to restrict auditors, but that there are occasions when this might be breached and that these have to do with moral obligations to others which might conflict. With regard to his assistant, the teacher gives the justification that 'she's a good professional teacher, she's a mother' (item 10). The respondent is also a professional teacher, but not a mother, which suggests that a different quality should be brought into the interaction, something that might help the child, thus also indicating that there is a possible moral obligation to enjoin someone else who might be qualified to help deal with the problem.

Bellman notes that, in relation to secrecy,

'Different cohorts of members can be identified by their respective rights to know. However, persons are included or excluded from knowing the secret according to their relationship to other cohorts who also possess an equivalent right. This suggests that social networks can be defined according to differential access to concealed knowledge and/or interpretative keys that elicit some alternate version of social reality. This attention to membership is crucial because often the very identification of whether some piece of information is or is not secret is a direct matter of membership identification.' (Bellman, 1981, p. 21)

Sacks (1992) similarly establishes that there are regulations about who can be told what:

'For some information it should be held within the family; for some information it should be told only to your doctor or your priest, etc. So some of these personal troubles can have extremely restricted legitimate audiences. There may be some troubles for which there's 'only one other person in the world' who has rights to hear it. Sometimes also, 'one other person in the world' who has rights to hear it first. If you're in such a trouble, turn to X first. Such a sequence can be quite important, and it can be quite standardized for all kinds of personal troubles.' (Sacks, 1992, p. 561)

Being sexually assaulted by one's father might well be deemed such a personal trouble.

However, neither Sacks nor Bellman indicates how members decide on who it is that can be told, although there must be certain rules in relation to it because members themselves do know, as the teacher did. Some of those rules are articulated in the teacher's interview talk: certain people ('the head', his wife), by virtue of their relationship, have certain 'rights to knowledge'. Furthermore, the interview data also displays a 'relative exclusion of persons' (Sacks, 1992) to certain information (anyone other than those mentioned), and also a 'relative sequencing for those who can be told' (. . . what we've got to do now is involve your assistant (item 19)).

The proposition that there is an order to telling, and that this is a socially organised and negotiated achievement on every occasion in which confidentiality is at issue, is of some consequence for dealing with child sexual assault. For example, this has particular relevance to the problems of legal evidence. There is an assumption that because children come into contact with people, for example a teacher, to whom they can tell such matters, and such opportunities to tell are not taken up, then this serves to invalidate or make less of the truth status of their statement, particularly in a court of law. This rests on two assumptions:

(a) that one feature of being a victim of sexual assault is that you would want to tell someone else, and

(b) that there are persons available to tell, such as teachers, in that they offer qualities which make them available in a conventional sense, e.g. they are trustworthy, or they are physically available, and it is a matter of routine for such persons to make opportunities in that they may be expected to greet children and ask them how they are.

In relation to the first point, Goffman's work on passing is particularly relevant. There is some indication that children who are victims see themselves as 'damaged goods' (Sgroi, 1982), thus knowledge of sexual assault may well be seen as stigma. Goffman makes the following comment on information control and personal identity:

> '. . . when his differentness is not immediately apparent, and is not known beforehand (or at least known by him to be known to others), when in fact he is a discreditable not a discredited, person, then . . . the issue is that of managing information about his failing. To display or not to display, to tell or not to tell, to let on or not to let on, to lie or not to lie, and in each case, to whom, how, when and where.' (Goffman, 1963, p. 57)

Norms regarding personal identity pertain to the kind of information control the individual can appropriately exert. In order to handle personal identity, Goffman asserts that it is necessary to know to whom the person owes much information and to whom he owes very little. This further endorses the sequencing referred to by Sacks, and the categorisation activity referred to by Bellman, though, again, it does not specify any rules or norms that might order 'telling'.

However, some inference can be drawn on the basis of studies on other topics. For example, in his examination of the social organisation of dying, Sudnow (1967) reports on his observations of conversational practices surrounding the breaking of bad news.

> 'In one instance, a morgue attendant was observed to arrive at the nurses' desk to secure a deceased patient's belongings and addressed the nurse, asking where the patient's things were, while the relative was standing alongside the nurses' station awaiting the physician. The nurse managed, by eye signal, to alert the attendant to the bystander's identity and inhibit further references to his relative's body. This sort of possibility is maximized when the news of a death spreads within the hospital to those occupationally involved in such matters faster than it spreads to kin.' (Sudnow, 1967, p. 126)

This extract indicates the social order of telling as it is managed in a hospital setting. In the case of death, doctors are the people who should break the news to relatives; it is not appropriate to overhear such news as occupational talk. The dead person's doctor would have been socially, if not practically, identified as the first source of identification of death for certain. The relatives are treated as having an entitlement to that 'first-hand' knowledge. Thus, there is a sense in which it is known, and shared as known, that some people should be told before others and, therefore, that until those people are told, others should not be told, or should not let it be known that they know. Both Sacks and Sudnow suggest that relatives are first in line for certain kinds of information. This might also be the case with sexual assault, particularly in relation to mothers, and especially where the perpetrator is the mother's partner. This aspect of the social organisation of telling has tremendous consequences for understanding the predicament of children who cannot tell those 'first in line', for whatever reason, and may be a reason why children do not tell at all. If the first in line cannot be told, then the second or third may not be told either, not at least until the first is told.

A further point of relevance to telling has to do with the impetus to 'pass'. Passing refers specifically to the concealment of discrediting information.[5] Goffman proposes that because there are great rewards in being considered normal, almost all persons who are in a position to pass will do so on some occasion by intent. In addition, he maintains that when stigma relates to parts of the body that would customarily be concealed in public places, then passing is inevitable, whether desired or not. If, instead of 'parts of the body' we substitute 'acts on the body' that the normally qualified must conceal, then it would follow that 'not telling' (passing) is inevitable. It is proposed that where a differentness is unapparent an individual must learn that, in fact, she can *trust herself* to secrecy. Starting with the feeling that everything is known, a realistic appreciation that it is not known, and need not be known, gradually develops.

> 'Similarly, there are records of girls who, having lost their virginity, examine themselves in the mirror to see if their stigma shows, only slowly coming to believe that in fact they look no different from the way they used to.' (Goffman, 1963, p. 101)

Thus, if child victims are sworn to secrecy, a facet which victim accounts support, then the propensity might be towards passing. More importantly, under ordinary conditions, without being sworn to secrecy, Goffman's work suggests that the impetus is to 'pass' if one can, to not tell, to be 'normal' and furthermore, that the obligation is as much to oneself as to others.

Professionals investigating cases of child sexual assault take for granted, as does any member, this level of social competence in terms of the social organisation of information exchange and use it to obtain information—for example, when professionals introduce themselves as 'friends', or 'friends of friends' (Wattam, 1992). The point I want to emphasise here is that, despite the fact that this is a massively routine part of conversation and interaction and is available for routine use by everyone including professionals doing the work of investigating sexual assault, its constraining features are not formally taken into account in relation to children and young people themselves. The rules can be used to manipulate children, and thus there is an implicit understanding of the child's competence in this regard, but children are not viewed as persons with equivalent entitlement to rule use.

The fact that it is not possible to tell something to just 'anybody' who might be available in a physical or social sense is evidenced by the confidentiality contract itself. This is particularly so in the case of teachers who have a professional responsibility to breach confidentiality imposed by a child in order to do what is organisationally expected of them. The receipt of the confidence as a 'trouble' places an onus on the recipient to 'do something' and this will generally require 'passing on' the confidence to others. As I have noted in a research report on the ways in which teachers deal with confidentiality (Wattam, 1989), there appears to be a key right involved in confidentiality, the right of the originator to be referenced for permission to pass on the information. Item 6 in the transcript above has the respondent trying to introduce his 'assistant' as a recipient of the same information and the child declines. Item 19 is a further acknowledgement of this right: 'We've got to get her to open up to her' (the assistant). The teacher could just as easily tell his assistant, but this is not sufficient, because the assistant cannot then say that she knows the confidential information unless she shows that there has been a clear breach of confidentiality. The 'passing on' of information is seen as a morally accountable matter requiring, in some sense, the permission of the original teller as the 'owner' of the information told 'in confidence', to be consulted before passing it on to other parties.

In the case of child sexual assault, if, as happens in the case above, the original teller asserts his or her right to deny the information, this places the auditor in a position of some moral conflict. The recipient is caught between a professional and possibly moral obligation to do something about the information, and a moral (but to a lesser extent professional) obligation to adhere to the 'confidentiality contract'. This dilemma can be described as the 'confidentiality trap' (Wattam, 1989) and was handled in various ways. Most of the teachers interviewed resolved it sooner or later, but did not always feel happy with the outcome.

CONCLUSION

The social organisation of passing on information is acutely relevant to the disclosure of child harm and injury by children. This is not just because they may request confidentiality, but because the very nature of sexual abuse is the enlisting of a child in a private act. Private means that it is not known to anyone else, other than those present, and that this is understood by those present. If the nature of the circumstances is inherently private, the passing on of information about it is never incidental, inconsequential *a priori* without meaning (unless a child does not understand that it is private as when very young children make announcements of it). Sexual abuse can be made public in three ways: through the existence of witnesses, the discovery of evidence (physical or material) or through the child's disclosure. The first two are relatively rare, and usually follow from the third as information most pursued post disclosure. Thus, more often than not, children are faced with the difficult and consequential task of breaching privacy, secrecy, a confidence. The act(s) and relationships that they have been a party to is known, and sometimes overtly stated, to be a 'secret' between the perpetrator and themselves· It is not so much that children do not have access to people who are available to tell, but that they are constrained by social processes, some of which are described above. If adults have difficulties with such transactions, so will, and so do, children. Like adults they will need time and help (just as the teacher sought help) to negotiate the breaching of confidences—confidences they hold with themselves and in relation to all those who know them. It is therefore a gross injustice that breaking confidentiality is treated in such a procedural fashion, in the same way (and documents) that discuss, for example, convening a case conference and joint working procedures.

One irony of this chapter is that it depends for its sense on explicating what everyone knows (to do with the passing on of information) which should be self-evident. However, because it is so much a taken for granted feature, a feature that implicitly allows information sharing to proceed, its force is not acknowledged explicitly. Because it is such a mundane feature of daily life the expectation is that it can be easily got over. Management of information in terms of disclosure and non-disclosure, and the emphasis on the importance of how information is shared, rather than what information is shared displays how child abuse can be transacted around without it ever needing to be stated (in so many words) or defined. Confidentiality is one method by which children and young people anticipate they might retain control over what is said and, thereby, what happens to them and those close to them. A breach of the request is a clear statement of their loss of that control. In addition, it also places them in a profoundly prejudicial position.

The sanctions for professionals breaching confidentiality are serious and job threatening. Yet professionals are licensed to breach the confidentiality of children on the basis of their best interests, on a *need to know* basis. The need to know rule is only applied in the context of other professionals. We do not start from the child and, from their point of view, ask who needs to know first, then second, and so on. The teacher had to tell his wife, his assistant, his head. The child will have to tell his or her carer, siblings, closest friends—those who know the child best. Of course, the child often cannot because the enormity of the problem will transform lives, change perceptions, alter everything. The child will no longer be able to 'pass', will be known as a 'victim', referred to as an 'abused' child, be someone other than he or she was before. Confidentiality provides a device that the child can use to hold onto his or her identity as 'normal', as someone who can 'pass'. As practice refocuses towards need this is a 'need' we should consider respecting: the child's need to remain who he or she wants to be, until such time as that child is ready to change.

NOTES

1. I have divided the transcript using the naturally occurring pragmatic connector 'and' (Stubbs, 1993). Stubbs (1983) points out that connectors may be used in symmetrical relation, such as 'he peels the potatoes and she chops the carrots', but they can also imply a temporal sequence as in 'and then'. He notes that 'a basic interpretative principle is that if 'and' can be interpreted temporally, as 'and then', it will be; and if, further, it can be interpreted causally, it will be' (p. 79). Thus the way I reproduce the text here shows each connected action as the production of a temporally bound 'causal' account.
2. A helpful analytic device, particularly in relation to big packages, and thus enabling general statements on text such as this, is derived from Wittgenstein (pp. 192–193):

    'We may thus regard the object as the correlate of a group of acts related to it or, reciprocally, we may regard that group of acts as the equivalent of consciousness of the object.

    In order to conceive of the object as the correlate of acts, we need not reduce it to consciousness. Even though in every particular act the object presents itself under one aspect or from one side, what is grasped in any such act is not an aspect, a side, or any part of the object but, rather, the whole object appearing in a *determinate* way.' (My emphasis.)

    This notion of determination is crucial to understanding the language game of 'confidentiality' since what is presented by the teacher is the way in which confidentiality (as a 'whole object') was used to explain his further talk and actions.
3. Watson's proposition about the use of pro-terms also gives a potential reading of item 20: 'Here is a problem that I can't really take any further.' The use of 'a problem' clearly indicates that the teacher is saying that this is not 'his' problem, nor is it precisely the girl's problem any longer, it has become 'a' problem in a general sense. Without the notion of possession it could be argued that it then becomes something which can be passed on.
4. This means that they cannot be disclosed to the public except under certain conditions, usually by order of court.
5. The concealment of positive information is referred to by Goffman as 'reverse' passing (Goffman, 1963).
6. A recognition of this is the development of 'preventive' materials for use in schools, and by parents, which are based on a general concern with such things as 'good and bad secrets' (see, for example, Michelle Elliot's *Kidscape*).

REFERENCES

Bellman, B.L. (1981) The paradox of secrecy. *Human Studies*, **4**: 1–24.

Besharov, D. (1990) Gaining control over child abuse reports. *Public Welfare*, **48**: 34–39.

Bittner, E. (1969) The concept of organization. *Social Research*, **32**: 233–239.

Butler, I. and Williamson, H. (1994) *Children Speak: Children, Trauma and Social Work*. Harlow, Longman.

DHSS (1988) *Working Together: A Guide to Interagency Cooperation for the Protection of Children from Abuse*. London, HMSO.

DoH (1991) *Working Together Under the Children Act, 1989*. London, HMSO.

DoH (1995) *Child Protection: Messages from Research*. London, HMSO.

DoH (1998) *Working Together to Safeguard Children: New Government Proposals for Inter-Agency Cooperation: Consultation Paper*. Children's Services Branch, Department of Health, London.

Finkelhor, D. (1979) *Sexually Victimised Children*. Beverly Hills, Sage.

Finkelhor, D. (1984) *Child Sexual Abuse: New Theory and Research*. New York, Free Press.

Garfinkel, H. (1992) *Studies in Ethnomethodology*, 2nd edition. Cambridge, Polity Press.

Goffman, E. (1963) *Stigma: Notes on the Management of Spoiled Identity*. Harmondsworth, Penguin.

Hughes, J.A. and Wattam, C. (1989) *Some Aspects of Confidentiality Talk and the Disclosure of Child Sexual Abuse*. Working Paper, Sociology Department, Lancaster University.

James, J., Womack, W. and Strauss, F. (1978) Physician reporting of sexual abuse and children. *Journal of the American Medical Association*, **240**: 1145–1146.

MacLeod, M. (1996) *Talking with Children about Child Abuse: ChildLine's First Ten Years*. London, ChildLine.

Nash, C.L. and West, D.J. (1986) *Sexual Molestation of Young Girls: A Retrospective Study in Sexual Victimisation*. Aldershot, Gower.

NCCAN (1988) *Study of National Incidence and Prevalence of Child Abuse and Neglect*. National Centre for Child Abuse and Neglect, Washington, DC, US Department of Health and Human Services.

NCCAN (1994) *Study of National Incidence and Prevalence of Child Abuse and Neglect*. National Centre for Child Abuse and Neglect, Washington DC, US Department of Health and Human Services.

Sacks, H. (1992) *Lectures on Conversation*, Vols I and II. Oxford, Blackwell.

Sedlak, A.J. and Broadhurst, D.D. (1996) *Third National Incidence Study of Child Abuse and Neglect*. Washington, DC: US Department of Health and Human Services.

Sgroi, S.M. (1982) *Handbook of Clinical Intervention in Child Sexual Abuse*. Toronto, Lexington Books.

Sorenson, T. and Snow, B. (1991) How children tell: the process of disclosure in child sexual abuse. *Child Welfare*, **70**(1): 3–15.

Stubbs, M. (1983) *Discourse Analysis: The Sociolinguistic Analysis of Natural Language*. Oxford: Blackwell.

Sudnow, D. (1967) *Passing On: The Social Organisation of Dying*. Englewood Cliffs, NJ, Prentice Hall.

Summit, R. (1983) The child sexual abuse accommodation syndrome. *Child Abuse and Neglect*, **7**: 177–193.

Waldby, C. (1985) *Breaking the Silence: A Report Based Upon the Findings of the War Against Incest Phone-In Surve*. Sydney, Honeysett Printing Group.

Watson, R. (1987) Interdisciplinary considerations in the analysis of pro-terms, in Button, G. and Lee, J. (eds) *Talk and Social Organisation*. Clevedon, Avon; Multilingual Matters, pp. 261–289.

Wattam, C. (1989) *Teacher's Experiences with Children who have, or who may have, been Sexually Abused*. Occasional Paper No. 5. London, NSPCC.

Wattam, C. (1992) *Making a Case in Child Protection*. Harlow, Longman

Wattam, C. (1996) Can filtering processes be rationalised?, in Parton, N. (ed.) *Child Protection and Family Support: Tensions, Contradictions and Possibilities*. London, Routledge.

Wattam, C. and Woodward, C. (1996) And do I abuse my children? . . . No!— Learning about prevention from people who have experienced child abuse. *Childhood Matters: The Report of the National Commission of Inquiry into the Prevention of Child Abuse. Vol. 2: Background Papers*. London, HMSO.

Wittgenstein, L. (1952). *Philosophical Investigations*. Oxford: Blackwell.

5

COMMUNICATION

Helen Westcott

'Looking after (children) would be easier and much more effective if we really heard and understood what they have to tell us'. (Utting et al., 1997, p. 7)

Ten years on from the Cleveland inquiry (Butler-Sloss, 1988), statements such as this represent a fairly damning indictment of the child protection and criminal justice systems, and of some professionals working within these systems. Communication with children, and especially children thought to have been abused, was a central theme throughout the Cleveland report, as it was also in the Orkney inquiry that followed later (Clyde, 1992). Scandals in public care have highlighted the failure to listen to children making allegations of mistreatment, including sexual abuse (e.g. Kirkwood, 1993). What is it about child sexual abuse that continues to makes it so difficult for us to hear and understand children?

Answers to this question are many and complex. Nevertheless, it is possible to identify important communication issues which arise from personal, professional and organisational factors. This chapter will discuss a number of such issues, drawing on research with children themselves (see Wade and Westcott, 1997, for a review), and on critiques of the current systems invoked in response to an allegation or suspicion of child sexual abuse (e.g. McGee and Westcott, 1996; Wattam and Woodward, 1996). The focus will be primarily on the initial stages of inquiries, and particularly investigative interviews conducted according to the *Memorandum of Good Practice* (Home Office/DoH, 1992), but in a framework which stresses the wider communicative context within which such inquiries occur. In highlighting different issues, the chapter at times presents a negative assessment of current policy and practice. I therefore wish to acknowledge at the outset those practitioners and policy makers who, against the odds (and the political and ideological structures weighted against them) do indeed carry out skilled and positive interventions with children.

SETTING THE COMMUNICATIVE CONTEXT: AN ECOLOGICAL APPROACH

Bronfenbrenner (1977, 1979) outlined an 'ecological approach' to child development. According to this approach, when we consider how a child develops we need to examine closely the different systems which surround the child, as well as the relationships between systems. Although theoretical, this framework can inform our practical consideration of inquiries, or investigative interviewing of children, as illustrated below.

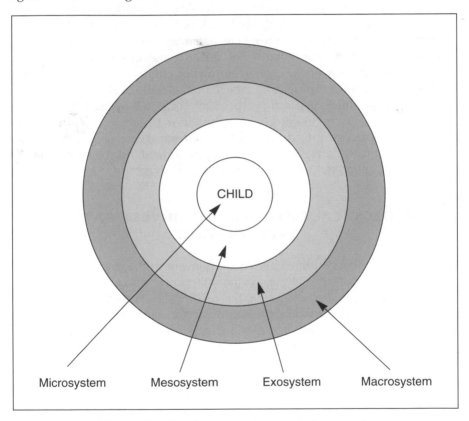

Figure 5.1   Bronfenbrenner's ecological approach

'Within the ecological approach there exist four inter-relating systems (or levels), with the child situated at the centre of all (see Figure 5.1). The most simple system is the *microsystem*, described by Bronfenbrenner as "a pattern of activities, roles, and interpersonal relations experienced by the developing person in a given setting with particular physical and material characteristics".' (1979, p. 22)

This includes fundamental relationships (e.g. mother–child), and different settings such as home, school, etc., where face-to-face interactions occur. The next level comprises the *mesosystem*, which is a system of microsystems created whenever an individual moves from one setting to another—for example, between the child's family, school and social life.

The third level of the ecological model is the *exosystem*, which 'refers to one or more settings that do not involve the developing person as an active participant, but in which events occur that affect, or are affected by, what happens in the setting containing the developing person' (1979, p. 25).

For a child, the exosystem might include a carer's work place, the school class of a sibling, or their parents' network of friends. Finally, there is the *macrosystem*, which refers to cultural consistencies among the micro-, meso- and exosystems, and underlying belief and ideological systems. This level, therefore, includes society-wide perceptions of children, women, minority groups, etc. The other important aspect of the ecological approach is its emphasis on the child's *personal* perspective. Thus, it is necessary to understand the child's environment as she or he views it, rather than attempt to identify any objective (or adult) reality. It encourages a child-centred approach, since professionals should attempt to understand the situation (e.g. investigation, interview) from the child's perspective.

ECOLOGICAL DIMENSIONS OF INVESTIGATIVE INTERVIEWING

The different systems outlined above are relevant to the investigative situation. At the *microsystem* level there is the interviewer and child in the *Memorandum* interview. In the *mesosystem*, the relationship between the interview and the child's home situation, the social support networks, and the school can be explored. The *exosystem* may include social services departments, police stations and Crown Prosecution Service (CPS) offices where decisions are made about interviewing and protecting children, prosecuting offenders, and developing related policies and procedures. Finally, the *macrosystem* will consist of current society-wide beliefs concerning children, and particularly their responses as witnesses and victims of abuse. These beliefs will also be reflected, in different ways, in the professional subcultures involved, such as social work, the police and the law.

Some illustrations reveal the value of this approach in sensitising us to the wider communicative context within which inquiries occur. As an example of the mesosystem, consider a child who sees his or her parents regularly portraying the police as interfering aggressors with whom contact should be avoided at all costs. If this child later comes to the attention of professionals as a suspected victim of child abuse, it may well be that he or she is expected to talk to a police officer about allegations involving highly intimate and illegal acts. The child's experiences at home could then act as a strong disincentive and stressor in the interview setting. Two young people described exactly this experience in their accounts of being interviewed for suspected sexual abuse (Westcott, 1996, p. 83):

'They don't make you feel natural. Don't seem natural because I know police people.' (Male, 17 years)

'Police uniforms just psych me out! I'm not used to the police being good. I felt like I'd done something wrong with them sitting there and all the uniforms, with the walkie talkies and that on.' (Female, 16 years)

As a second example (again of the mesosystem), consider the implications of 'no, go, tell' child abuse 'prevention' packages (such as *Kidscape*; e.g. Elliott, 1990) for disabled children who use non-verbal communication, who are physically immobile, or who are visually impaired. Concepts such as 'safe', 'private', 'uncomfortable' and 'touch' may be problematic for children with learning difficulties or children whose impairments result in frequent intimate body contact, which may be intrusive or painful. One teacher reflected on the introduction of *Kidscape* with their group of disabled children:

'*Kidscape* has also made us realise how few decisions the kids make. This is the biggest thing that has come out of it and we are as guilty as everyone else . . . until the kids realise they can have some control over their lives, they haven't got a chance with *Kidscape*.' (Trevelyan, 1988, p. 17)

Until disabled children experience choice and control over their bodies and what happens to them in their daily lives at home or at school, how can we expect them to think they have choice or control (however limited) in more abusive situations, or indeed in the investigations which may eventually follow (i.e. other settings)? Related arguments extend to all children concerning the value and generalisability of such prevention packages, which focus on the 'danger' from strangers, when most children are abused by relatives or people known to them (e.g. Sullivan *et al.*, 1997; Wattam and Woodward, 1996).

One final example is a comment made by a respondent (a social work trainer) in a survey of *Memorandum* training (Westcott, 1996; Westcott and Davies, 1996a). This comment highlights the relationships between the different systems in the ecological approach:

'Both design and delivery of training and operational management of child sexual abuse investigations are bedeviled by the perception that the MOGP is largely ineffective in protecting children or prosecuting offenders—however hard we try to do 'better' interviews . . . I guess I and others are reluctant to commit time and energy to MOGP work, when it doesn't seem to be doing any good.' (Westcott, 1996, p. 147)

The respondent is indicating that individual practice at interviews (the microsystem) and training and management (the exosystem) are being negatively influenced by the *Memorandum*'s failure to achieve protection or justice for children (the macrosystem). Further, the quotation emphasises the importance of personal perspectives, again in line with the ecological approach. It is the respondent's *perception* of the *Memorandum*'s ineffectiveness that is influential.

The remainder of this chaper uses the ecological approach as a framework to discuss communication issues. Research on children's perspectives of investigative interviews, and of the professionals who conduct them (the microsystem), will be reviewed. Service provision in this area (the exosystem) will then be discussed, with particular reference to disabled children, before fundamental questions around criminal justice and child protection (the macrosystem) are finally raised.

CHILDREN'S PERSPECTIVES ON INVESTIGATIVE INTERVIEWS AND INTERVIEWERS

The following extracts appeared in Westcott (1996):

> 'Do you know the people what go around the woods saving animals, it's a bit like that but saving children instead of animals.' (Female, 6 years; p. 137)

> 'Well I felt that she believed me but like . . . she weren't out to, you know like care for my feelings, she was just out to get this bloke, you know, she just wanted him put away, so yeah she did believe me. But you know like, I don't think she actually did 'cos she went over and over everything so she might have been just like not believing me, it felt like she did at the start.' (Female, 16 years; p. 35)

> 'The way he actually asked me things, he comforted me. He said you don't have to tell us if you don't want to, it's all right . . . and stuff like that.' (Male, 13 years; p. 34)

Perceptions of interviews and interviewers vary widely among children, but even young children can be very sensitive to factors associated with the style of the person interviewing them. A number of researchers have asked children and young people what it was like to be interviewed for suspected abuse, and generally their findings have highlighted common experiences (Barford, 1993; Berliner and Conte, 1995; Blagg, 1989; Butler and Williamson, 1994; Prior *et al.*, 1994; Roberts and Taylor, 1993; Wade, 1997; Wade and Westcott, 1997; Wattam, 1992; Westcott and Davies, 1996b; see also Wattam and Woodward, 1996). Communication issues are identified as particularly important. Children like interviewers who are caring, who listen and who have a sense of humour. They want interviewers to be interested, sensitive, supportive, understanding and trustworthy. Moreover, many children want professionals to give them non-judgemental advice about their situation and to treat their disclosures confidentially. It is very important for children and young people that they feel believed.

Overall, children and young people in the studies seem more positive than negative about 'speaking out' of their abuse; however, the experience is also described as a very difficult one. This difficulty arises both from the emotional intensity of the abuse experience and the interview situation, and from the prioritising of evidential requirements over children's needs—for example, the quest for specific details, questioning which is often interrogative rather than investigative. For example (Westcott, 1996):

> 'I mean it got easier as I went along but you still had to get down to the very nitty-gritty and actual wording for things like that, and that was very, very embarrassing.' (Female, 17 years; p. 32)

> 'Well, they were questioning me about dates and that, and I couldn't remember, that got to me, and times, I mean you don't remember that sort of thing really. How long it went on for an' all that.' (Female, 16 years; p. 32)

> 'I know I was really scared because I thought you know like it says you got to say it all correct otherwise you get sent to prison . . . I was so scared they was saying things like "what was you wearing" and I was thinking "oh my", 'cos it was over a year now . . . 'cos I used to change my clothes about five times a day.' (Female, 16 years; p. 29)

Another consequence of the prioritising of evidential requirments is the failure to consult with children, or to give them choices or control over the way in which the investigation and the interview proceed. It surely makes it more difficult for practitioners to hear and understand children if children themselves do not understand what they are being asked, why they are being asked it in such an unusual way, or why they are not able to have more control over the eventual outcome. These issues relate to the communicative context of the investigation and interview within which children find themselves, particularly the 'rules' of the interaction. Experimental psychological research has shown that if we start to make some of these rules explicit for children as they apply to the interview, such as explaining that they must describe their experiences without assistance from the interviewer, that children should signal that they do not understand the interviewer's question(s), then the evidential value of children's accounts of events can be improved (e.g. Mulder and Vrij, 1996; Saywitz *et al.*, 1993).

There is a danger that much current research on child witnesses overemphasises cognitive issues in communication (such as young children's suggestibility to leading questions; e.g. Ceci and Bruck, 1995), while underestimating the importance of social and motivational factors. Children who have participated in research studies about being interviewed indicate clearly that they do make decisions within the interview about what they will and will not say—decisions which go beyond simply responding to questions as put to them. They may withhold information to protect loved ones' feelings, because they feel that interviewers are being unhelpful, because they are afraid, or because they are not sure of what is happening. Other children may feel able and willing to give a full account of their experiences—for example (Westcott, 1996):

> 'Not relieved because of the way they were just like blunt or something, I couldn't say the whole story and I never did and haven't now.' (Male, 17 years; p. 31)
>
> 'It is better to talk to people about it. Knowing he would get to be put away, and he wouldn't be out doing it to any other little kid.' (Female, 16 years; p. 37)
>
> 'I liked it when Mum and Dad went out. When Mum and Dad was in there I wouldn't talk—I wouldn't say owt. No, I knew it would upset them and they would start crying, and I did not want that. (Female, 16 years; p. 38)

The difficulty facing children who give incomplete disclosures is that this may create problems for them and their advocates later in the investigative process, as it can easily be exploited by defence lawyers in court (see, for example, Wade and Westcott, 1997, pp. 58–59). This is one consequence of the *Memorandum of Good Practice* (Home Office/DoH, 1992) and the criminal justice system portraying disclosures of child sexual abuse as 'one-off' events, rather than part of a process of children's experiences. Having to treat disclosures as discrete events (which are nonetheless similar across children) makes it difficult for practitioners to respond effectively to individual abuse victims, and contradicts all that is known about the great variety of ways in which children and young people make allegations or disclosures of sexual abuse. For example, disclosure may be 'accidental' or deliberate; it may be verbal or non-verbal; it may be complete or incomplete; it may be immediate or delayed many years; it may later be denied, recanted or restated; it may be influenced by age and cultural factors (Bradley and Wood, 1996; Campis *et al.*, 1993; Elliott and Briere, 1994; Keary and Fitzpatrick, 1994; Nagel *et al.*, 1997; Petronio *et al.*, 1996; Sas *et al.*, 1995; Sorenson and Snow, 1991; Wattam and Woodward, 1996).

AN IDEAL SYSTEM . . . FOR PERPETRATORS?

Research findings therefore suggest that some key features of communication in an ideal system for responding to allegations or suspicions of child sexual abuse would be as follows:

- *Flexibility* Responses tailored to individual children's needs and requirements, which may change over time.
- *Empathy* Responses which recognise the multifaceted and changing nature of the child's position in relation to the abuser and other significant adults and children.
- *Honesty* Open answers and honest information about the likely outcome (or non-outcome) of the child's involvement.
- *Respect* Respect for the child as an active participant in the process, for the child's right to be heard, and for the child's ability to contribute in decision making and planning. Respect also for the different professions involved in child abuse work.
- *Confidentiality if desired* Advice sought and given confidentially, without automatically invoking a full investigation.
- *A 'human touch'* Sensitive listening to the child (or interpretation of the child's behaviour), even humour when appropriate—that is, natural and warm communication.

The reality, however, is that many of these features are often missing. The child protection system is increasingly bureaucratic and resource-driven. Confidentiality is inevitably compromised by authorities' fears in relation to risk assessment, and their desire to protect their own interests. Within investigations (and particularly interviews), empathy and the human touch are 'permitted' only within limits which do not threaten the evidential status. Current guidelines (DoH, 1991; Home Office/DoH, 1992) marginalise children as participants in the process, and overlook the degree to which older children actively co-operate or disengage from the investigation. Honesty would require explicit information about possible negative outcomes, including the poor chances of prosecution and conviction, and the inevitable disruption to the child's family and school life. Small wonder it is difficult for practitioners to hear and understand children within such a system, or that recent commentators have criticised the child protection and criminal justice systems as favouring perpetrators (e.g. Home Office, 1998; Utting *et al.*, 1997; Wattam and Woodward, 1996).

It is unfair to lay these charges solely at the feet of individuals operating the child protection system, since the system itself is constructed and constrained by wider societal structures, and the role of professionals is both essential and unenviable (Parton, 1996). However, it is clear that many problems remain in the management of child abuse. As an example, we will consider here the professional response to disabled children thought to have been abused, where communication factors assume even more importance—and where the child protection system appears weighted even more in favour of abusers.

CHILD ABUSE AND DISABLED CHILDREN

Research has emphasised the vulnerability of disabled children and young people to abuse, with disabled children more than 1.5 times as likely to be physically, sexually and emotionally abused than non-disabled children (Crosse *et al.*, 1993; Sullivan *et al.*, 1997). Detailed analyses of the reasons for the increased vulnerability of disabled children are available (e.g. Morris, 1995, 1998a, 1998b; Sobsey, 1994; Westcott and Cross, 1996), but in brief they include (Westcott and Cross, 1996, pp. 129–130):

- dependency, whether it is physical or social, necessary or created;
- multiple carers providing multiple opportunites for abuse;
- insensitive and inadequate professional practice and poor quality of care;
- use of residential care, which has its own dynamics creating opportunities for abuse;
- communication barriers, including the absence of vocabulary necessary to describe abuse;
- a lack of sex education and related materials designed to meet the requirements of disabled children.

Of course, at the macro-level, society's treatment of disabled children—the way it makes them 'invisible' second-class citizens—underpins all these issues (Sobsey, 1994; Westcott and Cross, 1996). Here we can unpick some issues in the context of the child protection system, and communication (failures). For example, disabled children are over-represented as victims of child abuse, yet they are under-represented among referrals to many social services departments. In some cases, medical or behavioural indicators of abuse are mistakenly attributed to the child's impairment instead, such as self-mutilation or masturbation among children who have severe learning difficulties (e.g. Kennedy, 1992). Alternatively, stereotypes of carers of disabled children (both parents and professionals) as 'saints' prevent practitioners from questioning what is happening to the child (e.g. Morris, 1998b). For some, the child's impairments are assumed to protect the child from victimisation.

Conversely, disabled children have been found to be highly over-represented on the child protection register (e.g. Morris, 1998b), yet until statistics were specifically examined in relation to a research project, this fact had not been detected by the system, or by those operating it. Both situations represent the failure of adults to 'hear'disabled children.

Communication is obviously a fundamental issue, especially for children who do not communicate verbally. For such children the problems are often two-fold: first, many artificial systems do not contain the necessary vocabulary to describe abuse, and, second, child protection workers (and many other practitioners) are usually unable to communicate via non-verbal systems. Morris (1998a; 1998b, p. 116) found that many of the 30 disabled young people living away from home interviewed for her project

- did not have access to a communication system which suited their needs;
- did not have routine access to people who understood the ways they communicated;
- did not have access to independent facilitors.

Professional inability to communicate with the child may be used to justify why services are inaccessible—often implicitly blaming the disabled child for not 'fitting' the services that are available. Marchant and Page (1992) give some examples:

- 'He can't get into the building.'
- 'She wouldn't have the understanding to cope with counselling.'
- 'He can't talk.'

Marchant and Page reframe these comments to locate the problem with the service providers who are unable or unwilling to hear and understand the disabled victim of abuse:

- 'Our building is not accessible.'
- 'We do not have the commitment, time, knowledge or confidence to work with disabled children.'
- 'We don't know how to communicate using Bliss/Makaton/Rebus or Sign Language.'

In fact, disabled children have shown themselves to exceed expectations in interviews for suspected abuse or research, and have been resourceful in overcoming communication barriers imposed by adults (see below). Marchant and Page again provide an eloquent example (1993, p. 7). One young girl made the following statement, using a communication board that did not possess the vocabulary she needed. She said:

'Nurse R cross she tell me up children up she mean cruel hurt leg her hand I cry.'

This was later clarified to mean

'Nurse (beginning with) R (got) cross. She tell me (to shut) up (that I would wake the other) children up. She (is) mean/cruel (she) hurt (my) leg (with) her hand I cry.'

In an ironic twist, as a result of giving this child and others the appropriate vocabulary via a special communication board, for the purposes of an investigation into suspected abuse, the professionals are then susceptible to suggestions that they had *led* the children to make allegations. Clearly, disabled children must have access to a wide-ranging vocabulary at all times, which may itself challenge some existing myths, e.g. that disabled children are asexual, that disabled children have important things to say about their lives.

Even disabled children who have profound learning and/or physical impairments are able to communicate, but it may only be those people who have regular contact and/or meaningful relationships with such children who are able to detect and recognise signs. These may include body posture, facial grimaces, particular behavioural responses, etc. Harnessing the intimate and detailed knowledge of the carers of children who have impairments is vital to the inquiry process.

In recent years much has been done to highlight both the vulnerability of disabled children and the inadequacy of most child protection service provision—for example, the development of the *ABCD* training and resource pack (ABCD Consortium, 1993). However, despite the efforts of the Children Act 1989 to bring disabled children within mainstream social services, their position as service users remains precarious (Middleton, 1998; Morris, 1998b). For example, they may fall in the communication gap between child protection teams, disability teams, and/or adult and children's services. It is also important to ensure that, given political pressures (e.g. DoH, 1995) to restrict child protection inquiries and place greater emphasis on family support (in itself no doubt valuable to many disabled children and their families), recent advances in awareness of the vulnerability of children who are disabled are not lost.

Marchant and Page (1992, 1993, 1997) have been at the forefront of training and practice initiatives to promote joint working relationships between child protection social workers and practitioners working with disabled children. The former need to receive education about different impairments, and about the host of other professionals routinely involved with disabled children who may be able to assist in the identification of abuse, and in the planning and carrying out of an investigative interview, e.g. speech therapists (Page, 1993). The latter—carers for disabled children—need training on the vulnerability of children who are disabled, and on action to take if concerns arise. Enhanced communication between the fields of child protection and disability is essential if service provision is to be improved and disabled children are to be protected from abuse. Empowerment of disabled children and adults is a key requirement (Westcott and Cross, 1996).

CHILD PROTECTION AND CRIMINAL JUSTICE

If improvements to the child protection system are essential, then even greater advances are necessary if justice is to be a realistic aim for disabled victims (e.g. Utting *et al.*, 1997). Despite the significant advances for children's welfare introduced as a result of recent Criminal Justice Acts, child witnesses as a group fare particularly badly within the criminal justice system. As many commentators have argued, contrary to Article 12 of the UN Convention on the Rights of the Child, children who are witnesses struggle for 'opportunities to be heard' (e.g. Brennan, 1994; Westcott, 1995). Further, and contrary to Article 39, many aspects of the system itself, notably connected with communication, cause children further distress. Examples include the language and style of cross-examination, the failure to liaise with children and their families post-verdict, or to offer support.

Macro-level issues about the balance between child protection and child welfare versus criminal justice (particularly 'protection' of the defendant) need to be addressed (e.g. Nelson, 1997; Home Office, 1998; Utting *et al.*, 1997; Wattam, 1997). Elsewhere I have argued that the advantages of the current system for dealing with children's evidence are still outweighed by associated disadvantages (Westcott and Jones, 1997), and that improvements wrought by the *Memorandum of Good Practice* are concerned with children's welfare rather than protection *per se*. It is also not clear how reforms such as videotaped interviews and videolinks promote children's access to *justice*—for example, there have been no apparent increases in prosecutions or convictions related to sexual offences against children (Davies *et al.*, 1995; Utting *et al.*, 1997).

This is not to disregard the improvements in practice following implementation of the Criminal Justice Acts of 1988 and 1991, most of which are visible at earlier stages of the inquiries process, and most of which are centred around communication issues—for example, better interviewing techniques and better inter-agency collaboration. Paradoxically, the macrosystem in the broadest sense is offering a more positive vision through these Acts, through the Children Act 1989, and through the UN Convention—that is, the importance of listening to children and taking what they say seriously. However, responses within the lower level systems are undermining this vision, and the macrosystem itself (e.g. government) is not then sufficiently active in supporting and defending the vision it offers. Piecemeal and limited improvements are the result, such as judicial discretion, resistance from legal professionals, and bureaucratic inertia nullifying recent reforms for child witnesses (e.g. Chandler and Lait, 1996; Plotnikoff and Woofson, 1995; Westcott, 1995). Also, local authorities have failed, in practice, to ascertain disabled children's wishes and feelings about placements in care (Morris, 1998a, 1998b).

LISTENING TO CHILDREN

The beginning of this chapter posed the question: 'What is it about child sexual abuse that continues to make it so difficult for us to hear and understand children?' No doubt the nature of the subject contributes: sexuality is still a taboo topic for many people; exploitation is an uncomfortable reminder of adults' disregard for children's rights; family relationships and the wish not to interfere with this enduring social institution. Whether at a personal or professional level, these characteristics can make it very difficult for adults to respond to children who may be trying to disclose abuse.

Throughout this chapter I have attempted to explore communication issues that may help us to understand why we are not very good at listening to sexually abused children, and may also provide pointers for improving our practice in this area. If we want to look after children (to hear and understand them), then first we have to listen to them. This sounds like a truism, but the brief research review of disabled children and child protection offered here is a salient reminder of one group of children for whom opportunites to be listened to are rare indeed. Similarly, the casual statement in *Messages from Research* (DoH, 1995, p. 8), shows how easy it is to disregard the perspectives of children from many sections of society:

> 'It is also the case that important groups, such as children with disabilities, those placed for adoption or those living in residential or specialist foster care are not specifically dealt with. Similarly, issues of race, gender and rights may not be as salient in the studies as some readers might wish. . . .'

We need to translate the philosophy of listening into practice—that is, into face-to-face communication with children and their advocates, and into action informed by that communication. Although this chapter has concentrated on implications at the professional level, listening is also required at the personal level. This means individual adults—parents and professionals—opening up channels of communication with children about routine, day-to-day activities, and really trying to understand children's perspectives on their lives. Crucially, however, listening is required at the societal level, such that influential organisations and governing bodies wield their power to ensure that children's perspectives are incorporated and respected.

Change at this macro-level is essential if listening to abused children is to become more than rhetoric. There are already too many examples in the child welfare field of the consequences of failing to instigate deep-seated structural reforms. For example, discussions about the prevention of institutional abuse stemming from inquiries in the 1990s mirror many of those in the Kincora report (Hughes *et al.*, 1986), and will continue to do so until underlying issues about the status of residential care work and children looked after are properly addressed. Contemporary criticisms of the way children are treated within the court system (Home Office, 1998; Utting *et al.*, 1997) repeat recommendations made years earlier by many commentators (e.g. Royal Commission on Criminal Justice, 1993; Pigot, 1989).

Power—reflected in authority and resources—is the underlying issue, as illustrated by the three themes highlighted above: sexuality, exploitation and family relationships. Changes at the macro- or societal level to facilitate communication with children who have been abused will only come about when existing power dynamics within this and other levels (see Figure 5.1) are challenged. Undoubtedly awkward questions about the balance of power between adults and children, defendants and witnesses, perpetrators and victims will be raised (see Nelson, 1997). Beliefs about child protection, criminal justice and the distribution of resources will also be called into question (Westcott and Jones, 1997). But we must be ready to support listening to children with the power to act on what children say. Fundamentally it is difficult for us to listen to and understand sexually abused children because power dynamics in the *status quo* (i.e. in the micro-, meso-, exo- and macrosystems) keep it that way.

REFERENCES

ABCD Consortium (1993) *The ABCD (ABuse and Children who are Disabled) Training and Resource Pack*, available from NSPCC Child Protection Training Group, Leicester (tel. 0116 234 0804).

Barford, R. (1993) *Children's Views of Child Protection Social Work*. Norwich, University of East Anglia.

Berliner, L. and Conte, J. (1995) The effects of disclosure and intervention on sexually abused children. *Child Abuse and Neglect*, **19**: 371–384.

Blagg, H. (1989) Fighting the stereotypes—'ideal' victims in the inquiry process, in Blagg, H., Hughes, J.A. and Wattam, C. (eds) *Child Sexual Abuse: Listening, Hearing and Validating the Experiences of Children*. Harlow, Longman.

Bradley, A.R. and Wood, J.M. (1996) How do children tell? The disclosure process in child sexual abuse. *Child Abuse and Neglect*, **20**: 881–891.

Brennan, M. (1994) The battle for credibility—themes in the cross examination of child victim witnesses. *International Journal for the Semiotics of Law*, **7**: 51–73.

Bronfenbrenner, U. (1977) Toward an experimental ecology of human development. *American Psychologist*, **32**: 513–531.

Bronfenbrenner, U. (1979) *The Ecology of Human Development: Experiments by Nature and Design*. Cambridge, Harvard University Press.

Butler, I. and Williamson, H. (1994) *Children Speak: Children, Trauma and Social Work*. Harlow, Longman.

Butler-Sloss, E. (1988) *Report of the Inquiry into Child Abuse in Cleveland*. London, HMSO.

Campis, L.B., Hebden-Curtis, J. and Demaso, D.R. (1993) Developmental differences in detection and disclosure of sexual abuse. *Journal of the American Academy of Child and Adolescent Psychiatry*. **32**: 920–924.

Ceci, S.J. and Bruck, M. (1995) *Jeopardy in the Courtroom: A Scientific Analysis of Children's Testimony*. Washington, American Psychological Association.

Chandler, J. and Lait, D. (1996) An analysis of the treatment of children as witnesses in the Crown Court, in *Victim Support, Children in Court*. London, Victim Support.

Clyde, J. (1992) *The Report of the Inquiry into the Removal of Children from Orkney in February 1991*. Edinburgh, HMSO.

Crosse, S.B., Kaye, E. and Ratnofsky, A.C. (1993) *A Report on the Maltreatment of Children with Disabilities*. Washington, DC, National Center on Child Abuse and Neglect.

Davies, G., Wilson, C., Mitchell, R. and Milsom, J. (1995) *Videotaping Children's Evidence: An Evaluation*. London, Home Office.

DoH (1991) *Working Together under the Children Act 1989: A Guide to Arrangements for Inter-Agency Cooperation for the Protection of Children from Abuse*. London, HMSO.

DoH (1995) *Child Protection: Messages from Research*. London, HMSO.

Elliott, M. (1986) *Keeping Safe: A Practical Guide to Talking with Children*. London, Bedford Square Press.

Elliott, M. (1990) *Teenscape: A Personal Safety Programme for Teenagers*. London, Health Eduction Authority.

Elliott, D.M. and Briere, J. (1994) Forensic sexual abuse evaluations of older children: disclosures and symptomatology. *Behavioral Sciences and the Law*, **12**: 261–277.

Home Office (1998) *Speaking Up for Justice. Report of the Interdepartmental Working Group on the Treatment of Vulnerable or Intimidated Witnesses in the Criminal Justice System*. London, Home Office (Procedures and Victims Unit).

Home Office/DoH (1992) *Memorandum of Good Practice on Video Recorded Interviews with Child Witnesses for Criminal Proceedings*. London, HMSO.

Hughes, W.H., Patterson, W.J. and Whalley, H. (1986) *Report of the Committee of Inquiry into Children's Homes and Hostels*. Belfast, HMSO.

Keary, K. and Fitzpatrick, C. (1994) Children's disclosure of sexual abuse during formal investigation. *Child Abuse and Neglect*, **18**: 543–548.

Kennedy, M. (1992) Children with severe disabilities: too many assumptions. *Child Abuse Review*, **1**: 185–187.

Kirkwood, A. (1993) *The Leicestershire Inquiry 1992*. Leicester, Leicestershire County Council.

Marchant, R. and Page, M. (1992) Bridging the gap: investigating the abuse of children with multiple disabilities. *Child Abuse Review*, **1**: 179–183.

Marchant, R. and Page, M. (1993). *Bridging the Gap: Child Protection Work with Children with Multiple Disabilities*. London, NSPCC.

Marchant, R. and Page, M. (1997) The *Memorandum* and disabled children, in Westcott, H.L. and Jones, J. (eds) *Perspectives on the Memorandum: Policy, Practice and Research in Investigative Interviewing*. Aldershot, Arena.

McGee, C. and Westcott, H.L. (1996) System abuse: towards a greater understanding from the perspectives of children and parents. *Child and Family Social Work*, **1**: 169–180.

Middleton, L. (1998) All the running you can do . . . *NAPSAC Bulletin*, **23**: 4–13.

Morris, J. (1995) *Gone Missing? A Research and Policy Review of Disabled Children Living Away from their Families*. London, The Who Cares? Trust.

Morris, J. (1998a) *Still Missing? (Vol. 1) The Experiences of Disabled Children and Young People Living Away from their Families*. London, The Who Cares? Trust.

Morris, J. (1998b) *Still Missing? (Vol. 2) Disabled Children and the Children Act*. London, The Who Cares? Trust.

Mulder, M.R. and Vrij, A. (1996) Explaining conversation rules to children: an intervention study to facilitate children's accurate responses. *Child Abuse and Neglect*, **20**: 623–631.

Nagel, D.E., Putnam, F.W., Noll, J.G. and Trickett, P.K. (1997) Disclosure patterns of sexual abuse and psychological functioning at a 1-year follow-up. *Child Abuse and Neglect*, **21**: 137–147.

Nelson, S. (1997) The Memorandum: Quest for the impossible?, in Westcott, H.L. and Jones, J. (eds) *Perspectives on the Memorandum: Policy, Practice and Research in Investigative Interviewing*. Aldershot, Arena.

Page, M. (1993) Child protection investigations, in the training and resource pack. *ABuse and Children who are Disabled.*

Parton, N. (1996) Child protection, family support and social work: a critical appraisal of the Department of Health research studies in child protection. *Child and Family Social Work,* **1**: 3–11.

Petronio, S., Reeder, H.M., Hecht, M.L. and Ros-Mendoza, T. (1996) Disclosure of sexual abuse by children and adolescents. *Journal of Applied Communication Research,* **24**: 181–199.

Pigot, T. (1989) *Report of the Advisory Group on Children's Evidence.* London, Home Office.

Plotnikoff, J. and Woolfson, R. (1995) *Prosecuting Child Abuse: An Evaluation of the Government's Speedy Progress Policy.* London, Blackstone.

Prior, V., Lynch, M. and Glaser, D. (1994) *Messages from Children: Children's Evaluations of the Professional Response to Child Sexual Abuse.* London, NCH Action for Children.

Roberts, J. and Taylor, C. (1993) Sexually abused children and young people speak out, in Waterhouse, L. (ed.) *Child Abuse and Child Abusers: Protection and Prevention.* London, Jessica Kingsley.

Royal Commission on Criminal Justice (1993) *Report.* London, HMSO.

Sas, L.D., Cunningham, A.H., Hurley, P., Dick, T. and Farnsworth, A. (1995) *Tipping the Balance to Tell the Secret: Public Discovery of Child Sexual Abuse.* London, Ontario, The London Family Court Clinic.

Saywitz, K., Nathanson, R., Snyder, L. and Lamphear, V. (1993) *Preparing Children for the Investigative and Judicial Process: Improving Communication, Memory and Emotional Resiliency.* Final Report to the National Center on Child Abuse and Neglect (Grant No. 90CA1179).

Sobsey, D. (1994) *Violence and Abuse in the Lives of People with Disabilities: The End of Silent Acceptance.* Baltimore, Maryland, The Paul H. Brookes Publishing Company.

Sorenson, T. and Snow, B. (1991) How children tell: the process of disclosure in child sexual abuse. *Child Welfare,* **70**, 3–15.

Sullivan, P.M., Knutson, J.F., Scanlan, J.M. and Cork, P.M. (1997) Maltreatment of children with disabilities: family risk factors and prevention implications. *Journal of Child Centred Practice,* 4: 33–46.

Trevelyan, J. (1988) When it's difficult to say No. *Nursing Times,* 84: 16–17.

Utting, W., Baines, C., Stuart, M., Rowlands, J. and Vialva, R. (1997) *People Like Us: The Report of the Safeguards for Children Living Away from Home.* London, HMSO.

Wade, A. (1997) *The Child Witness and the Criminal Justice Process: A Case Study in Law Reform.* University of Leeds, Unpublished PhD thesis.

Wade, A. and Westcott, H.L. (1997) No easy answers: children's perspectives on investigative interviews, in Westcott, H.L. and Jones, J. (eds) *Perspectives on the Memorandum: Policy, Practice and Research in Investigative Interviewing.* Aldershot, Arena.

Wattam, C. (1992) *Making a Case in Child Protection.* Harlow, Longman.

Wattam, C. (1997) Is the criminalisation of child harm and injury in the interests of the child? *Children and Society,* **11**: 97–107.

Wattam, C. and Woodward, C. (1996) And *do* I abuse my children? . . . No!—Learning about prevention from people who have experienced child abuse, in *Childhood Matters: Report of the National Commission of Inquiry into the Prevention of Child Abuse. Vol. 2: Background Papers.* London, HMSO.

Westcott, H.L. (1995) Children's experiences of being examined and cross-examined: the opportunity to be heard? *Expert Evidence,* 4: 13–19.

Westcott, H.L. (1996) *The Investigative Interviewing of Children.* University of Leicester, Unpublished PhD thesis.

Westcott, H.L. and Cross, M. (1996) *This Far and No Further: Towards Ending the Abuse of Disabled Children*. Birmingham, Venture Press.

Westcott, H.L. and Davies, G.M. (1996a) Memorandum training in ACPCs: a survey. *Journal of Practice and Staff Development*, **5**: 48–64.

Westcott, H.L. and Davies, G.M. (1996b) Sexually abused children's and young people's perspectives on investigative interviews. *British Journal of Social Work*, **26**: 451–474.

Westcott, H.L. and Jones, J. (1997) The Memorandum: considering a conundrum, in Westcott, H.L. and Jones, J. (eds) *Perspectives on the Memorandum: Policy, Practice and Research in Investigative Interviewing*. Aldershot, Arena.

6

TREATMENT

Judith Trowell

INTRODUCTION

Child abuse (CA) and child sexual abuse (CSA) are among the major mental health problems of the last decade. Considerable resources are being put into identifying and investigating the causes of abuse. However, there has been concern about: the lack of *treatment* resources; the lack of knowledge about treatments; the treatments that are most effective; to whom they should be provided; and the symptoms or problems that are most likely to be influenced by treatment.

WHY TREAT THE SHORT- AND LONG-TERM EFFECTS OF CHILD SEXUAL ABUSE?

There have been reviews of follow-up studies of children who have been sexually abused. Beitchman *et al.* (1991) looked at 42 studies for short-term effects, and, in brief: reached the following conclusions:

1. Victims of child sexual abuse are more likely to develop some form of inappropriate sexual or sexualised behaviour than those not abused.
2. The frequency and duration of sexual abuse is associated with more severe outcome.
3. CSA involving force and/or penetration is associated with greater subsequent psycho-pathology.
4. Sexual abuse perpetrated by the child's biological father or stepfather is associated with greater psychological problems.

Victims of CSA are more likely than non-victims to come from families with a higher incidence of marital separation/divorce, parental substance abuse and psychiatric disorder.

In an allied review Beitchman *et al.* (1992) conclude in relation to long-term effects that there are three major sets of sequelae:

1. In comparison with women not reporting CSA, women who do report a history of CSA more commonly show evidence of anxiety and fear, and depression or depressive symptoms which may be related to force or threat of force during CSA. They also show evidence of re-victimisation experiences, suicidal ideas and suicidal behaviour.
2. Previously, there was insufficient evidence to show a relationship between CSA and a specific post-sexual abuse syndrome, though there was an association; however, there is evidence to show a link between multiple personality disorder and borderline personality in adults and a history of childhood physical and sexual abuse.
3. Looking at the relationship between facets of abuse and particular or specific outcomes: more evidence exists to support a traumatic impact of post-pubertal than pre-pubertal abuse; longer duration of abuse is associated with greater impact; the use of force or threat of force is associated with negative outcome; penetration (oral and vaginal) is associated with greater long-term harm; and abuse involving father or stepfather is also associated with greater long-term harm.

Other reviews indicated that there were likely to be more links with mental health problems (Browne and Finkelhor, 1986; Tong and Oates, 1990; Mullen, 1990; Palmer *et al.*, 1992). Symptoms included affective disorders, eating disorders, somatisation disorders and borderline personality disorders. Follow-up studies also show behavioural difficulties such as anger control as well as depression and anxiety (Herman, 1986; Oates and Tong, 1987; Conte and Schuerman, 1987). Random community samples showed a relationship between child sexual abuse and increased psychopathology (Bagley and Ramsay, 1986; Mullen *et al.*, 1988; Bifulco *et al.*, 1991; Bushnell *et al.*, 1993). However, there is a view that sexual abuse is a marker, an event for other factors which contribute much more to adult psychopathology, and that all these factors originate in a disrupted and disorganised childhood (Mullen *et al.*, 1993; Finkelhor and Baron, 1986; Russell, 1986). Bifulco *et al.* (1991) reported that parental violence and extended institutional care were also potent predictors of sexual abuse and subsequent adult psychopathology.

The impact of sexual abuse on children has also been an area of intense study. Browne and Finkelhor (1986) consider the type of sexual abuse that is harmful to children. Conte and Schuerman (1987) and Kolko *et al.* (1988) have shown that abused children display more psychopathological symptoms than non-abused children, but this finding is not consistent.

Johns (1997) in a review states that 'depression and anxiety measures appear to produce different results for younger children than for adolescents', and Berliner and Elliot (1996) state that:

'As a group, sexually abused children do not self-report clinically significant level of distress on symptom checklist measures of depression, anxiety, and self-esteem and often do not differ from comparison groups of non-abused children on these measures.'

It has been suggested that this may be because the generic measures are not sufficiently abuse-specific (Briere and Runtz, 1993), hence the advocacy of more abuse-specific measures by Finkelhor and Berliner (1995), or it may be because these symptoms take time to develop. However, there appears to be something of a tautology in the use of abuse-specific measures, in that they appear to compare how closely a child's symptomology matches a predetermined set of symptoms correlated with sexual abuse. This suggests that they may be of less use as a tool to research the effects of abuse.

Children who have been sexually abused appear more likely to display the symptoms of post-traumatic stress disorder (PTSD) and more likely to display sexualised behaviour. However, most do not meet PTSD diagnosis levels (McLeer, et al., 1992) and most do not engage in sexualised behaviour (Freidrich, 1993).

The interpersonal effects seem to be that sexually abused children are more aggressive and withdrawn than children who have not been abused (Freidrich, et al. 1987) and also tend to have a greater self-blame and reduced trust (Mannarino and Cohen, 1996).

Thus, there is a body of research which suggests that sexually abused children tend to display a range of symptoms, and the key variables affecting the severity of the response appear to be (Johns, 1997):

- the frequency and duration of abuse;
- the amount of force used;
- the nature of the abuse acts (particularly if penetrative or not); and
- the closeness of the abuser's relationship to the victim.

Children themselves react differently to similar abusive events. A particularly strong factor appears to be the family context of the child. The fact that children can display a range of symptoms, including being asymptomatic, suggests that focusing on groups of children displaying similar symptoms may be a better way to structure analysis rather than any specific abuse type.

It is highly relevant that recent research has demonstrated that the symptoms exhibited by those who have been sexually abused fall into certain categories—in children, post-traumatic stress disorder, chronic stress and trauma and, in adults, severe personality difficulties (Deblinger et al., 1989;

Terr, 1991; Herman *et al.*, 1989). For example, in the sample of McLeer *et al.* (1988), about half the children who had been sexually abused met the full criteria for PTSD, while many of the remaining children met at least some of the criteria. Trowell *et al.* (1999, and in preparation) provide more comprehensive information about such links in a sample referred for a therapy outcome project.

Finkelhor and Berliner (1995) usefully suggest that we are beyond the stage of considering whether one therapeutic modality is better than another. What is now required is more refined, personally related therapy in accordance with the abuse history and past and current circumstances of each child.

Given the body of literature on the effects of CSA it is important to consider treatment interventions that could contribute to the amelioration of both the short- and long-term effects. Individual, group and family approaches have been considered as relevant models for dealing with the trauma and subsequent disturbance or distress. However, it is not just the disruptive influence of the abuse; as important may be pre-existing difficulties in the mother–daughter relationship. Frequently, it has been shown that a lack of availability, either physically or emotionally or both, has affected the daughter's capacity to relate to her mother and left the daughter more vulnerable and less able to share her worries or distress. Thus, symptoms and problems may result from a combination of pre-existing difficulties, the effects of abuse and events post disclosure rather than just the abuse *per se.*

Recently, more attention has focused on cognitive behavioural treatment for sexually abused children, especially those suffering from PTSD (Deblinger *et al.*, 1990). Although changes were demonstrated over time on the post-treatment measures, this was again an uncontrolled study. Further studies using cognitive behavioural treatments with more rigorous methodologies are being reported, but improvements are limited (Berliner and Saunders, 1996).

It is also important to consider the contribution of Tebbitt *et al.* (1997). In their study, children were followed up five years after their initial assessment post-sexual abuse. Initially, the children presented with depression, self esteem and behaviour problems; five years later, there had been no significant changes in any of these. While some children improved, an equal number had deteriorated, and treatment had shown no effect on the overall rates of depression, self-esteem or behaviour problems. Predictors of a poor outcome are children who are sad or depressed and have low self-esteem at intake.

ASSESSMENT

Once the child protection procedures have been followed and the child is in a safe enough setting, a careful assessment of the child and his or her family is needed. The child needs to be considered physically, psychologically, emotionally and socially, and his or her functioning within the family and in school.

It is important to take a full history from all those involved so that any physical or mental health problems are clarified, giving a vital social history. All too often there are gaps in the background knowledge of the child or family, and this information can be extremely helpful in thinking about how best to intervene.

Domestic violence, intergenerational abuse, or substance or alcohol abuse, must be recognised and appropriate help offered. In our Young Family Centre (MYFC), of 159 families seen, 61% had mental health difficulties, 51% were experiencing domestic violence, 50% had been abused in their own childhood, 38% had drug and alcohol problems, 27% had been in care as a child, and 20% had a criminal record (Trowell and Hodges, 1997).

It is also important, as part of the assessment, to clarify what is and is not possible as a treatment outcome. Treatment does not provide answers to remaining questions; it cannot change the personality of children or young persons or transform them into socially conforming citizens. It also does not provide substitute parenting. It does, however, provide a setting in which to work on symptoms, behaviours and issues arising from the abuse, and also any disruptions, disturbances or losses before and after the abuse emerged.

WHEN TO OFFER TREATMENT

Some children and young people want and need help immediately after the allegations emerge, but many, once the child protection process has occurred, want time to recover to get on with their lives, perhaps in a new place within a different family structure. Many report that they want to feel human again, get on at school and find their friends. Generally, children and young people do need to remember and it may take some time in treatment to develop sufficient trust to be able then to work on the issues. But they also need to be allowed to forget so that having done some work they can move on and not be made to go over the abuse again and again.

It seems, therefore, that some want help immediately, some when settled in their placement, and some at the onset of puberty or when involved in an intimate relationship. (Some sexually abused survivors come for help when pregnant and others when their child is the age they were when abused.)

The timing is important; the person needs to know that treatment is available, and it needs to be offered. In response to a request for help it should be found, but help should not be forced, and genuine refusal needs to be respected. It is also important that those who have accepted treatment, and those who have declined treatment, should know that it is right and appropriate to seek further help at any time. 'Top ups' seem to be a vital part of any long-term treatment.

For many children and young people, there are few statutory services available and often the most appropriate and useful will be that provided by voluntary organisations or community groups. What can be offered varies enormously but can be extremely helpful as most of these sources of help are based in the community and so are local, not off-putting and not stigmatising. There are first the larger voluntary organisations, next the small local charities and, last, the self-help groups.

Treatment interventions

There are a number of treatment options that can be considered. Group therapy, which has been the treatment offered most frequently, is generally a focused therapy with all the participants having experienced sexual abuse. The groups are banded for age. Groups are not always easy to set up, as there may be insufficient children of a particular age, in which case many children are offered individual therapy. As more adolescents are often known to the services, group therapy is more often available for those in their teens. Whether the person is offered group or individual therapy, it is usually important to ensure that the carer(s) are also offered help. This may be in the form of carers' groups or individually. Group therapy may be successful even where the carers are in different situations—for example, one child with a single mother, the abuser having been excluded; one child with a parental couple, the abuser being outside the immediate family; one child in foster care or in a residential unit. Where the carers form a reasonably homogeneous group, group therapy seems to be of value (Hildebrand and Forbes, 1987).

Family work and family therapy are important at certain stages of the treatment. If a child or young person has been removed from the family and is due to be placed back at home, if the non-abusing parent and the sibling group need to work on shared issues, or if the alleged abuser is to remain or return to the household, then, in all these situations, family work or family therapy can be helpful. It is rarely the first intervention, but it may be prudent to consider family work or family therapy as part of the treatment package. It is vital that child protection issues are not seen as being the responsibility of the non-abusing carer or even of the child or young person.

As well as seeing the whole family, there are often major issues between mother and daughter if the daughter has been abused by a family member. The mother may have been unavailable emotionally or physically, or another child may have been the preferred child. The child or young person may be triumphant and very difficult or depressed, anxious and either clingy or avoidant. Work with the mother–daughter couple in such situations can be essential.

Some young people or children may need help through medication. Young people over 16 years may benefit from the newer antidepressants if there is clinical depression. A very small number of children and young people present with what appears to be attention deficit hyperactivity disorder ADHD) and so it may be useful to try methyl phenidate for a short period to see if there is some relief. Some children and young people may have such severe post traumatic stress disorder (PTSD) that they can almost appear psychotic, and it is important to assess the child or young person carefully. If the flashbacks or re-experiencing are too overwhelming, medication may be helpful, although talking the person through the episode is probably preferable.

Forms of psychological treatments

Psychological treatments, frequently referred to as the talking treatments, have different theoretical frameworks although abused children frequently require practitioners to be able to draw on a range of concepts. The main useful frameworks are cognitive behavioural, psychodynamic, attachment and systems theory.

Cognitive behavioural treatments can include debriefing, social skills training, anger management and sexualised behaviour management. A particular problem is identified and this is explored and worked on in a systematic way taking individuals through a planned programme and this may be individually or in a group.

Psychodynamic therapy may be brief focused, may be once weekly open ended or several times weekly open ended. It may draw on attachment theory, psychoanalytic theory or cognitive analytic. Change in children or young persons, whether they are seen individually or in a group, is brought about by focusing on the relationship between the therapist and the person, seeing in this microcosm a repetition of the past symptoms, behaviours and relationships that are causing distress. These are put into words and discussed but the main therapeutic agent is the therapeutic relationship where the children or young persons experience the other as responding in a different way from earlier relationships and where they can try out different responses themselves. It is well known that children abused physically can be so used to this style of interaction that when it doesn't happen in a new relationship, they can be more and more defiant—apparently seeking the usual response from adults, i.e. physical abuse. When this fails to happen, they can be confused and in a panic; through this, they learn about themselves and others. In many small and large incidences like this, sexually abused children and young people learn about themselves, their thoughts, feelings and responses and how the therapist(s) can provide an experience of another that responds differently and also can enable them to think about what is happening to make them feel differently and to show it verbally and non-verbally. The practitioner also frequently is acting as a secure base and is providing a model of an attachment relationship—a concerned empathic adult that can be trusted to maintain an appropriate emotional and behavioural environment.

Educational treatment can take place in a clinic or a school setting and is an applied therapeutic intervention. The child or young person is seen and the focus is the school tasks, but when difficulties emerge, the tasks are explored to discover the emotional, behavioural or relationship issues that are inhibiting or blocking learning and functioning. By identifying problems as they emerge in the learning environment, it is immediately possible to make the links between family issues, internal mental state and thinking, remembering and understanding. Practitioners working this way need to draw on cognitive behavioural, psychodynamic and attachment theory.

Creative arts interventions can involve art, music, drama or sand tray work; movement or dance is also used. These non-verbal therapies are often very helpful for young people and those who lack the confidence or the social and verbal skills to manage the 'talking treatments'. Music evokes feelings, sand tray work, painting, drawing and clay form another means by which individuals or groups can express abstract thoughts and feelings. Dance and drama therapy can be applied using someone else's 'script' or can be improvised at the time but again personal experience is distanced and, hence, made manageable or perhaps even made thinkable. Once again, the main theoretical frameworks used are psychodynamic and attachment theory alongside appreciating creative skills.

Clearly, all these interventions use play as a means of communication. How the play is used in the treatment depends on the therapeutic task. Play therapy is an intervention in its own right, drawing on the creative arts, psychodynamic understanding and cognitive behavioural learning theory, and the practitioner may be seen as a secure base and offer the experience of an attachment figure.

It is important when selecting an intervention to be clear about the tasks to be addressed. These may include:

- working on abuse issues;
- working on current disruptions, losses, separation;

- working on earlier childhood issues;
- ameliorating psychopathology frequently:
  — post-traumatic stress disorder
  — depression and suicidal thoughts
  — anxiety and panic attacks
  — separation anxiety
  — atttachment disorders
  — conduct disorders
  — eating disorders;
- working on future plans, self-confidence self-esteem;
- working on family and social relationships.

PROBLEMS WHEN OFFERING TREATMENT

When sexual abuse has occurred, a number of issues need to be considered. Some children and young people are apprehensive about being seen individually and prefer group treatment—probably because individual work involves being in a closed room with one adult, and may resemble the abuse situation. Some individuals do not want, or refuse, to be treated by a male therapist; others decline a female therapist. This also needs to be taken seriously, but has advantages and disadvantages; whichever gender the therapist may be the individual may change his or her view during treatment. It is important to be as sensitive and as thoughtful as possible. The race and culture of the therapist is very important and matching as far as possible is appropriate.

Where there are language differences, work with a translator changes the treatment. Similarly, where the child or young person is deaf and a signer is required, it may change the treatment but it can also enrich the treatment to have the child or young person witness and experience two adults able to co-operate and work together to further his or her best interest.

Children and young people with learning disabilities, physical disabilities or chronic illness are over-represented among those who have been abused. Good access to the treatment premises are vital and the therapists need to have learned the modifications to their techniques to make the interventions appropriate (Turning Points, 1997).

When offering treatment, it is crucial to be clear about consent from the child or young person, his or her carer and anyone with parental responsibility, e.g. parent or social worker. The issue of confidentiality and its limits must be explored. It must be made clear that if there are serious concerns about current abuse, they will need to be shared. This sounds straightforward but, in fact, it is one of the most complex and difficult issues when working with an abused person. During the treatment, post-traumatic stress disorder may emerge or it may be present from the start. Flashbacks of the abuse, or re-experiencing the abuse, or very vivid dreams that are an abuse enactment, need to be carefully distinguished from real current abuse. If the individuals are to build up their trust, they will want to be given time to explore, but it is all too easy for the therapist to be caught in an optimistic state of mind, convinced that re-abuse cannot be happening. Holding on to uncertainty and exploring the possibilities often need to be part of good supervision to ensure that there is no collusion or precipitate action.

When children or young persons who have been abused are offered treatment, their carers need support to bring the children and also to think about fluctuations in the children's behaviour or emotional state. The abuse may also have evoked memories of their own abuse and they may also need to be rebuilding their own lives. Finding colleagues to work with the carers is often a big problem but is essential. Children often cannot change unless their home environment allows it and can manage to support tentative new ways of interacting.

But, perhaps, the major issue is the emotional impact on the person providing the treatment, in whatever form. Often, the material brought to treatment is very distressing—guilt and shame—but also excitement, sexual innuendo and repeated sexualisation of words, behaviour, interaction. Many people who work with sexually abused children and young people do not have good-quality regular supervision. This is vital to be able to stay in touch with the child, to be able to bear what is heard and seen, and not to allow the abuse to enter one's personal life and relationships. This latter is extremely difficult, given that the material is intrusive and provokes revulsion, intense compassion and violent and sexual thoughts.

PSYCHOTHERAPY OUTCOME STUDY WITH SEXUALLY ABUSED GIRLS

Finkelhor and Berliner, as reported earlier, have reviewed treatment programmes that have been evaluated and were offered to sexually abused children and young people. It seemed important to continue this outcome research, and in 1993 the Psychotherapy Outcome Study was funded by the Department of Health and the Mental Health Foundation. The study was based at the Tavistock Clinic, Maudesley Hospital, Royal Free Hospital, Guy's Hospital and Camberwell Child Guidance, all in London, UK. Design and method issues are reported elsewhere (Trowell *et al.*, 1995). This study was for sexually abused girls, and a parallel study for abused and abusing boys was conducted at Great Ormond Street Hospital (Skuse *et al.*, 1998).

After baseline assessment the girls (6–14 years) were randomly allocated to group or individual psychotherapy. The individual therapy consisted of

up to 30 sessions of psychodynamic focused therapy which was child centred, so that issues were discussed as the child raised them. The group
therapy was psycho-educational and psycho-therapeutic with a set agenda
prior to each group. The group had a male and a female as co-leaders, with
the number of participants varying between 12 and 18. The girls were
banded for age, the older girls having more sessions. Both the individual
and the group members addressed the relationship that evolved with their
therapist, and all the therapists had regular highly skilled and experienced
supervisors.

The girls were seen for follow-up one and two years after the start of
therapy. Much of the earlier part of this chapter has been crystallised from
the experience of this project which has both confirmed and contradicted
clinical experience.

Each girl had frequent symptoms and problems, particularly post-
traumatic stress disorder, major depressive disorder and the anxiety disorders, and this was confirmed by the high number of co-existing disorders.
This means that many or most children with mental health problems do not
have just one disorder, but often, two or three. In this sample of sexually
abused girls, there were four to six disorders in 50% of the girls. This was
compared with a community sample of non-abused mental health referrals,
where the average number of disorders was two (Trowell *et al.*, 1999).

Similarly, these sexually abused girls were more seriously impaired by
their symptoms and disorders than had been recognised in previous studies
of referred sexually abused girls (Trowell *et al.*, in preparation)

Of the girls referred, 81 were assessed; referrals were excluded where a
girl was not adequately protected in her current placement, or where a girl
was too disturbed to cope with outpatient individual or group therapy.
Some girls refused to participate in the outcome study and were offered
alternatives.

Only two girls discontinued their treatment. Many of the girls were traced
for the one-year follow-up, and the majority for the second year follow-up.
Some girls refused to be seen for follow up, wanting to put the abuse behind
them. At baseline, the girls were very distressed: three-quarters had post-
traumatic stress disorder; half were clinically depressed, many with suicidal
thoughts and behaviour; and two-thirds were experiencing anxiety, panic
attack and separation anxiety.

Alongside the work with the girls, carers were offered support, frequency
was negotiated, and these workers were also supervised. It must be remembered that these girls were referred to a particular project and this is not to
imply that all sexually abused girls have this level of difficulty. All these
girls had symptoms as well as an abuse history.

Overall, the girls improved considerably, the depression and anxiety di-
minished and post-traumatic stress disorder reduced considerably. The

girls' educational functioning in school also improved considerably, almost reaching the same level as our non-abused control group. Differences in outcome between individuals and groups are not apparent in the psychopathology (PTSD, depression, anxiety, etc.). Other measures are currently being analysed, such as self-esteem, coping strategies, child behaviour check list (CBCL) and family functioning. There is also a considerable amount of qualitative data such as drawings, clinical assessments, a structured clinical interview and the therapy notes.

Preliminary data analysis on the outcome has suggested some interesting variables that influence change. Approximately one-quarter of the girls were fostered and all of them entered therapy. They, at baseline, were less troubled by PTSD despite the abuse having been for longer, starting at an earlier age and involving more abusers. However, by the two-year follow-up, they had not done so well, and PTSD had improved less than other psychopathology. The impact of the disruption and loss of their family, school and friends—and, for some, frequent moves—seemed to have counteracted the initial benefit gained from their removal from the abusive environment. But it must be remembered that these were the most severely abused girls with the most disturbed family background.

Where the child remained with a parent, the overall improvement continued in the year after the end of therapy. The girls reported much improved relationships with their mothers and most felt closer to and could talk to them. The mothers and foster carers had all worked in the project but the mothers seemed able to use this to continue to facilitate their daughters' improvement after the professional intervention ceased.

The notes and records of the individual work have been analysed (the group notes await analysis). The topics of concern to the girls, given that the treatment was child led, were in two main areas. First was the disturbance, disruption or loss of the relationship with the mother. A few mothers had died, others had had a major psychiatric illness, and many were depressed or involved in situations of domestic violence (54%). Many mothers had been the subject of physical or sexual abuse in their own childhood (68%). The second issue was the sexual abuse itself which was either dominating the child's thoughts and/or actions; or it was denied, leaving the child cut off, flat, and unresponsive.

How well both these issues (which were often intertwined) could be covered, partly seems to have determined the outcome. But interestingly, how the girls' relationship with the therapist developed and could be talked about also seemed important. When the therapist could acknowledge the girls' rage and pain in the room, and they could talk about the ensuing treatment, progress followed. If the rage and pain were outside with the abuser, progress was slower or absent.

For both the girls and the therapist, chaos and confusion reigned frequently, as did a sense of mindlessness—a lack of capacity to think or remember. For example, most girls could not even remember the way to the treatment room after five sessions, although almost all could after 20 sessions. The capacity to remember the way to the room seems to be linked to outcome—that is, the capacity to think and remember was emerging or re-emerging.

Where the girls had had some experience of good enough parenting, they could respond to, and use, the treatment. But for some girls, the abuse had followed early experiences of an absent or unavailable (physically or mentally) main carer and they seemed to have nothing inside to build on—the therapist's report feeling that there was a void, an emptiness. If this was present, it seems to be also linked to outcome. Some girls did well despite severe early deprivation when the current carer could support and respond, but some carers lacked this capacity even when they engaged in and tried to use their own parent support work on the project.

Many of these girls would not have been offered help outside the project and some of them would have been seen as unlikely candidates. Their capacity to attempt to engage was very well supported by their referrer, usually the social worker, and this commitment was essential. Because of it, many girls improved and many of them have since been able to ask for or seek out more help as they felt they needed it. The interest and support of the social worker in these very disturbed girls made all the difference in terms of what the girls could obtain from the project.

Parallel work with the carers was also vital as it helped them to understand the girl and themselves and to accept the changes. As indicated, many of the carers were preoccupied with their own issues from their childhood or with current issues. The work with the carers focused on encouraging them to bring the girls on management issues and, where appropriate, on their own preoccupations. Many carers were in a state of shock and loss themselves, as well as in touch with their own experiences and seized the time to discuss their own situations.

Most of the carers were seen individually because of the range of topics they wished to raise. Some parents were much more preoccupied with family issues where the abuser was from the extended family or a close friend. Some foster carers had many issues of their own, while other foster carers were very experienced specialist carers. Some carers were seen in groups, giving some advantages when the carers had common problems. The effectiveness of the carers' groups varied with the extent to which they could share concerns. Where each member had a particular issue, it was difficult to manage the group to make it helpful to the carers. The main management issues that arose were how to manage the changes in the girls. Girls who had been angry and rebellious often became sad and depressed, and girls who were dissociating, blank and flat first became more aware of their situation then became angry or sad and depressed. Often, carers found these changes difficult to accept, but it was important that this process should be understood.

CONCLUSION

This project confirms that where sexual abuse has occurred, the situation for the children or young persons can be improved if they request help. It also stresses the need for a careful assessment of the problems and difficulties after the child abuse issues have been dealt with. It is unclear how many abused children and young people need help.

The form of therapy or intervention, and who is available to do the work, will depend on resources. But this project also demonstrates that some severely damaged abused girls needed specialist help and this help may need to be lengthy. However, many girls made good use of what was available and could get on with their lives.

SUMMARY

Assessment

Child sexual abuse (CSA) is not a disorder, it is an event and so assessment is a complex process preferably involving a multidisciplinary team. Aspects of the child's behaviour, functioning and story alongside a picture of the family and the alleged abuser are considered. The past history of each individual is also important and slowly the pieces of the jigsaw make up the process of the assessment.

Treatment

This involves a range of intervention for the sexually abused survivor, the family, the abuser and the professionals. The impact of CSA is always profound and needs to be acknowledged whenever it emerges—that is, all the time or subsequently.

Given the complexity, treatment always involves a range of intervention and considerable resources, but we now have evidence that it can help to improve overall function and school performance, and can also reduce distress.

REFERENCES

Bagley, C. and Ramsay, R. (1986) Sexual abuse in childhood: psychological outcomes and implications for social work practice. *Journal of Social Work and Human Sexuality*, **4**: 33–47.

Beitchman, J.H., Zucker, K.J., Hood, J.E., Da Costa, G.A., and Akman, D. (1991) A review of the short term effects of child sexual abuse. *Child Abuse and Neglect*, **15**: 537–556.

Beitchman, J.H., Zucker, K.J., Hood. J.E., Da Costa, G.A., Akman, D. and Cassaria, E. (1992) A review of the long term effects of child sexual abuse. *Child Abuse and Neglect*, **16**: 101–118.

Berliner, L. and Elliot, D.M. (1996) Sexual abuse of children, in Briere, J., Berliner, L., Bulkley, J., Jenny, C., and Reid, T. (eds) *The APSAC Handbook on Child Maltreatment* Thousand Oaks, CA, Sage, pp. 51-71.

Berliner, L. and Saunders, B. (1996) Treating fear and anxiety in sexually abused children: results of a controlled 2-year follow-up study. *Child Maltreatment*, **1** (4, November): 294-309.

Bifulco, A., Brown, G.W. and Alder, Z. (1991) Early sexual abuse and clinical depression in adult life. *British Journal of Psychiatry*, **159**: 115–122.

Briere, J. and Runtz, M. (1993) Child sexual abuse: long term sequalae and implications for assessment. *Journal of Interpersonal Violence*, **2**: 367–379.

Browne, A. and Finkelhor, D. (1986) Initial and long term effects: a review of the research, in Finkelhor, D. (ed.) *A Source Book on Child Sexual Abuse*. Beverly Hills, Sage.

Bushnell, J.A., Wells, J.E. and Oakley Browne, M. (1993) Long term effects of intrafamilial sexual abuse in childhood. *Acta Psychiatrica Scandinavia*, **85**: 136-142.

Conte, J.R. and Schuerman, J.R. (1987) Factors associated with an increased impact of child sexual abuse. *Child Abuse and Neglect*, **11**: 201–211.

Deblinger, E., McLeer, S.V., Atkins, M.S., Ralphe, D.L., and Foa, E.B. (1989) Post-traumatic stress in sexually abused, physically abused and non-abused children. *Child Abuse and Neglect*, **13**: 403–408.

Deblinger, E., McLeer, S.V. and Henry, D. (1990) Cognitive behavioural treatment for sexually abused children suffering post-traumatic stress: preliminary findings. *Journal of American Academy of Child and Adolescent Psychiatry*, **29**: 747–752.

Finkelhor, D. and Baron, L. (1986) Risk factors for child sexual abuse. *Journal of Interpersonal Violence*, **1**: 43–71.

Finkelhor, D. and Berliner, L. (1995) Research on the treatment of sexually abused children: a review and recommendations. *Journal of American Academy of Child and Adolescent Psychiatry*, **34**.(11): 1408–1423.

Freidrich, W.N. (1993) Sexual victimization and sexual behaviour in children and a review of recent literature. *Child Abuse and Neglect*, **17**: 59–66.

Freidrich, W.N., Beilke R.L. and Urquinza, A.J. (1987) Children from sexually abusive families: a behavioural comparison. *Journal of Interpersonal Violence*, **2**: 391–402.

Herman, J.L., Perry, J.C. and Vander Kolk, B.A. (1989) Childhood trauma in borderline personality disorder. *American Journal of Psychiatry*, **146**: 490–495.

Herman, J., Russell, D. and Trochi, K. (1986) Long term effects of incestuous abuse in childhood. *American Journal of Psychiatry*, **143**: 1293–1296.

Hildebrand, J. and Forbes, C. (1987) Group work with mothers who have been sexually abused. *British Journal of Social Work*, **17**(3): 285–303.

Johns, M. (1997) *NSPCC Study of Children's Recovery Process*. London, NSPCC.

Kolko, D.J., Moser, J.T. and Weldy, S.R. (1988) Behavioural/emotional indicators of sexual abuse in child psychiatric inpatients: a controlled comparison with physical abuse. *Child Abuse and Neglect*, **12**: 529–541.

Mannarino, A.P. and Cohen, J.A. (1996) A follow up study of factors that mediate the development of psychological symptomalogy in sexually abused girls. *Child Maltreatment*, **1**(3): 246–260.

McLeer, S.V., Deblinger, E., Atkins, M.S., Foa, E.B. and Ralphe, D.L. (1988) Post-traumatic stress disorder in sexually abused children. *Journal of American Academy of Child and Adolescent Psychiatry*, **27**: 650–654.

McLeer, S.V., Deblinger, E., Henry, D. and Orvaschel, H. (1992) Sexual abused children at high risk for post-traumatic stress disorder. *Journal of American Academy of Child and Adolescent Psychiatry*, **31**: 875–879.

Mullen, P.E. (1990) The long term influence of sexual assault on the mental health of victims. *Journal of Forensic Psychiatry*, **1**: 13–34.

Mullen, P., Martin, J., Anderson, J., Romans, S. and Herbison, G.P. (1993) Childhood sexual abuse and mental health in adult life. *British Journal of Psychiatry*, **163**: 721–732

Mullen, P.E., Romans, S., Clarkson, S.E., and Walton, V.A. (1988) Impact of sexual and physical abuse on women's mental health. *Lancet*, **1**: 841–845.

Oates, R.K. and Tong, L. (1987) Child sexual abuse: an area with room for professional reforms. *Medical Journal of Australia*, **147**: 544–548.

Palmer, R.L., Chaloner, D.A. and Oppenheimer, R. (1992) Childhood sexual experiences with adults reported by female psychiatric patients. *British Journal of Psychiatry*, **156**: 261–265.

Russell, D.E.H. (1986) *The Secret Trauma: Incest in the Lives of Girls and Women* New York, Basic Books.

Skuse, D., Bentovim, A., Hodges, S., Stevenson, J., Williams, B., New, M., Lanyado, M. and Andreou, C. (1998) Risk factors for the development of sexually abusive behaviour in sexually victimised adolescent males. *British Medical Journal*, **317**: 175-179.

Tebbitt, J., Swanston, H., Oates, K. and O'Toole, B. (1997) Five years after child sexual abuse: persisting dysfunction and problems of prediction. *Journal of American Academy of Child and Adolescent Psychiatry*, **36**(3): 330–339.

Terr, L.C. (1991) Child traumas: an outline and overview. *American Journal of Psychiatry*, **148**: 10–70.

Tong, L. and Oates, R.K. (1990) Long term effects of child sexual abuse, in Oates, R.K. (ed.) *Understanding and Managing Child Sexual Abuse*. London, Saunders.

Trowell, J., Berelowitz, M. and Kolvin, I. (1995) The design and methodological issues in setting up a psychotherapy outcome study with girls who have been sexually abused, in Aveline, M. and Shapiro, D. (eds) *Research Foundations for Psychotherapy Practice*. London, Wiley.

Trowell, J. and Hodges, S. (1997) Emotional abuse: the work of a young family centre. *Child Abuse Review*, **6**: 357–369.

Trowell, J., Sadowski, H., Kolvin, I., Berelowitz, M., Weeramanthri, T. and Leitch, I. (in preparation). Abuse characteristics as risk factors for psychiatric impairment in sexually abused girls – findings from the Tavistock/Maudsley Treatment Outcome Study.

Trowell, J., Ugarte, B., Kolvin I., Berelowitz, M., Sadowski, H. and Le Couteur, A. (1999) Behavioural psychopathology of child sexual abuse in school girls referred to a tertiary centre – a North London study. *European Journal of Child and Adolescent Psychiatry*.

Turning Points (1997) *A Resource Pack for Communicating with Children*. NSPCC Publication.

7

COPING, SURVIVING AND HEALING FROM CHILD SEXUAL ABUSE

Clare Woodward and Donal Fortune

> 'He adjusted himself to beams falling and then no
> more of them fell, and he adjusted himself to them
> not falling.' DASHIELL HAMMETT

The sexual abuse of children represents one of the most invidious violations of the rights of the child. Despite the well-documented pervasiveness of the social taboo surrounding discussion of the occurrence and extent of child sexual abuse (CSA) (Draucker, 1992; Rush, 1980), and the understandable desire to believe that CSA represents a small clinically discrete subcategory of socioeconomic disadvantage and individual pathology, CSA is nonetheless increasingly coming to the attention of professionals working in the field and also in epidemiological or survey investigations of incidence and prevalence (see Baker and Duncan, 1985; Kelly *et al.*, 1991). In a relatively recent survey conducted by the NSPCC (June, 1995), one in six adults reported having experienced sexual 'interference' as a child.

CSA also undermines our expectancies about what constitutes acceptable behaviour towards children. The fact that, in many instances, the perpetrator and victim are either known to each other or are of the same family can often make it difficult for us to comprehend how healing from abuse may be possible at all, given the wider emotional and attachment issues that ramify from the actual abuse acts. It can be relatively easy to believe that abuse in childhood is so traumatic that the abused individual, remain locked forever within the abuse experience, interpreting the world from a vantage point built upon damage, anger and pain: never able to free themselves from the abuse perhaps to the point of acting out their own abuse on their children. Yet in the majority of cases, people abused in childhood do not go on to inflict damage on themselves or others. Prospective follow-up studies of parents who were victims of child abuse show that only a small minority go on to abuse their own children (Browne and Herbert, 1995). For this small minority of people who do go on to repeat patterns of abuse, this is likely to be the result of failure of the process of attachment in their own childhood and of the lack of appropriate care-giving role-models within the context of the survivor's development to adulthood. While the rate of child abuse attributed to individuals with a history of abuse is higher than in the general population, the inevitability of intergenerational abuse has not been substantiated. The beliefs of people abused as children both about themselves and the abuse—while certainly prone to characteristic distortions and unhelpful feelings of stigma, shame or disgust from time to time—can be conceived in the majority of cases as being relatively normal responses to the abnormality of their experiences. Children who were victims of abuse do heal from their abuse and survive in creative and heroic ways and indeed, for many, survive also in the face of considerable psychological and social adversity.

This chapter will look at the ways that children who have been sexually abused go on to heal from their abuse. It adopts a salutogenic perspective recognising that disclosure is central to beginning the process of healing, and, using the words of adults abused as children, shows that despite the undertow of pain and distress that sexual abuse brings with it both in the immediate and in the longer term, healing is possible. The chapter also examines some of the more systemic effects and moderators of abuse and healing, recognises that abuse occurs within family and social systems, and suggests the importance of support for both the child and the family. In the second half of this chapter we will use the personal accounts of healing from respondents to the National Commission of Inquiry into the Prevention of Child Abuse (NCIPCA) to illustrate the range of experiences of healing.[1]

CHILDREN'S STRENGTHS

Children have often been perceived by adults as being in the possession of some intrinsic resilience that protects them from acutely stressful events. On exposure to trauma, there was the expectation that, at worst, they would develop a short-lived reaction and then the whole nasty business would be forgotten. It has become well recognised that such simplistic considerations do not change the fact that children experience debilitating reactions that may not be forgotten over time (Yule, 1996). However, it is also important to stress that within the pain and distress that results from abuse, children do show remarkable resilience in the face of such adversity. This allows us to focus on the salutogenics of survival while also recognising the pain and distress that will invariably be enmeshed within it.

THE INEVITABILITY OF LONG-TERM NEGATIVE EFFECTS OF CSA?

Research from the past two decades has drawn attention to the pervasive and long-lasting negative effects of CSA on individuals with regard to a range of psychological, social and physical perturbations that have been linked to histories of abuse. Adults who were sexually abused in childhood have been shown to experience raised levels of psychological distress (Jehu *et al.*, 1988), including symptoms of post-traumatic stress disorder (McNew and Abell, 1995) as well as a number of other psychological difficulties such as depression and low self-esteem (Cahill *et al.*, 1991), feelings of guilt and self-blame (Ussher and Dewberry, 1995), general difficulties in relationships due to feelings of isolation, alienation and stigmatisation (Briere, 1989; Finkelhor and Browne, 1985), and sexual problems (Gold, 1986). These studies have tended towards the use of clinical samples which may not be generalisable to non-clinical populations. More recently meta-analytic reviews have suggested that certainly in the general population, CSA is not necessarily associated with significant psychological maladjustment (Rind and Tromovitch, 1997), and that associations between histories of CSA and adult symptomatology are significantly stronger among clinical populations (Neumann *et al.*, 1996). A number of factors have been suggested as mediating the possible deleterious effects of CSA on subsequent psychological functioning. These include: (1) the age of the child at onset; (2) frequency and duration of the abuse; (3) relationship of the child to the abuser; (4) if the sexual activity is severe, such as penetration; (5) whether the child participates in the sexual abuse; (6) the negative reactions of parents/significant others to disclosure (including blaming the child and saying disclosure would split the family) (Friedrich, 1987; Russell, 1986). However, these factors have primarily been extracted through research on clinical populations. There is therefore a need to examine the stories of healing from community samples of adults abused as children.

THE IMMEDIATE EFFECTS OF CSA ON CHILDREN

Holmes *et al.* (1997) make the point that it is only when the topic of the long-term consequences of childhood abuse gains a firm footing that there is a development of a comprehensive literature on the more immediate effects of, and responses to, such trauma in childhood.

There is some debate about whether there are always identifiable consequences of child sexual abuse. This question is of related importance to whether there exists a pattern of behaviours that may permit more certainty in the diagnosis or recognition of abuse. There are a number of behavioural signs which are associated with child sexual abuse, but which could also be due to other kinds of stressors, such as marital conflict and divorce, school difficulties and so on. The British Psychological Society's working party on child sexual abuse (1990) stated that behaviours which *may* signify child sexual abuse in younger children are: wetting and soiling, aggressive outbursts, sexualised behaviour, verbal statements, and avoidance of bedtime or bath-time. In older children, behaviours may include running away from home, demarcated changes in performance at school, withdrawal, eating disorders, and reduced or excessive inhibition in areas such as the sports changing room.

More general immediate psychological distress has also been found once the abuse has come to light. Depression (Stern *et al.*, 1995), Anxiety (Spaccarelli and Fuchs, 1997), low self-esteem (Jehu et al, 1988), perceptions of interaction difficulties with peers, aggression, and sensitivity to negative statements (Young *et al.*, 1994) are consistent findings in the literature. Psychological distress of course occurs within family contexts and systems and attention has been given to events and conditions which may increase the likelihood or frequency of psychological distress in abused children. Of overwhelming importance to healing from CSA is the issue of disclosure and, more specifically, initial and ongoing reactions to disclosure.

REACTIONS TO DISCLOSURE

A number of variables have been shown to be significant predictors of the child's response and adjustment to abuse. These factors relate both to the physical characteristics of the abuse, such as type or severity of abuse, age at onset and frequency or duration of the abuse, and to issues pertaining to the family environment, such as the relationship of the abuser to the victim (Finkelhor and Browne, 1986; Mian *et al.*, 1996). Elizabeth Monck (1997) draws attention to probably the most important factor in deciding whether the abused child will show patterns of adjustment to her abuse—whether the child is believed by significant others following disclosure. This issue is a critical factor in enabling a child to feel sufficiently secure to begin the process of healing. In Monck's study of 161 children, 15% of the sample of mothers either believed only in part what their child had disclosed or rejected the child's claim completely. Looking at risk factors for psychological adjustment to abuse in 48 teenage and pre-teenage girls, Spaccarelli and Fuchs (1997) found that children who reported lower support from non-offending parents had significantly higher rates of psychological distress. In many studies that explicitly investigated maternal support, the availability of such support and willingness to believe the statement of the child has been shown to be dependent upon the strength of the relationship between the mother and the abuser. In the 1989 study by Everson and colleagues, 44% of mothers were classified as providing consistent support following disclosure with the remainder being ambivalent, unsupportive or rejecting. This lack of support is equivalent to poor safeguarding, as the child thus suffers a second victimisation and in some instances is actively encouraged to collude with the abusing parent in denying the abuse. Not surprisingly, a consistent finding is that support from the non-abusing parent is the most important predictor of child psychopathology resulting from abuse.

Disclosure of abuse in childhood is a matter of the interaction of opportunity, availability, decision and—particularly in younger children—accident. The process of disclosure has been viewed as a type of developmental process involving issues of denial and recanting (Jones and McGraw, 1987; Gonzalez et al., 1993). Summit (1983, 1992) coined the term Child Sexual Abuse Accommodation Syndrome (CSAAS) to describe a putative five-stage model (secrecy, helplessness, entrapment, and accommodation, delayed unconvincing disclosure, and finally retraction) through which the process of disclosure may occur. Similarly Sorenson and Snow (1991) also propose a five-stage model of disclosure built upon the examination of 116 cases where objective evidence of abuse was also present (medical evidence, confession of the abuser, or criminal conviction). According to this model, stages involved: (1) initial denial of the occurrence of abuse; (2) tentative disclosure with reluctance towards discussion; (3) active disclosure; (4) recantation; and (5) reaffirmation of the abuse allegation. The issue of recantation has obvious implications for whether children perceive they will be believed. Rates of recantation in clinical or practitioner settings have been reported as lying between 4% (Bradley and Wood, 1996) and 27% (Gonzalez et al., 1993). Moreover, Bradley and Wood's study has been cited as evidence against the stage or gradual unfolding model of disclosure, at least in their sample of child protection cases. Indeed, the use of only externally validated cases in this study does not rule out the possibility that the picture of disclosure in the population of abused children who have not come to the attention of child protection agencies may, in all probability, be quite different because of the lack of external validation.

The results of the National Commission suggest that the picture of disclosure may indeed be quite different in people who do not come to the attention of child protection agencies. In many cases survivors stated that the abuse did not stop because of any intervention, but as a result of proactive behaviour on the part of the person who was being abused. In the letters describing the abuse and its aftermath forwarded to the inquiry, 21% of respondents felt that they had to move away in order for the abuse to stop. Only one in ten stated that they had felt able to tell someone about the abuse directly. Many participants wrote that while they couldn't verbally disclose what was happening to them, they felt that they had given sufficient signals for any interested person to act upon, but no one asked them if they needed help.

Disclosure of abuse can bring about major upheavals in the world of the child. Rounds of questioning, accusations, distress, arguments, perhaps removal of a parent or sibling from the home, and the involvement of professionals, will all mean that this is a time fraught with uncertainty and anxiety. There is some evidence that children use what are termed 'boundary access rules', such as selecting the best circumstances to tell, and seeking tacit permission and incremental disclosure to reveal their experiences of abuse within the family (Petronio *et al.*, 1996). In a similar manner, abused children also use such rules to evaluate and anticipate the potential consequences that may ramify from their disclosure, and often decisions on whether to tell are based upon an appraisal of the consequences that the disclosure may present.

Shame may also influence whether the child discloses the abuse. Research by Wyatt and Mickey (1988) found that a self-blaming attributional style was associated with not having disclosed the abuse. The relationship between non-disclosure and shame is likely to be bidirectional. Non-disclosure may lead to shame through a lack of opportunity to talk about and re-present the abuse scenario to the self. In the absence of external reinforcement of worth of the self, the survivor may rerun the abuse interoceptively, and not receive or be unable to generate any challenges to inappropriate feelings of stigma, guilt and shame.

In children for whom disclosure information is available, the majority of children tend to disclose to their mothers (Monck, 1997). Bradley and Wood (1996) found that 72% of their sample of 234 children had already made an explicit disclosure to a family member prior to child protection involvement, and that only 4% of children recanted their abuse allegation—usually as a result of care-taker pressure.

It was found within the NCIPCA sample that for the adults who told about the abuse as children (32%) told those most available to them, particularly their mothers (34%).

Findings from NCIPCA

In looking at the telling process it was possible to code the responses the person received according to whether they were (a) positive, (b) negative or (c) neutral. A positive response was recorded where it was clear that the writer had felt supported through the process of disclosure; a negative response was one in which the respondent was punished in some way as a result of telling, while a neutral response was coded where it was reported that the information was given but the teller neither felt supported nor punished but may be upset by the ambivalence of the response received. It was found that negative or neutral responses were more common than positive responses, with children in particular being less likely to get a positive response to disclosure.

One clear distinction found between respondents who told as adults and those who told as children was that those who told as children were more likely to be younger at the time of writing. While those who told covered all age groups, they were over-represented in the 25 and under group. This suggests that the recent decade of publicity and heightening of awareness concerning child sexual abuse has had some effect in relation to telling. It is also applicable to adults, many of whom had themselves told within the last ten years. Jennie illustrates the benefits of telling:

> 'Since disclosing to a very trusted friend I have got some professional help with coping with my past . . . I am 16 years of age and it is almost a round year since I disclosed and because of the support and love of a friend I am coping with what happened so much better. My flashbacks are not so violent as they were 18 months ago and I no longer live in fear that (a) no one will believe me, and (b) that I would be blamed.'

The majority of respondents to the National Commission were not able to disclose the abuse they were experiencing within childhood. Many felt that they were giving off signs and signals but no one seemed interested or intervened. Most (86%) reported not having received any help as children to deal with the abuse or the associated feelings which arose. Children often therefore had no choice but to cope with the abuse in any way they could. This was clearly illustrated by Sam:

> 'From the age of 8 years until my teens I was sexually abused by my stepfather, my mother knew the abuse was going on but did nothing to stop the abuse . . . She told all the family I was a compulsive liar, out of control and not to listen to me. I used to get blamed for everything that went wrong . . . it didn't take my sister and brother long to realise that if they had done something wrong and blamed me they got away with it and I got the beating. From the age of 12 when my dad died [he didn't know] my mother carried on with a vengeance. I had to take care of myself so I became a survivor in anyway I could.'

COPING

It is often difficult to disentangle attempts by the child at coping with abuse from challenging or problem behaviours. For example, sexualised behaviour may be an attempt to normalise the abuse act; coping through cognitive avoidance can lead to distraction from active images or thoughts about the abuse, and while having some short-term benefits, can lead to school work difficulties and difficulties in peer interactions; kicking up a ruckus and refusing to go to bed is an attempt to avoid the abuse happening, but is also likely to lead to categorisation as a 'difficult' child and the use of additional punitive measures to deal with such problem behaviours. According to Jenny Kitzinger (1990, p. 166):

> 'The survival strategies . . . are, in the mainstream literature, labelled symptoms of abuse or listed as a catalogue of sickness illustrating the terrible consequences of incest. Activities that could be recognised as attempts to resist, or cope with the abuse are instead . . . cited as evidence of deep psychic scarring. Such disease terminology obscures the child actively negotiating her way through the dangers of childhood. She is recast as a submissive object of victimisation.'

Children have been shown to cope with traumatic events by the use of a wide range of strategies—some of which will be adaptive, while others will be less so. Coping attempts will undoubtedly be shaped by the ongoing environment as well as particular characteristics of the child. There has been an increasing interest in processes of cognitive appraisal (how children assess the abuse impact against their ability to cope), coping strategies (what children engage in to deal with the abuse and its effects) and attributional processes (what they attribute their abuse to) and their relationship to outcome. Following the transactional account of stress and coping, wherein individuals will appraise the significance of a stressor against the resources that they can draw upon, children are seen as active processors of information rather than passive objects upon which the trauma impacts. Chaffin *et al.* (1997) looked at the strategies used by 84 7–12 year olds who experienced CSA. They reported four main strategies of coping: avoidance, internalised, angry and active/social.

These four main strategies and more subtle levels within these strategies can be clearly seen within some of the ways reported by writers to the National Commission.

- *Behavioural strategies of avoidance*
  'I avoided ever being alone with [father] and many nights I put a chair behind my bedroom door so if he visited my room, it would make a noise and hopefully disturb my stepmother.' [Jean]

- *Cognitive strategies of avoidance dissociation*
  'My way of coping with the abuse was to pretend that it was not really happening to me. I could not tell anyone because then it would become real. I had to keep it all to myself. During the actual acts I would draw my inner self out leaving my body so that I could not feel what was happening to me. I would just watch from the ceiling then go back to my body when it was all over.' [Fran]

- *Internalised*
  'I suppose I dealt with my abuse by internalising my feelings and blaming myself for letting it happen. After all I went to [the abuser's] house on more than one occasion. I also liked him—I did not like what he made me do but at least he gave me attention and in a strange way I did feel loved. Despite the pain it has caused me I could never be angry at him—at me yes.' [Linda]

- *Anger and the release of pain*
  'I became very angry and rude with everyone and anything, my mum could not understand me at all. To get rid of the hurt and frustration I felt inside I used to hit out at my dolls and teddies. I felt no one loved me and I hated the world.' [Rebecca]

- *Active/social*
  'I began going out a lot, just to get away from him and the house. I joined a gang and used to stay out virtually all the time. I would make sure that I left home before he came back from work and would not come back until very late at night. He tried to prevent me from going out but it didn't work, I would not obey him. Eventually I got a boyfriend and was married at 17.' [Carol]

Other coping strategies adopted by respondents included challenging the perpetrator which in several instances resulted in the abuse stopping. For example,

'When I was 13, I suddenly connected what he was doing to me with playground dirty jokes and next time he abused me, I asked him to stop and, to my surprise, he did.' [Jane]

The coping responses used and the beliefs that respondents had concerning how they 'lived through' and 'survived' the abuse is likely to have an impact in terms of how they feel about themselves. For those respondents who were able to take some form of control over what was happening to them at the time, through for example, putting a chair against the door to prevent the perpetrator from entering the bedroom, or marrying at a young age to escape the family home, are all powerful actions which are in contrast to much of the literature which has tended to focus predominantly on the powerlessness of the child in the abusive situation. Obviously, by recognising the strengths that many respondents illustrated within their narratives, it is not to say that those who did feel powerless at the time of the abuse, and indeed afterwards, could have done anything differently at the time. However, for some respondents it was evident that they felt that they should have done something differently, and prevented the abuse from either beginning in the first place or continuing to occur, for example, by disclosing that the abuse was happening. Given all the difficulties that surround being able to disclose and talk about one's experiences of abuse, one possible coping strategy is to write about the abuse and one's feelings.

> 'I have found that writing about what happened to me when I was younger very helpful. Every time I begin to think about the abuse I write my thoughts down in my diary. I then shut the book and feel better. It does not take all the pain away but it does help when I feel angry, confused or frustrated and have no one to turn to.' [Alice].

FORMAL HELP WITH HEALING IN CHILDHOOD

The most cursory of glances at the provision of psychological services for abused children suggests a considerable mismatch between what is available and what is required (Sharland et al., 1996). While there has been increasing emphasis on the rights of the child now enshrined in law in the 1989 Children Act (DoH, 1991), the Act does not cover all children or provide services where they are not already extant. Links with health services are problematic under the Act because a health authority must comply with the request for help from a local authority 'only provided that the request is compatible with its own statutory or other duties and does not unduly prejudice the discharge of its function' (Kurtz, 1995). Probably in most cases, whether due to temporal factors, access to services, non-disclosure or family issues, the majority of survivors only receive help in adulthood rather than childhood.

There have been initiatives since the early 1990s to attempt to redress this imbalance in service provision. Children are more likely now to be able to receive professional help at the time of their abuse than children abused at any other time. From 1991 the Department of Health allocated funds for the development or expansion of services for sexually abused children and adolescents to a number of voluntary agencies and also provided funding to evaluate the efficacy of such services (Monck et al., 1996; Monck and New, 1996). Some studies have reported improvement on measures of mood, self-esteem, and behaviour as a result of the intervention (Monck et al., 1996) while others have not (Kendall-Tackett et al., 1993), and at this early stage sufficient follow-up data is unavailable. The lack of consensus on outcome may have to do with particular therapeutic orientations used and also may be related to a difficulty in certain interventions in conceptualising children's difficulties in functional terms (locating distress and behaviour in context) rather than being guided by overly restrictive structural or diagnostic concerns (Persons, 1986).

RESPONDENTS TO THE NCIPCA: EXPERIENCES OF HELP RECEIVED AND HEALING

In addition to asking 'victims' for their 'experiences' of childhood abuse, NCIPCA also provided a list of questions on which respondents could give their views if they wished. Of interest to this chapter were the questions: If you need help where would you go? If you have experienced the 'child abuse system' run by professionals, what are your impressions of it? From the total sample of letters, 28% of respondents commented on the first question concerning the availability of help for those who had experienced childhood abuse. For over a third the view was that either respondents *did not know where to go for help* or *that they felt no one was interested*. Twenty-eight per cent of respondents also commented on the question concerning their views on the 'child abuse system' and the help that they had received. As the help received by respondents varied and was not always stated, help was coded as one broad category, which includes help received from mental health professionals, doctors, police and social workers. Thirty-three per cent of respondents wrote that they were critical of the help given, a further 30% were critical of the legal system and 16% were critical of Social Services.

For the respondents who wrote that they were currently receiving help, help was defined in two ways: formal and informal. *Formal help* referred to counselling, social work, medical, psychiatric and psychological services and voluntary organisations such as Rape Crisis, ChildLine, NSPCC and Relate; *informal help* referred to help given by family, friends and self-help through books, writing and other sources. Half of those who used counselling services commented that they were of most help, and approximately two-thirds of those who went to survivors groups and other voluntary organisation found them beneficial. Other key findings were (see Wattam and Woodward, 1996, pp. 104–106):

- In 44% of cases the respondents had not received any formal help.
- For 41% of respondents who had not received formal help and for 21% who did, informal help was listed as their greatest source of support (32% of the total sample).
- In 32% of cases, the respondents stated that their partners had helped them most.
- Of the 31% of respondents who made no comment on formal or informal help, it was clear that for over half (52%) no one was offering to help. In the remainder of cases it was not clear.
- Of the total sample, 27% felt that no one or nothing was helping.

Respondents' beliefs and feelings regarding the healing process often reflected whether they had received any help for their abuse and the type of

help they had received. Receiving help that enables individuals to undermine unhelpful or inappropriate beliefs and assumptions will obviously
have an impact upon how they feel about themselves. In addition to any
formal or informal help received, significant changes or turning point events
for the individual can come about in a number of different ways. For example, meeting a supportive partner or having a child. This view is illustrated by Lesley who writes:

> 'As the years went past I became a very difficult teenager, my father and I did
> not get on so I got many a good hiding, whenever my brother came home I
> found it very difficult to look at him. I was raped when I was 14, again I never
> told anybody. I ran away from home three times, and eventually married a
> man who used to beat me and abuse me. Then something wonderful happened
> I had my son. I was only 19 but he gave me a purpose and someone to love. I
> found the strength through my son to leave my abusive husband and start
> afresh.'

ADULTHOOD: COMING TO TERMS WITH THE ABUSE AND FINDING ACCEPTANCE

It is apparent from the research reviewed that healing is a long-term process
that involves choosing, discarding, adapting and assimilating different ways
and means of accepting one's self and the past. In general, healing from
abuse only occurs in adulthood, and only occurs in adulthood for a number
of reasons, which may have to do with opportunity, resources, geographical
distance, social change and so on. However, the most important factor is
also the simplest one—healing takes time.

> 'The legacy of pain that abuse carries doesn't just go away—although now I
> can honestly say that things have certainly become easier. I can remember a
> time when all I ever thought about was the abuse—blurred memories that felt
> so unreal. I thought I was going crazy, "it didn't happen, I must be making it
> up". At times it was so hard just to get through each day. I often felt that when
> in public I was wearing a mask—I couldn't just be me, for one thing I didn't
> know who "me" was, and for another I was scared how people would react if
> they really knew about me and my past. Today, I no longer need my mask—I
> don't blame myself for the abuse and I refuse to carry the shame—the abuse
> wasn't my fault. The key to my happiness I see as being more accepting of
> myself—and in achieving this I thank firstly ME.' [Mary]

Coming to terms

> 'I was sexually abused by my father until I was 15 years old, when I finally
> managed to say something about it. I, however, regard myself as one of the
> lucky ones as all along the line I have found understanding, and when I finally

admitted needing it, help to come to terms with the legacy left over . . . I think the most notable aspect of my healing is the fact that I can now discuss things with my mum on an equal footing. I've come to the conclusion that, okay, she wasn't wonder mum but funnily enough so has she. We talked a lot over the past few months and cleared up a lot of things and although I have lost my pretence of a perfect family I have gained a very good friend in my mum. I still get down occasionally and I know I've still got a way to go, but I can finally see the end of the tunnel and I know that soon I'll be the person I could have been for many years, and that's even without the happy ever after bit.' [Janice]

. . . and finding acceptance

'My sense of self at the moment has really shifted. I suppose it was only till very recently that I stopped seeing [the abuse] as very negative. In the beginning it really felt like I have got to root it out – take it out, get rid of and feel it. I think gradually over the last few years I have become much more about accepting and coming to terms and realising that it is so much part of who I am, that I can't root it out. I don't want to root it out. I want to acknowledge it and work with it, and more recently I suppose I have been starting to feel it as a gift. You know I actually feel quite pleased with the things about who I am in terms of having been abused and being a "survivor".' [Kerry]

VICTIM AND SURVIVOR IDENTITIES

One way to explore how people feel about themselves as they move through the process of healing is to ask those individuals who have adopted the label either 'victim' or 'survivor', to explain what these terms actually mean for them. In some instances this may have no significance, while for others it can be very symbolic in terms of how they currently perceive themselves and often reflects differences between individuals in terms of, for example, help received or denied, beliefs and feelings regarding the abuse, coping responses used, the healing process and one's sense of Self. Identities such as 'survivor' or 'victim' had many different meanings for respondents, from feeling like a victim because they perceive themselves to be a 'nothing person' to the use of the survivor identity to indicate that they are in control of their life having 'come to terms' with their past experiences. Several respondents also wrote about how they were once victims and how they are now survivors, and in doing so described how this 'transformation of self' had taken place. Often within the literature people who have experienced CSA are seen either as all victims or as all survivors, and while both these terms are shorthands to the phrase 'people who have experienced sexual abuse in childhood', it does not take into account the differences that can exist between individuals and indeed within the same individual over time. People can occupy a number of standpoints simultaneously engaging in identification with others who have been abused and also wishing not to because of the difficulty in accepting that adults can be capable of inflicting such pain on those they purport to love.

> 'These are the years in which I came to terms with the knowledge that I am a survivor of childhood sexual abuse. Even now its hard to use the term "survivor". I want to stand tall with the many women and men who have experienced abuse of all forms, but at the same time I still don't really want to believe that it happened to me—but what choice do I have?' [Mary]

Simply asking why people feel that they are victims or survivors or neither can provide a subtle means whereby individual differences in terms of how they feel about themselves in relation to their past experiences of abuse can be revealed. In addition, by not taking into account the various connotations that these labels might have, may lead some individuals to feel further abused by being misrepresented. Of course, some people do not use either of these labels or, if they do, they do not attach any real meaning to the terms used. But, for some respondents, being described in a certain way is an important issue. For example:

> 'I hope that [by telling of my experiences] it is clear that I was not simply a "victim" at any stage—I did well at school and was generally well liked. I was very independent and had the ability to cope with life—qualities which are shared by many adult survivors. I find the stereotype of the victim helplessly drifting through life, allowing her own children to be abused and often alcoholic, etc., etc., not only offensive, but it also prevented me from speaking out for many years and I know this is common to many survivors. The research on which this stereotype is based is often on a small minority of people who have remained victims and have not been able to cope. Of course they exist—as do those who don't make it at all, but are murdered or commit suicide because they can't cope with the pain—but they are not the majority. The majority— who must number hundreds of thousands—do cope despite the pain, have careers and marriages, friends and hobbies just like other people.' [Chris]

CONCLUSION

This chapter has attempted to take a broad approach to the issue of healing from child sexual abuse. Disclosure has been given a prominent place and in a sense is the pivot around which healing can begin in the first instance. Children are resilient and deal with their abuse in a wide range of ways. This resilience in no way detracts from knowledge about (a) the immense pain and distress of ongoing abuse, and (b) that such abuse can have real lasting effects on the child. However, it is important not to superimpose our own absolutist notions of what it is in terms of behaviour, emotion or cognitions that constitutes adaptive coping. There is a relatively unique phenomenological quality to the form that coping with the abuse and its aftermath takes. Certain children and adults will have opportunities to use and develop different ways of dealing with their abuse. Notions of right and wrong ways of coping are often unhelpful and can lead to internalising value judgements and impossible comparisons with others whose tale of abuse will be quite different, and this, in turn, can only lead to negative self-evaluation. Coping occurs, like so many other psychological variables, within the concrete contexts and material conditions of everyday lives. It is subject to patterns of constraint, change, choice, availability and so on. In the simplest terms, children use what they can in a value-free sense to cope with their abuse.

The research reviewed in this chapter—from empirical quantitative studies and qualitative experiential data—has suggested that initial negative or ambivalent reactions to disclosure can represent a significant risk factor for the emergence of subsequent distress, ongoing psychological difficulties and for the development of a coherent sense of self in the survivor of child abuse. External validation, which can only be received through disclosure, assists healing in that it permits a re-presentational challenge to the abuse and its associated thoughts and feelings. Significant others and the wider society have an important role to play in this by validating, recognising and above all listening to children who have been abused. The National Commission data on disclosure suggests that we have become more likely to listen to children in that a higher percentage of people who disclosed were under 25 years of age. However, this is tempered by the knowledge that a considerable number who do disclose report that their disclosure has been met with something significantly less than acceptance by care-givers and weak implementation of the rights of the child to be protected from abuse. It would appear that there is little room for complacency. While children may feel more able to disclose abuse today, acceptance and publicity of its occurrence function at a very superficial level, leading children to believe that they will not be listened to. Listening and hearing are, of course, two very different things requiring different responses in both responsibility and action.

Throughout this chapter we have advocated that the process of healing is just that—a process that occurs over time and changes in the light of new experience. There is no clearly defined discontinuity involved such that one day there is a victim and the next there is a survivor, having forever put the past behind. Given the best of circumstances, support and belief on disclosure in childhood, children can begin the process of healing while still in childhood. However, circumstances during childhood are often something less than that necessary for healing. The overwhelming majority of people who were abused in childhood report that they can only truly begin their process of healing in adulthood. Acceptance of the abuse and, more importantly, realisation of the strengths and creativity that one sets in place in dealing with the abuse and its outcome are essential in this process. So, too, is the knowledge that although some days may go well and other days not, this is all right and will probably be good enough for the present. Stories of surviving have shown that expectancies of a glorious end stage where healing is attained like some mystical nirvana is unlikely to be helpful in healing. These stories show healing as a gradual acceptance of oneself in the ebb and flow of everyday life—an acceptance that recognises both pain and resilience.

'Looking back, I can't quite believe how different I now feel about myself and the abuse I experienced as a child, and despite the difficulties I encountered, I feel I am now a much stronger and better person. If I could offer hope to others who are presently struggling (some days I still do) with the knowledge that they too were sexually abused in childhood, it would be to say that there is no one set procedure to follow—each person is unique and everyone has had different experiences, as well as different ways in which they might be coping (for me drinking was one of the ways I coped until I was able to find alternative ways, which were less damaging). I also feel it is important to go at your own pace, and to find help where you can. Finally, and if at all possible, to believe in yourself, to be kind to yourself, because like me, you also deserve to find some inner peace and happiness.'

NOTE

1. NCIPCA was originally set up by the NSPCC to make recommendations for developing a strategy for reducing the incidence of child abuse. Part of its remit involved collecting information from people who had experienced childhood abuse, which attracted over 1,000 written submissions (in the form of letters) mostly about child sexual abuse. This chapter draws, in part, upon the analysis of letters conducted for the NSPCC (see Wattam and Woodward, 1996) and also draws upon PhD research undertaken by the first author entitled: 'Being visible: representations of self and identity within personal experience narratives of child sexual abuse.'

REFERENCES

Baker, A. and Duncan, S.P. (1985) Child sexual abuse: a study of prevalence in Great Britain. *Child Abuse and Neglect*, **9**: 457–467.
Bradley, A.R. and Wood, J.M. (1996) How do children tell? The disclosure process in child sexual abuse. *Child Abuse and Neglect*, **9**: 881–891.
Briere, J. (1989) *Therapy for Adults Molested as Children: Beyond Survival*. New York, Springer Publications.
British Psychological Society Working Party (1990) Psychologists and child sexual abuse. *The Psychologist*, **8**: 344–348.
Browne, K.D. and Herbert, M. (1995) *Preventing Family Violence*. Chichester, Wiley.
Cahill, C., Llewelyn, S.P. and Pearson, C. (1991) Long-term effects of sexual abuse which occurred in childhood: a review. *British Journal of Clinical Psychology*, **30**: 117–130.
Chaffin, M., Wherry, J.N. and Dykman, R. (1997) School-age children's coping with sexual abuse: abuse stresses and symptoms associated with four coping strategies. *Child Abuse and Neglect*, **21**: 227–240.

DoH (1991) *The Children Act 1989*. London, HMSO.

Draucker, C. (1992) *Counselling Survivors of Childhood Sexual Abuse*. London, Sage Publications.

Everson, M.D., Hunter, W.M., Runyon, D.K., Edelsohn, G.A. and Coulter, M.L. (1989) Maternal support following disclosure of incest. *American Journal of Orthopsychiatry*, **59**: 197–206.

Faust, J., Runyon, M.K. and Kenny, M.C. (1995) Family variables associated with the onset and impact of intrafamilial childhood sexual abuse. *Clinical Psychology Review*, **15**: 443–456.

Finkelhor, D. and Browne, A. (1985) The traumatic impact of child sexual abuse: a conceptualisation. *American Journal of Orthopsychiatry*, **3**: 28–42.

Friedrich, W.A. (1987) Behaviour problems in sexually abused children. *Journal of Interpersonal Violence*, **2**: 381–390.

Gold, E. (1986) Long-term effects of sexual victimisation in childhood: an attributional approach. *Journal of Consulting and Clinical Psychology*, **54**: 471–475.

Gonzalez, L.S., Waterman, J., Kelly, R.J., McCord, J. and Oliveri, M.K. (1993) Children's patterns of disclosures and recantations of sexual and ritualistic abuse allegations in psychotherapy. *Child Abuse and Neglect*, **17**: 281–289.

Holmes, G.R., Offen, L. and Waller, G. (1997) See no evil, hear no evil, speak no evil: why do relatively few male victims of childhood sexual abuse receive help for abuse-related issues in adulthood? *Clinical Psychology Review*, **17**: 69–88.

Jehu, D., Gazan, M. and Klassen, C. (1988) *Beyond Sexual Abuse: Therapy with Women who were Childhood Victims*. Chichester, Wiley.

Jones, D.P.H. and McGraw, J.M. (1987) Reliable and fictitious accounts of sexual abuse in children *Journal of Interpersonal Violence*, **2**: 27–45.

Kelly, L., Regan, L. and Burton, S. (1991) *An Exploratory Study of the Prevalence of Sexual Abuse in a Sample of 16–21 year old*. Child Abuse Studies Unit, Polytechnic of North London.

Kitzinger, J. (1990) Who are you kidding? Children, power and the struggles against sexual abuse, in James, A. and Prout, A. (eds) *Constructing and Reconstructing Childhood: Contemporary Issues in the Sociological Study of Childhood*. Basingstoke, The Falmer Press, pp. 157–183.

Kendall-Tackett, K.A., Williams, L.M. and Finkelhor, D. (1993) Impact of sexual abuse on children: a review and synthesis of recent empirical studies. *Psychological Bulletin*, **113**, 164–180.

Kurtz, Z. (1995) Do children's rights to health care in the UK ensure their best interests? *Journal of the Royal College of Physicians of London*, **29**: 508–516.

McNew, J.A. and Abell, N. (1995) Post-traumatic stress symptomology—similarities and differences between Vietnam veterans and adult survivors of childhood sexual abuse. *Journal of Social Work*, **14**: 115–126.

Mian, M., Marton, P. and LeBaron, D. (1996) The effects of sexual abuse on 3–5 year old girls. *Child Abuse and Neglect*, **20**: 731–745.

Monck, E., Sharland, E., Bentovim, A., Goodall, G., Hyde, C. and Lewin, R. (1996) *Sexually Abused Children: A Descriptive and Treatment Outcome Study*. London, HMSO.

Monck, E. (1997) Evaluating therapeutic intervention with sexually abused children. *Child Abuse Review*, **6**: 163–177.

Monck, E. and New, M. (1996) *Report of a Study of Sexually Abused Children and Adolescents and of Young Perpetrators of Sexual Abuse Who Were Treated in Voluntary Agency Community Facilities: Monitoring the Progress of Abused and Abusive Children*. London, HMSO.

Neumann, D.A., Houskamp, B.M., Pollock, V.E. and Briere, J. (1996) The long-term sequelae of childhood sexual abuse in women: a meta analytic review. *Child Maltreatment*, **1**: 6–16.

Persons, J.B. (1986) The advantages of studying psychological phenomena rather than psychiatric diagnoses. *American Psychologist*, **41**: 1252–1260.

Petronio, S., Reeder, H.M., Hecht, M.L. and Ros-Mendoza, T.M. (1996) Disclosure of sexual abuse by children and adolescents. *Journal of Applied Communication Research*, **24**: 181–199.

Rind, B. and Tromovitch, P. (1997) A meta analytic review of findings from national samples on psychological correlates of child sexual abuse. *Journal of Sex Research*, **34**: 237–255.

Rush, F. (1980) *The Best Kept Secret*. Englewood Cliffs, Prentice Hall.

Russell, D.E.H. (1986) *The Secret Trauma: Incest in the Lives of Girls and Women*. New York, Basic Books.

Sharland, E., Jones, D., Aldgate, J., Seal, H. and Croucher, M. (1996) *Professional Intervention in Child Sexual Abuse*. London, HMSO.

Sorenson, T. and Snow, B. (1991) How children tell: the process of disclosure in child sexual abuse. *Child Welfare*, **70**: 3–15.

Spaccarelli, S. and Fuchs, C. (1997) Variability in symptom expression among sexually abused girls: developing multivariate models. *Journal of Clinical Child Psychology*, **26**: 24–35.

Stern, A.E., Lynch, D.L., Oates, R.K. and O'Toole, B.I. (1995) Self esteem, depression, behaviour and family functioning in sexually abused children. *Journal of Child Psychology and Psychiatry*, **36**: 1077–1089.

Summit, R.C. (1983) The child sexual abuse accommodation syndrome. *Child Abuse and Neglect*, **7**: 177–193.

Summit, R.C. (1992) Abuse of the child sexual abuse accommodation syndrome. *Journal of Child Sexual Abuse*, **1**: 153–163.

Ussher, J. and Dewberry, C. (1995) The nature and long-term effects of childhood sexual abuse: a survey of adult women survivors in Britain. *British Journal of Clinical Psychology*, **34**, 177–192.

Wattam, C. and Woodward, C. (1996) And do I abuse my children? . . . No!—Learning about prevention from people who have experienced childhood abuse, in *Childhood Matters, Vol. 2: Background Papers*. London, HMSO.

Wyatt, G.E. and Mickey, M.R. (1988) The support of parents and others as it mediates the effects of child sexual abuse: an exploratory study, in Wyatt, G.E. and Powell, G.J. (eds) *Lasting Effects of Child Sexual Abuse*. Newbury Park, CA, Sage.

Young, R.E., Bergandi, T.A. and Titus, T.G. (1994) Comparison of the effects of sexual abuse on male and female latency-aged children. *Journal of Interpersonal Violence*, **9**: 291–306.

Yule, W. (1996) Post-traumatic stress disorder in children, in Salkovskis, P.M. (ed.) *Trends in Cognitive and Behavioural Therapies*. Chichester, Wiley.

8

'DON'T JUST DO IT': CHILDREN'S ACCESS TO HELP AND PROTECTION

Mary MacLeod

There is a moment in the film *Kindergarten Cop* when the hero (Arnold Schwarzenegger) has discovered that a boy is being beaten at home and will be beaten again if he tells on his father: he sees the father in the playground and advances on the man slowly and threateningly, to tell him that any more injuries to the boy (or his mother) will mean the offender has to deal with 'Arnie'. Seeing the satisfaction this moment engenders in young watchers suggests that, for children, access to child protection means an 'Arnie' in every school.

And indeed, the scenario reflects the circumstances of, and fulfils wishes expressed by, many children ringing ChildLine about physical and sexual abuse: a stop to the violence without everything in the family being turned upside down; action to end the violence without the child having to 'tell'; and safe retribution – the father is not beaten, 'only' threatened and controlled – access to protection without 'agency'.

> 'I just wish he'd stop.'
> 'I wish I could beat him up.'
> 'I don't want him to go to prison.'
> 'I don't want the family to break up.'

These are the wishes of many children reflecting the circumstances of a considerable group; but not all. Children who are beaten and sexually assaulted are not homogeneous; their circumstances, and the dynamics within their families, are as individual as they are. And so, the 'Arnie' scenario suffers from the same problem as so many of the social care solutions to parental violence against children. It assumes that the problem—and therefore the solution—is one-dimensional. Consider the struggles between apologists for 'family support' and 'child rescue': one camp cannot accommodate sadism; the other despair. As if something so complex, so impervious to straightforward categorisation, so hard to discover with certainty, so symbolic of the tensions between the private and public—the family and the state—could ever be simple and clear. Solutions are bound to be elusive.

Other children's voices tell a different story; they cannot wait to get rid of the abuser:

> 'I don't want to see him again . . . I wish he would leave and never come back . . . I hate him . . . I want to kill him . . .'

> 'I found him lying drunk. I thought about killing him and about killing myself.' [A girl, 12]

So responses have to be complex, reflecting the child's experience, the child's context and the psychology of the abuser. There can be no one-way street to help.

For many children, there is no road at all; only 6% of child callers describing sexual abuse had any contact with 'the authorities' prior to their call. When the abuser was a parent or parent figure, the proportions were even lower; and those who did call on social services had a hugely difficult journey ahead (MacLeod, 1996a; Keep, 1996; Wattam, 1996). Yet ChildLine callers are the children *most* likely to be able to engage help for themselves – mainly older (85% of callers who give their age were between 11 and 18 years of age), verbal (though there is a text telephone service) and able to get to a telephone.

Babies, young children, those with communication difficulties or physical dependency, and many psychologically entrapped children have no conceivable way of accessing help themselves. Much as we might want to solve the problem of child sexual abuse by leaving it in the hands of children and young people themselves, we cannot do so. A child-centred practice cannot stand or fall by whether it attends to the wishes of an individual child. It has to take account of the needs of the community of children and young people, as well as the particular circumstances of each child. Nor can we settle for prevention strategies in schools as the way forward—self-protection, when it comes to adult violence towards children, is often no protection. Formal mechanisms of intervention, too, are deeply flawed.

Nor can we hide behind rhetoric about the social construction of child abuse as a category. Of course it is slippery and hard to define; of course, it is relative. But just because categories are not stable (which categories are absolute, after all?) does not mean they are not useful or usable. The term 'child abuse' must always be invoked self-consciously, and with an acute awareness that children's own definitions should have a place; but we must never lose sight of the fact that real children experience real assaults. Children cannot be left by child welfare to be assaulted with impunity. This, in the end, is a matter of human rights.

The medicalisation of child abuse has been problematic, in that sexual abuse has been seen as a diagnosis with symptoms which can be recognised and treated, so reducing options and limiting understanding of the problem (MacLeod and Saraga, 1991). Yet medical metaphors usefully illuminate the difficulties in intervening. Being abused by a parent can be like having a brain stem tumour; how do you get rid of the tumour without destroying other essential parts of the brain? How are helpers to know which intervention will secure the best outcome? They cannot know with certainty. Even so, it is perturbing to discover the extent to which chance appears to be a factor in whether children are protected or not (Hunt and MacLeod, 1998), the system's reliance on children's willingness to make a statement and withstand a forensic process (Gibbons et al. 1995), and the unavailability of therapeutic and less formal help (Wattam, 1997; Farmer, 1997; Farmer and Pollock, 1998). How can we, then, widen the options available to those affected—children and adults—so that less depends on chance and there is more room for agency, including children's?

The existence of a confidential, anonymous form of help which children and young people use in large numbers offers access to information about children's definitions of child abuse and their ideas about how they might be helped. This chapter examines calls to ChildLine from children and young people suffering abuse to discover how access might be increased. 'Help' is not confined to protection and counselling; and 'access' is not limited to children's own agency. I draw on a number of ChildLine studies alongside an analysis of calls from children about sexual abuse (in particular abuse by parents or parent figures) in the year up to 31 March 1998. The views expressed are my own.

EVIDENCE FROM CHILDLINE CALLERS

ChildLine counsellors write a note of the conversation with the child immediately following the call. The conversation is for the child, not research. The information emerging from it is variable: children may not reveal aspects of their lives; and the record is not a verbatim account of everything the child has said, but a succinct narrative of a complex conversation which may have lasted 30 minutes or more. This research cannot provide complete demographic information or representative samples. Yet, because so many children feel freed from many of the constraints of ordinary conversations, it can report that what they say when talking is *their* idea, not a researcher's, journalist's, investigator's, clinician's or parent's. In that sense, their testimony is, perhaps, uniquely unmediated by adult agendas.

In the 1997–98 period, 115,146 new contacts were made by children and young people; 12,146 (10.5%) of these children described ongoing, recent or past sexual assault: 9,222 (10%) girls and 2,924 (12%) boys—around 1,000 children a month. Sexual abuse was named as their *main* problem by 9,608 (8%) child callers – 8% of girl callers and 11% of boys: 1 in 1,000 children aged between 5 and 18 in the UK in that year. Over 2,500 children talked about sexual assault precipitating or contributing to the problem they called about—for example, family relationship problems, physical abuse, running away, suicidal feelings, eating problems, among others.

Fewer boys than girls called about sexual violence – a ratio of just under 3:1 overall, and 2:1 in calls about parental abuse. The ratio has steadily fallen in the past five years from nearly 5:1 in 1993/94—a reflection of either more boys feeling able to use ChildLine, or boys feeling more able to name or 'admit to' being abused.

Who was responsible for assaults?

A total of 4,621 children (48%) described assaults by a parent, both parents or parent figures as their main problem: 3,050 girls and 1,571 boys. Sexual violence is gendered, according to these reports: the overwhelming majority of the sexual assaults were done by men or boys. But there were gender differences: a much higher proportion of boys than girls were assaulted by their mothers (18.5% compared with 1.6%). In 2% of cases (4% of boy callers and 1.7% of girls), children described both parents assaulting them; in these families, violence seemed to be a way of life.

As can be seen in Table 8.1, children were most likely to be assaulted within their immediate families; relatively little reported abuse was by strangers. This can mask the complexity of risk, seeming to divide sex

Table 8.1 Perpetrators of violence to children

Perpetrator	Total	Percentage of known data
Adult	7,919	82
Immediate family (including siblings)	5,057	52
Children/young people (including siblings)	1,383	14
Acquaintances/neighbours (96% male)	1,207	13
Extended family/foster family/close adult friends	1,221	13
Teachers	382	4
Strangers	403	4
Other authority figures	96	1

Note: Percentages in this table do not add up to 100 because categories overlap.

offenders into two camps: strangers and family members. Offenders target children in families as well as in residential or group settings (Dobash *et al.*, 1993; Conte, 1990; Colton and Vanstone, 1996), and men who abuse their own children also abuse others:

> 'Jackie, 12, called because she is being threatened at school and by local people because her Dad, who sexually abused her, also assaulted other children, including her friend Kristy.'

> 'Helen (14) called to talk about an imminent court case: her grandfather was going to court for assaulting her, her younger sister and eight other children.'

Children sexually assaulted by parents, step-parents or parent's partners were less likely than those assaulted by others to report other agencies being involved: just 5% of girls and only 1% of boys where the father or father figure was said to be the abuser; and 4.3% of girls and 0.6% of boys where the mother was the alleged abuser, compared with 6% overall. Boys were less likely than girls to be in touch with any authorities when they phoned. Only 1% were willing to be referred to other agencies, usually only as a last resort (MacLeod and Barter, 1996); children wanted rather to talk through what they could do.

How long had abuse been going on?

Assaults were rarely one-off (see Table 8.2). Just under one in three callers described assaults which were ongoing or happening over years; one in ten callers described a pattern of abuse over five years. More children and young people now call in the early weeks and months. In ChildLine's first

Table 8.2 Duration of sexual abuse by parents or parent figures: 1 April 1997–31 March 1998

n: 2,537	Total	Percentage of known data
Ongoing	342	14
Past	28	1
Recent	109	4
Less than 1 week	372	15
Less than 1 month	387	15
1 month to one year	813	32
1 year to 5 years	247	10
5 years +	239	9

Note: No information duration was recorded on 2,084 (45%) of the 4,621 children ringing about parental abuse.

year (1986–87) 65% of children and young people had been assaulted for more than one year, and nearly half of these talked of assaults going on over five years. Even as recently as 1993–95, the proportion was 54%, with one in five callers talking about assaults over five years. This suggests that access to information about abuse increases access to help and argues for broad public awareness campaigns.

Three-quarters of callers alleging abuse by parents gave specific details about the assaults. More than half described vaginal, anal or oral rape; more than one in three talked of sexual touching, and one in ten reported harassment or indecency (flashing, being made to watch masturbation or pornography, sexual comments or threats, or being watched naked).

> 'A 13-year-old boy talked about what had happened in his family since his mother had died three years before. His father had gone 'mad', smashing things and hitting him and his two younger sisters. His father regularly got drunk and sexually abused him or his sisters. While the abuse is going on, he just closes his eyes and hopes it's soon over, wishing he were dead. If they try to stop their father he beats them with a belt.'

> 'Dad does things . . . it happens when Mum is working . . . when I say to stop, he just hits me . . . I want to tell my mum but I'm scared.' [Jack, 9]

> 'She gets into bed with me and starts touching me. I tell her not to.' [Peter, 15]

> 'I want someone to come and take me and my sister away. My Mum has a boyfriend . . . he hits us and touches us where he shouldn't. My sister and me sleep in the same room . . . so we put something against the door to keep him out . . . it's been going on for a year . . . we both want to leave.'

> 'Dad comes into my room and touches me when he's drunk . . . I feel dirty and angry . . . I couldn't face telling the family . . .' [This 13-year-old girl eventually said she had taken vodka and pills and gave her name and location so an ambulance could be sent for her.]

Physical pain and injury, intrusive memories, nightmares, flashbacks, fear, guilt, fear of pregnancy or Aids, shame, anger, and feeling trapped all featured in children's accounts. Some effects were short-lived, relating to particular episodes, others pervasive. But lists of symptoms or outcomes can become yet another set of meanings restricting the possibilities for people to live their lives differently. While it is important to be alive to the possible range of impacts on children and young people, prescriptions can limit the expectations helpers have of children and they have of themselves.

There are tomes of research on the characteristics of so-called abusive families, but much research emerges from small clinical samples (MacLeod and Saraga, 1991; Kelly, 1999). Here there were no simple connections. The family circumstances children described were as 'normal' and 'abnormal' as those of children calling about other issues like divorce, family problems, or bullying. The abuse itself was the main distinction between those where abuse occurred and others. But that did not mean that the families were all alike. Whatever the broad causes of abuse, the presence and effect of it is individual to each family.

Children's explanations

Incest has been described as an attack on meaning; bewilderment and confusion were prevailing themes in the calls. If, as I argue, the meaning the child takes for what has happened is important in defining outcomes, it would be useful to discover more about children's explanations of violence. For most, the violence 'just is'; they could not explain it. Some saw the violence as a part of the person: 'My father's a bastard.' Boys, more commonly than girls, described physical violence accompanying sexual assaults and felt 'attacked' rather than exploited or used. They were more likely to feel angry and worried that they might turn out like their fathers.

A small proportion of young people talked about sexual violence occurring in the context of alcohol abuse (4% of children complaining about sexual abuse) or domestic violence. They said it happens *when* he's drunk rather than *because* he's drunk. Drink, drug use, bereavement, unemployment, parental separation were seen as a context or trigger to the violence rather than an explanation of it, though some excused their father (or their mother) by saying he was unhappy and the abuse had begun to happen because he was having a difficult time. Other children saw two parents: the normal loving one and the hurting one. Some felt special. Some, particularly boys abused by their mothers, talked explicitly about their confusion about liking what happens and feeling ashamed and dirty afterwards. They were more likely, then, to feel implicated in the abuse: *'I can't stop myself, but I feel awful afterwards.'*

TELLING AND SEEKING HELP

It is assumed that children do not get help because they do not tell about sexual assaults, but the picture is much more complex. Though the vast majority of children and young people calling ChildLine had not yet been in touch with any authority; three-quarters had told someone, according to those callers about whom information was recorded (one in five boys and one in two girls). Friends were most likely to be told, followed by parents, other family members and teachers.

Boys were twice as likely as girls to have told no one, as Table 8.3 shows. One in four girls and one in five boys had told their mothers about paternal abuse; while one in ten had told fathers about maternal abuse. Involvement

Table 8.3   Who children confided in over sexual abuse by
parent or parent figure

	Girls	Boys
Relative	283 (20%)	44 (14%)
Friend	447 (31%)	93 (30%)
Mother	336 (24%)	48 (15%)
Teacher	47 (3%)	7 (2%)
Police	48 (3%)	5 (1.5%)
Social services	43 (3%)	3 (1%)
Father	20 (2%)	11 (4%)
No one	216 (17%)	109 (35%)
Totals	1,431	320

Note: Percentages come to more than 100 because some children had
confided in more than one person.

by the authorities was even rarer where the abuser was a parent. Very few
mentioned any formal counselling or therapeutic help.

Despite all the advice and guidance, adults and other children tend to
'maintain' the secret, at least from the authorities. They, like the children,
fear the consequences of involving authorities, having little idea about how
social services would conduct an inquiry (MacLeod, 1997). They have little
confidence in the effectiveness of child protection—with some reason, according to research (Gibbons *et al.*, 1995; Farmer, 1997). And the stigma,
upheaval and distress provoked by invoking the child protection system
means that concerned adults or parents, as well as child protection professionals, require the most unequivocal evidence of assault. So telling is not
enough, it has to be the right kind of communication.

> 'My seven-year-old has a friend. He has just given me a graphic account of
> sexual assault by his stepfather. I don't know what to do. I'm worried about
> bringing the world crashing down about people's ears.'

> 'I want to know how I can protect her without calling the police.'

WIDENING ACCESS

Any attempts to widen access to mainstream services must be based on the
assumption that there is every reason to avoid the 'authorities' unless driven
to it.

Getting children more secure protection and help is the aim of everyone.
Improving the court process is widely recommended (Keep, 1996; Plotnikoff
and Woolfson, 1995; Home Office, 1998; NSPCC, 1996; Utting, 1997). Police
are becoming more committed to intelligence-led policing as a way of

detecting assaults and securing convictions with less emphasis on children's evidence. There is also, of course, the DoH-led initiative to 'refocus' child protection and emphasise family support.

However, to increase children's access to protection from assault would require a transformation of the way we think of children and conceive of them as users of help. Helplines have made a start here. Their existence has changed the relationship between children and help from passive recipients of services—when adults see something amiss—to users. How far can we conceive of this extending?

HELPLINES

Helplines have now become so much part of society's response to child assault that they are recommended in the Implementation handbook for the Rights of the Child (Hodgkin and Newell, 1998) by the Utting report (1997), and required in Department of Health and Department for Education and Employment guidance to residential homes and boarding schools. They have sprung up across the world. Yet, whole groups of young people are excluded from using them through age, communication difficulty or lack of access to a private, safe telephone. They do not necessarily secure protection, but at least children are heard and cared for, even if only to help them 'give sorrow words'.

They cannot be seen as 'the answer' to children's access to help, only a partial answer. But examining why they work for young people can tell us about barriers to help and what children require to find a service accessible.

What makes helplines unique is, first, their direct accessibility to children—a function of the technology but also of the decision (taken by most children's helplines) that calls are free to the caller, thus making the technology available; and, second, that children wanted to use them. Why?

Communication on the telephone is limited to voice and ear (or read text on minicoms) a limitation which offers children freedom. They can give their name or not, call when they want, say what they want, and put the phone down if they want. They are safe from physical abuse or interference from the adult with whom they talk. They are not the object of anybody's gaze or touch. No one need know they have called. They can talk without committing themselves to the consequences, to a point of view, to the 'whole' truth. A phone call need not make things worse; even so some callers are very fearful that their parent will somehow 'know' they have phoned.

Children and young people have a different kind of conversation on a helpline, breaking the conventions of loyalty around family life, community and peer group. They are not confined by the 'rules' of social work, counselling or therapeutic practice about how their contact will be organised. They decide whether or not to pursue conversations; so the decisions that are usually taken by the adult about the nature, frequency and duration of contact are not the adult's to make. Young people may want to work in a haphazard and desultory way or in quick and fast bursts of contact: brief encounters.

There is an audience—counsellors—whose responses have an impact on what callers say and how they feel they have been received. Child callers have, over the years, given clear messages about what kind of audience they require—especially about the intervention they want. They are offered an almost absolutely confidential service; it is something they check up on constantly: 'You're not going to tell anyone?'; 'My mum won't know I've rung, will she?'; 'I don't want anyone to know about this.' At children's request, ChildLine contacts police social service, other agencies or parents, to invite intervention on the child's behalf. In cases of threat to life, if a child's location is known, a referral will be made without the child's consent. Most helplines in other countries work in this way, but some, like Allo Enfance Maltraite in France, and the NSPCC in England, cannot because of their statutory role.

There is anecdotal evidence (personal communication with members of Icelandic, Danish and Swedish helplines) that children elsewhere are more willing to be referred to services than children in the UK. (Willingness also varies in different parts of the UK—for example, children in Northern Ireland appear least willing to consider referral (Mason, 1998), possibly because of the pressures of vigilante justice.) These Nordic helplines, their workers suggested, work in an environment where children's human rights are taken more seriously so family privacy is less 'sacred' and state services are less feared. More and better comparative research is required to establish how UK helplines could be more of a gateway to social services. But the message from children's use of helplines is that they want more say in what happens and how it happens. They do not want adults to rush in and take over. As one boy put it when reporting why he would call ChildLine (Barford, 1993):

> '. . . they give advice . . . social workers don't tell you what to do, it just happens, they don't tell you there and then, it just happens . . . ChildLine tells you what social workers do and you understand.'

STATUTORY AND LEGAL ROUTES TO CHILD PROTECTION

Callers who had experience of the statutory services mainly described what went wrong. The indignities suffered by child witnesses in court are well reported (Keep, 1996; Utting, 1997; NSPCC, 1996). The law is too blunt an instrument for achieving child protection. But everything is not wrong: children generally find interviews with social workers or police supportive: 'the social worker was nice', 'the policeman was OK, I could talk to him'. Even video interviews are rarely complained of by children (though medicals are): telling in a formal way and being treated seriously seemed to be a validation. Barford's study (1993) and Dempster's (1993) show that over time many children come to feel that, difficult though intervention was, it was better than suffering the abuse.

The aftermath of disclosure in the family network, the court process, and having to go into care are hugely stressful; though care can be an intense relief: 'It was like being on another planet being in my foster home; I felt safe.'

Shaw's study found that 15% described coming into care as great, and 12% said the best thing was being with someone who cared (Shaw, 1998). It is dangerous to demonise care and imply that being with the family is always the preferred option. Again and again children say on the phone:

'I want to go in a children's home.'
'I wish I could be adopted.'

But what of the rest? There is no doubt that fear of care silences children. Both children and adults are fearful of making things worse. Children are locked in their families. They have nowhere else to go. The possibility of losing them and losing everything with them is all too real.

'I read something in MIZZ about a girl being abused and she told and it was OK. Well that didn't happen with me. My mum didn't believe me. I ended up in care and I've lost everyone.'

'Dad is coming home from prison today after 18 months,' Jim said. 'He sexually abused me for over a year. Mum wants him to come home. I've begged her not to let him, but she won't listen.'

'My life has gone to pieces since my father went to court. Mum and Dad split up. I stayed with my Mum, but we kept rowing so I went into care. I still get nightmares.'

'The family all blame me.'

'My Dad looked really sad in court. I hate what he did; but I don't hate him.'

'It was easier to talk than I thought . . . I did talk to Mum and it's better now.'

'Thank you for talking to my daughter last weekend. She is safe now and feeling better.'

'I rang to tell you that my uncle was found guilty. I'm glad I went through with it.'

Most children are reliant on the mother (the father, if the mother is violent) to end their exposure to violence—that is, until they reach a point of running away or escaping themselves. But non-abusing parents get little support through the process of protecting their child using family law, which could be a route to securing a child's safety without invoking care or criminal proceedings; indeed, allegations of assault are often taken to be a mother being malicious.

Children and young people have no idea how to get access to a court to say what they think. Courts have been reluctant to appoint solicitors and *guardians ad litem*, even when sexual abuse allegations exist. Children's access to protection would be significantly widened if this were to happen automatically, as it could if s. 64 of the Family Law Act 1996 were implemented. Where courts are prepared to be open to children, and hear from them on the child's terms, safer decisions can be made. One 7-year-old girl who refused to allow anyone in the family to know she was being assaulted by her father, finally agreed to let ChildLine tell the judge. Here was a judge willing to listen, even though the communication was unconventional and, consequently, this child was protected.

The picture is mixed. Some children feel they get justice and that makes a difference. So limiting, but not eliminating, the 'forensic' gaze offers most. What children say suggests that the conventional course of an inquiry moves too fast and too definitively for them and for their families. Everyone needs time to absorb the enormity of what is alleged to have happened. They need to be able to consider how they can manage matters as individuals and as a family without having everything taken out of their hands. It is relatively easy to conceive of a protected mediation and treatment space where admissions of guilt and involvement in treatment are rewarded by avoidance of the criminal route.

But this could be a dead-end for children if the form of intervention euphemises incidents of abuse: 'only one little broken bone' (quote from Catherine Marneffe of Kind in Noor at European Family Therapy Conference, London, 1992); or assumes that sexual violence is either a symptom or a 'condition' of family dysfunction rather than a behaviour with a multitude of differing meanings; or sentimentalises families: 'Parents are the experts on their children' (Hearn, 1997). One can as well say, and perhaps with more authority, that children are the experts on their parents.

In fact, when adults do attempt to act as experts by taking action, they are taken less seriously than professionals (Gibbons *et al.*, 1995; MacLeod, 1997) and they get little support to manage (Farmer and Owen, 1995). If the professional sphere is to become more inclusive towards those it serves, it has to share responsibility for judgements as well as care with adults and with children and young people. Otherwise, young children and those dependent on adult intervention will not get early help or even any help. Family conferences promise a great deal here, if children have an advocate in them: for, what is good for the family may not necessarily be good for the child.

Recent research (Hunt and MacLeod, 1998) into parental responses to changed practice since the Children Act found that some parents resent focus on children (children were not interviewed). Of course they do, they may be deeply envious of care and nurture given to children and desperate for their own emotional needs to be met. But that does not mean that children should be left out. According to Frost (1997), short, intensive teamwork which makes partnerships with the entire family, parents and children, is highly successful in averting crises and promoting parents and children's well-being. Clearly good working models exist.

But what of the fathers? The invisibility of fathers and men in child protection work is a major weakness. If men and fathers are peripheral to the practice of family support or of child protection, they remain the problem but not the solution, continuing a discourse which excludes men from responsibility and confines them to the category 'beyond control'.

EXTENDING CHILDREN'S FREEDOM

Child callers talked about ways they try to protect themselves: going to friends, calling in their relatives, asking to go into care, telling the offender to stop, crying, saying no, threatening to tell, leaving ChildLine material around, locking bedrooms, running away, getting ill, or attempting suicide.

'I've told my friend and I sometimes stay over so I don't have to be there.'

Children confide most in their own friends. This argues for programmes in school which involve young people in talking about how they can help each other. Having the conversation about abuse in the third person might also be much less punitive to boys and young men by focusing on their capacity to help rather than problematising masculinity; so perhaps they might be less likely to blank off—a feature of current prevention programmes (Suderman et al., 1993).

If child access is to mean anything at all, it has to be considered broadly, from the provision of information and public awareness campaigns through to the detail of court and therapeutic process. Above I have indicated how some changes in current policy and practice might extend access to protection. Could more be done? If we consider the predicament of a child facing the imminent likelihood of another sexual assault at home, how do we imagine they can be allowed to seek help? At present they are allowed to find their own strategies and they are also allowed to complain to 'the authorities' and hope that this produces protection.

But can we imagine something which offers children greater agency: a family conference, for example, providing a child with a help-call arrangement—like elders who want independence, and to stay in their own home, but want to do it safely? Can we imagine refuge provision open to young people in times of danger? Or respite care arrangements agreed as part of a child safety plan? Could we see such help being organised co-operatively by families with similar problems or by non-abusing parents? Can we imagine contact orders only being made if help call arrangements were agreed? Or a house wired to alert help if a risky situation develops? Already, it would be possible to control the activities of some sex offenders through electronic monitoring and confine people to the equivalent of 'house arrest' linked to treatment instead of to prison. The technology is there. Children can often predict the dangerous times. But such solutions would imply acceptance of the reality of sexual violence instead of denial framed round sex offenders as 'other' kinds of people.

The single biggest contribution to improving services for children and families would be to make therapeutic help widely available. At present the position is infamous (Farmer and Owen, 1995; DoH, 1995; MacLeod, 1997; Farmer, 1997). Even children in care receive little help. Non-abusing parents can be left to get on with it, and most offenders avoid treatment because they are not formally convicted. Therapy does make a difference to outcome, so, too, do less formal means of offering support: young people's initiatives, befriending, and self-help among parents and families.

Access to individuation and meaningful help

Help becomes accessible when it is appropriate to the individual. Children are a group of people united by their status as children and divided by almost anything else you can name—age, gender, class, family structure, race, culture, sexual orientation, health, religion, beliefs, and education, among others. Yet children more than any other group are seen as homogeneous with similar needs and wishes. Responses are packaged for them, irrespective of their differences.

Evidence suggests that boys are more likely to externalise distress and girls to internalise it: boys acting out by attacking others and girls by attacking themselves or others by forcing them to witness their self-attacks. Boys appear to be less willing to seek help early, and less able to wait for help when they have decided to ask for it; they get more quickly alienated by a slow or uncertain response (MacLeod and Barter, 1996). They require help tailored to their concerns not only for their own sakes but for their future behaviour as men and fathers.

And what of other aspects of identity, like race, colour, class, culture, disability? How do these impact on the process of victimisation and of seeking and receiving help and finding meaning? Significance has to be given to the right things, without ever confining a child to a box because of assumed ideas about his or her identity and what it implies. Working with children of a colour or culture different from the worker's own or the majority does not signify a different approach, but different thinking. It is more difficult to make fine judgements about the significance of matters. The meaning abuse has for the child and the family may be affected, and the options open or felt to be open to the child and family may differ. The principle is never to reduce any child's or family's options on the basis of what it is assumed they might be able to consider.

The tasks of helping are not different for any child: trying to stop the abuse; validating the experience; supporting the child's resistance; challenging internalised oppression; making the child safe; dealing with feelings; allowing the story to be told; discovering a meaning that is not destructive. Children and young people value an approach which is explicit about difference without labouring it, recognises what the helper may represent and works with the impact the relationship, attends to likely feelings of callers towards the helper without being preoccupied with it, is alive to when difference should be acknowledged and when not, and is prepared to offer choice.

Access to a helper of choice

Children and young people may wish to speak to people of specific gender or cultural identity, but not necessarily predictably. Helpers cannot escape what they represent to others by virtue of their gender or race identity: being white involves being representative of what is done in the name of whites; being a male of what is done by men. This can raise emotional business in the helper and can profoundly affect the quality and dynamics of the 'helping' relationship.

Children say that the kind of person has an impact, too. Children in children's homes and foster homes feel particularly aggrieved when they cannot get on with their social worker or key worker and yet are supposed to talk with them about their concerns. Of course, they do not. Limiting choice can mean that children opt out.

Access to naming and explaining

None of us is neutral when considering questions about child sexual abuse—not even researchers, be we are ever so careful and scientific; we come with agendas which affect what we perceive as the 'problem' and as 'the solution'. These agendas are reflected in the debates about theory, knowledge and approach. Underneath the struggle between 'family support' and 'child rescue' approaches, two debates still dominate the way child abuse, especially sexual abuse, is theorised, researched and understood. Is violence gendered? Is violence transmitted across generations?

There is still considerable uncertainty about which mechanisms produce people who, whatever the stress, the gender, even ideology and every encouragement to be violent, refuse to participate, while others seem to attack with impunity. Yet the 'cycle of violence' has reached the level of received truth in both professional and lay worlds. Theories affect children's explanations and expectations about how they will be affected; callers commonly worry that they are going to be damned to perpetuate the violence they suffer.

That the process of naming something as abusive is important is shown by recent research in the USA on the physical punishment of children. When adults defined their own experience of parental punishment or care as abusive, they were more likely to report less violence to their own children than those who did not, even though they had been assaulted the same number of times (Hemenway et al., 1994). The objective reality would need to be tested before confidently accepting this. Yet it does suggest the place of meaning in mediating the past; and it suggests that meaning and agency are connected: that how you see something has an impact on how you behave. It suggests that in naming something as 'abusive'—as a problem—children and young people are taking a step towards agency.

But naming the problem also means being exposed to the prevalent discourses about what it means to have this problem, which is why, no doubt, the title of Wattam's analysis of survivor's letters to the NSPCC commission was entitled: *And do I abuse my children? . . . No!*

The major contribution that theoretical developments in cultural studies have made to the study of child welfare is to undermine notions of certainty, of objectivity and subjectivity, therefore widening the possibilities for naming and identifying experience, and creating a place for children, perhaps, to be subjects. With recognition that there are subjectivities, we can begin to see that the story of an event is told from differing points of view. This puts emphasis on who gets to tell the story, whose story gets told, and whose story informs the theory.

Whatever other therapeutic interventions are made for individuals and families, a necessary part of the process of coping with trauma is telling what happened: the need to bear witness. Children need a place to tell the story even if they cannot yet face the consequences of 'telling'.

Access to hope

All children reported here will make their own journey towards meaning—a meaning that might imprison them in the past and past relationships, or one that might enable them, in the words of one adult survivor, to play the cards life had dealt to the best advantage. We need to be able to convey to children that because the history cannot be erased does not mean it cannot be differently felt and differently understood.

I have argued here for a much more flexible response to child sexual abuse, based on the reality that abuse is not 'one thing' and that help, as currently organised, is far too difficult to face for many adults and children, thus excluding people from the safe care they need. If people use confidential services, like helplines, to seek help and advice, it seems absurd to rule such approaches out of the mainstream completely. Surely it should be possible to have structured, protected spaces where professional discretion can be exercised for the long-term benefit of children and their parents.

I have also argued that children and young people should have not only a right to help independent of the interests or will of their families, but also that they should have greater capacity to direct, along with others, the way help and protection are delivered to them. Even quite young children are perfectly capable of entering a discussion about what they would like to change and how. If they are provided with the space to think and consider, they can begin to feel that they are taking some control, that they are resisting what is happening to them, which, in itself, can produce a transformation, a sense of agency. As one 14-year-old boy said at the end of his call to ChildLine: 'I feel I've taken a step. . . . '

REFERENCES

Barford, R. (1993) *Children's Views of Child Protection Social Work*. Norwich, Social Work Monographs.

Barter, C., Keep, G. and MacLeod, M. (1996) *Children at Crisis Point*. London, ChildLine.

Colton, M. and Vanstone, M. (1996) *Betrayal of Trust: Sexual Abuse by Men who Work with Children*. London, Free Association Books.

Conte, J.R. (1990) The incest offender: an overview and introduction, in Horton, A. *et al*. (eds) *The Incest Perpetrator*. London, Sage.

Dempster, H. (1993) The aftermath of child sexual abuse, in Waterhouse, L. (ed.) *Child Abuse and Child Abusers*. London, Jessica Kingsley.

DoH 1995) *Child Protection: Messages from Research*. London, HMSO.

Dobash, R.P., Carnie, J. and Waterhouse, L. (1993) Child sexual abusers: recognition and response, in Waterhouse, L. (ed.) *Child Abuse and Child Abusers*. London, Jessica Kingsley.

Epstein, C. (1996) *Listening to Ten-year-olds*. London, ChildLine.

Epstein, C. (1996) You can do therapy on the telephone, *Young Minds Magazine*, issue 29.

Farmer, E. and Owen, M. (1995) *Child Protection Practice: Private Risks and Public Remedies: A Study of Decision Making, Interventions and Outcomes in Child Protection Work*. London, HMSO.

Farmer, E. (1997) Protection and child welfare: striking the balance, in Parton, N. (ed.) *Child Protection and Family Support*. London, Routledge.

Farmer, E. and Pollock, S. (1998) *Sexually Abused and Abusing Children in Substitute Care*. Chichester, Wiley.

Frost, N. (1997) Delivering family support: service development, in Parton, N. (ed.) *Child Protection and Family Support* London, Routledge.

Gibbons, J., Conroy, S. and Bell, C. (1995). *Operating the Child Protection System*. London, HMSO.

Hearn, B. (1997) Putting child and family support into practice, in Parton, N. (ed.) *Child Protection and Family Support*. London, Routledge.

Hemenway, D., Solnik, S. and Carter, J. (1994) Child-rearing violence, *Child Abuse and Neglect*, **18**: 1011–1020.

Hodgkin, R. and Newell, P. (1998) *Implementation Handbook for the Convention on the Rights of the Child*. Geneva, UNICEF.

Home Office (1998) *Speaking up for Justice*. London, The Stationery Office.

Hunt, J. and MacLeod, A. (1998) *Statutory Intervention in Child Protection*. Bristol, Centre for Socio-Legal Studies, University of Bristol.

Keep, G. (1996) *Going to Court: Child Witnesses in their Own Words*. London, ChildLine.

Kelly, L. 1999) *No Easy Answers: Managing Sex Offenders in the Community*. London, ChildLine, NCH Action for Children, NSPCC (forthcoming).

MacLeod, M. (1996a) *Talking with Children about Child Abuse*. London, ChildLine.

MacLeod, M. (1996b) *Children and Racism*. London, ChildLine.

MacLeod, M. (1997) *Children Living Away from Home*. London, ChildLine.

MacLeod M. and Barter C. (1996) *We know it's tough to talk* London, ChildLine.

MacLeod, M. and Saraga, E. (1991) Clearing a path through the undergrowth: a feminist reading of recent literature on child sexual abuse, in Carter, P., Jeffs, T. and Smith, M.K. (eds) *Social Work and Social Welfare Yearbook*. Milton Keynes, Open University Press.

Mason, A. (1998) *Children Calling from Northern Ireland*. London, ChildLine.

NSPCC (1996) *Childhood Matters: Report of the National Commission of Inquiry into the Prevention of Child Abuse*. London. HMSO.

Plotnikoff, J. and Woolfson, R. (1995) *Prosecuting Child Abuse*. London, Blackstone Press.

Shaw, C. (1998) *Remember My Messages*. London, Who Cares? Trust.

Suderman, M., Jaffe, P.G. and Hastings, E. (1993) *A.S.A.P.: A School-based Anti-violence Programme*. London, Ontario, London Family Court Clinic.

Utting, W. (1997) *People Like Us*. London, The Stationery Office.

Wattam, C. and Woodward, C. (1996) And do I abuse my children? . . . No!— Learning about prevention from people who have experienced child abuse, in *Childhood Matters: The Report of the National Commission of Inquiry into the Prevention of Child Abuse. Vol 2: Background Papers*. London, HMSO.

9

FAMILY SUPPORT

Linda Colclough, Nigel Parton and Mark Anslow

Recent years have witnessed a major debate termed the 'refocusing' of children's services. Most recently the consultation on the revision of Working Together (DOH, 1998) has argued that the government wishes to shift the balance in the provision of children's services and aims to promote the central message that child protection work must be placed firmly within the context of wider services for children in need and that children should not be routed inappropriately into the child protection system as a means of gaining access to services. It is argued that many families who find themselves enmeshed in the child protection system suffer from multiple disadvantages and that they need help at an earlier stage to tackle their problems before 'parenting difficulties escalate into abuse'. A more holistic view of the needs of vulnerable children and their families is required. The development of what has come to be called, 'family support' has taken on a strategic significance for bringing about these changes.

This chapter is primarily concerned with analysing the way in which family support policies and practices might develop if they are to take seriously the challenges they are expected to address in the area of child sexual abuse (CSA). The chapter is informed by both current research and also the experiences of the mothers and children who have taken up the services and advice of a small registered charity called MOSAIC (West Yorkshire). MOSAIC stands for Mothers of Sexually Abused in Charge. At various points in the chapter we draw directly on the comments and experiences of mothers in the group to illustrate the current problems with family support services and how these might develop in the future. Our quotes are taken directly from the mothers themselves.

The group was started in 1995 following the efforts of the now Project Coordinator following her own experiences of being a mother of a sexually abused child and the feelings of isolation and the severe lack of advice, help and general support she and her own children had found once the sexual abuse had been discovered.

The objects of MOSAIC are 'to relieve the mental and physical distress of mothers whose children have suffered from sexual abuse, by the provision of an advice, counselling and support service' and more generally 'to further the prevention of the sexual abuse of children'. Referrals are received directly from mothers or via the police, social services, probation, general practitioners, or other mainstream services. Since starting, over 60 mothers have received a service either individually and/or through the regular group that operates. The mothers have been responsible for over 100 children ranging in age from young babies to 16 year olds. The mothers themselves have been aged from their early twenties to mid-forties and have come from all social classes, including professionals, but have been predominantly white—just two being of Asian origin.

Well over half the perpetrators were the male father/carer and others included a teacher, step-grandfather and neighbour. In every case the perpetrator was well known to the family, illustrating the importance of power and (mis)trust in child sexual abuse. The experiences of the mothers and children in MOSAIC of both child protection and family support vividly illustrate the main findings in available research and the literature more generally. They also illustrate some key problems which need to be addressed if we are serious about developing family support in the future but are in great danger of being missed and overlooked in the current debates about 'the refocusing of children's services'.

The two catalysts for the recent debates on the 'refocusing of children's services' were the publication in 1994 by the Audit Commission of *Seen But Not Heard: Coordinating Community Child Health and Social Services for Children in Need* and the launch the following year by the Department of Health of *Child Protection: Messages from Research*. Both suggested that the central principle of the Children Act 1989—that the child in need can be helped most effectively if the local authority works closely with other agencies and in partnership with parents in order to provide a range and level of services appropriate to the child's needs—was not being developed and in some cases was being actively undermined (see Parton, 1997, for a more detailed discussion).

While the Department of Health research programme summarised in *Messages from Research* arose directly from concerns about the reactions of the investigative agencies in Cleveland (Secretary of State, 1988) to cases of alleged sexual abuse and a number of the studies had this as a central focus (Ghate and Spencer, 1995; La Fontaine, 1994; Monck and New, 1995; Monck *et al.*, 1995; Sharland *et al.*, 1996; Smith and Grocke, 1995), it is important to recognise that the research programme and *Messages from Research* itself had a much wider remit so that the more specific issues and concerns associated with sexual abuse almost get lost among other agendas and priorities.

The central policy recommendation in *Messages from Research*, and supported by the Department of Health since then, is to refocus child protection work in terms of family support and thereby prioritise section 17 and Part 3 of the Children Act 1989. 'An approach based on the *process* of Section 47 enquiries and the *provision* of Section 17 services (including those for children looked after away from home), might well shift the emphasis in child protection work more towards family support' (DOH, 1995, p. 55; original emphasis).

FAMILY SUPPORT: THE LEGISLATIVE AND POLICY FRAMEWORK

The development of family support is thus seen as not only being central to the Children Act 1989 but as the most productive way of responding to actual and potential cases of child abuse and the 'refocusing of children's services'. However, it is important to recognise that the notion of family support has a very brief and recent history.[1] While it does not figure in the Children Act 1989, it is key in the associated *Guidance* (DoH, 1991a).

Section 17 of Part 3 of the Act gives local authorities a general duty to safeguard and promote the welfare of children in need and to promote the upbringing of such children by their families by providing an appropriate range and level of services. Similarly, Schedule 2 of the Act contains further provisions designed to help children in need to continue to live with their families and generally prevent the breakdown of family relationships. The definition of 'children in need' is contained in section 17(10) and as the *Guidance* stresses is 'deliberately wide to reinforce the emphasis on preventive support and services to families'.[2]

The Guidance is clear that the introduction of the term 'family support' indicates an important change of emphasis. Whereas previously the notion of prevention was restricted to the provision of services in order to prevent a child coming into care—a *negative* interpretation of prevention—the emphasis in the Children Act 1989 is on providing *positive* support to a child and their family. This includes the use of *accommodation* when children are *looked after* by the local authority in *partnership* with the parents where their *parental responsibility* is maintained.

Family support is thus potentially open-ended in scope, where it is implied the views and preferences of users will be given considerable weight. It is by definition diffuse and its potential range only limited by its dependence, in operational terms, on the concept of *children in need* (Tunstill, 1996, 1997).

FAMILY SUPPORT AND 'REFOCUSING': SOME CENTRAL PROBLEMS

However, all the available evidence suggests that the development of family support services has been very slow and patchy (Aldgate and Tunstill, 1996; Colton *et al.*, 1995; Giller, 1993; DoH, 1994).

More recently a Social Services Inspectorate report (SSI, 1996) of inspections of eight social services' family support services between 1993 and 1995 concluded that:

> 'the quality of the service being provided to children and their families was extremely varied. Only a small number of LAs provided a consistently good service, and in a similar sized minority the services were rather poor. In seven of the eight LAs it was very difficult to gain access to services unless child protection concerns were expressed. Only one LA was consistently able to intervene early to provide services to support the family with a view to averting a more serious and costly demand for services at a later date? (p. 1)

Similar findings were found in inspections that took place in another eight social services departments in England between October 1996 and April 1997 when it was concluded that 'departments continue to respond to child protection and looked after children cases to the exclusion of support to other families of children in need' (SSI, 1997, para. 1.4).

Thus while the development of family support is actively supported across the political and professional spectrum it is also clear there are a number of fundamental difficulties and tensions in such a process of refocusing (Parton, 1997; Parton *et al.*, 1997) not least of which is a severe lack of resources and a hostile climate which is still likely to blame organisations and front-line practitioners when things are seen to go wrong, particularly where a child dies.

In the current debates child abuse is conceptualised as a 'continuum' so that services should be differentiated to meet different levels of need and the form of intervention should recognise different thresholds of intervention. In seeing the relationship between family support and child protection in this way, it is assumed that not only will the provision of family support services at an earlier stage prevent parents maltreating their children, but that it will *divert* many cases and situations away from the child protection system rather than the latter be used as the point of entry for most child welfare cases as at present. In the process it is assumed that the primary concern is to provide a qualitatively different type and level of response and thereby recategorise cases that currently come into the system as child protection requiring an investigatory response. The key is therefore to ensure that cases are assessed (or categorised) and managed properly and, in particular, that the 'high-risk' situations which may indicate actual or potential significant harm are not missed and, similarly, the autonomy and privacy of families are not undermined by unnecessary child protection intervention. In particular, the model that underpins the proposals for change is a social stress model of child abuse so that if support or help could be provided to the family at an earlier stage child abuse could be prevented. While such an approach has many attractions how far is it appropriate for cases of child sexual abuse?

It seems to be assumed that the family consists of a 'naturalised' hetero-sexual couple and their natural children where the man is responsible for the financial support and the woman is responsible for the emotional support and care of the children (Van Every, 1991/2). Children are seen as passive receivers of socialisation, education and love and are thereby dependent, vulnerable, innocent and in need of protection (James and Prout, 1997). The 'family' is seen as the key building block of society offering nurturance and requiring support.

It is in this context that the 'refocusing of children's services' debate takes on a wider social and political significance. Not only is the family seen as a 'good thing' but it is not disaggregated and thus does not recognise that the interests of mothers, fathers and children may be different. While given a greater 'voice' than previously, children have their 'welfare' defined and mediated by adults, primarily parents and occasionally outside profes-sionals and the courts. This is quite explicit in the Children Act 1989 (Lyon and Parton, 1995). However, once we disaggregate the family in 'family support' and the parents in 'parental responsibility' by looking separately at the views, experiences and wishes of the women, children and young people involved in sexual abuse, a much more complex picture emerges—one which has quite different implications for what we might understand by 'support' and 'responsibility' and thereby quite different implications for policy and practice. Ironically, many of these issues were evident in a num-ber of the original Department of Health child protection research studies but barely figured in *Messages from Research* and thus have been mar-ginalised in much of the debate about the 'refocusing of children's services' since. The final sentence of the overview in *Messages from Research* is most instructive. 'It is argued that if policy and practice changes are to follow from this round of research, it should be to reconsider the balance of services and alter the way in which professionals are perceived by *parents* accused of abusing or neglecting their *offspring*' (DoH, 1995, p. 55, our emphasis). Mothers and fathers are seen as 'parents' and children are seen as 'off-spring'. This is quite inadequate.

A second major problem is that there is a failure to recognise the complex-ities and interrelationships between the criminal justice system, exemplified by the role of the police to investigate a crime, and the child welfare system, exemplified by the role of social workers to pursue the welfare of the child. It is this failure—and the wider social, political and organisational factors which reinforce it—which means that the latter is dominated by the former such that child welfare work, as experienced by the professionals, carers and children involved has become essentially a narrow forensic activity (Parton, 1997; Parton *et al.*, 1997). This is not simply concerned with where on the 'continuum' we locate the threshold for intervention but that we have two competing discourses in operation which cannot be easily integrated—conceptually or practically (Parton, 1997).

As Christina Lyon (1995, p. 153) has argued:

> 'except for minor provisions amending the orders which may be made in respect of children in criminal proceedings under the Children and Young Persons Act 1969 (s. 90 and Sched. 15) and the criteria which must be satisfied before accommodation orders may be made (s. 25), the Children Act does not deal in any way with the criminal justice system.'

The decision whether or not to prosecute an adult or juvenile perpetrator is the responsibility of the public authority charged with making such decisions within the criminal justice system, the Crown Prosecution Service. This refusal to acknowledge any interface between the criminal and civil systems places children, their carers and the professionals who work with them in an invidious position. On the one hand, parents should be worked with in 'partnership' in accordance with the principle of parental responsibility, and the fact that children are best cared for by their parents. On the other, there is the potential for prosecution and punishment of (at least one of) those parents.

Yet clearly there have been some major changes particularly in the area of child sexual abuse such that these tensions have become even more sharply focused in recent years. In particular, the police have taken on a central role such that, following Cleveland, they have been identified, along with Social Services, as the key statutory agency for the purposes of investigation. This was formalised further in *Working Together under the Children Act 1989* (DoH, 1991b). Rather than the police, and hence the criminal justice system, being involved at the point of a case conference, as previously, they are now involved from the beginning. This was further reinforced by the publication of the *Memorandum of Good Practice on Interviewing Children for Criminal Proceedings* (Home Office/DoH, 1992). These shifts in the decision-making processes have brought police involvement to the point of referral. As Wattam (1997a) has argued, referrals have effectively become complaints to the police so that prosecution is a consideration from the very beginning. The persuasive influence of the criminal justice system on child protection policy and practice is fundamental to any attempts to fundamentally 'refocus children's services'.

A third problem is that there is an assumption at the heart of current 'refocusing' that we have 'netted' all potential cases of child abuse, including sexual abuse. The problem is that we respond inappropriately and would be much better to define cases as 'children in need'. However, retrospective studies of adult survivors indicate that the vast majority of incidents of child sexual abuse go unreported to agencies of any kind (see, for example, Wattam and Woodward, 1996). Similarly, incidence studies demonstrate that the experience of child sexual abuse is much wider and more prevalent than official figures would suggest (Finkelhor, 1986; Kelly *et al.*, 1991; Queen's University, Belfast, 1990) and that official reports tend to be biased towards the poor and lower socio-economic classes while prevalence studies suggest that child sexual abuse is not class specific (La Fontaine, 1990). If we are serious about developing family support in relation to child sexual abuse, it is clear that refocusing or rebalancing what we currently do is insufficient. At present, current services are obviously not reaching those for whom they are designed.

THE CENTRALITY OF THE NON-OFFENDING CARER: THE ROLE OF MOTHERS

To a large extent, while child sexual abuse is perpetrated predominantly by men, the protection of children falls mainly on women. In the context of child sexual abuse, mothers are the key adult actors in child protection so that developing services which are supportive of mothers should be central, particularly in the aftermath of disclosure. We must never forget that it was women's groups who were among the first to 'hear' and 'believe' survivors' accounts and thereby bring the issue of child sexual abuse to public attention, and many have subsequently demonstrated the importance of trying to build alliances between professionals and mothers in order to develop appropriate policies and practices (Dempster, 1993; Hooper, 1992; Mullender, 1996).

Not only are mothers more likely to be told of abuse than professionals, but the way mothers respond to professionals and demonstrate their 'ability to protect' and co-operate with official agencies are the most important factors in children's recovery. Support from the non-offending carer is the most significant factor in trying to minimise both the short and longer-term effects of abuse (Wyatt and Mickey, 1987; Conte and Berliner, 1988; Everson *et al.*, 1989; Gomes-Schwartz *et al.*, 1990; Print and Dey, 1992).

It is evident from the research, however, that rather than construct a supportive, ongoing partnership with the mother, typically the prime concern of professionals and statutory investigatory agencies is whether evidence can be pieced together to substantiate the allegations of abuse and whether the mother is able to protect the child now and in the future: Is she a 'safe' parent? Once this question is addressed, very little support or service is forthcoming. Mothers do not just find professional responses unhelpful, they find them positively undermining and alienating (Hooper, 1992; Dempster, 1993; Farmer and Owen, 1995; Sharland *et al*, 1996; Walton, 1996).

This is thoroughly explicable when we recognise that professional decision making is primarily concerned with assessing, managing and ensuring against 'risk', and that this takes a particular form because of forensic concerns. There is a process underpinning professional responses to child sexual abuse which acknowledges that it is almost impossible to prove sexual abuse one way or the other, even though this is the central rationale for child protection work. As a result, methods for resolving the practical concern of the professional are substituted. These methods, which include the use of the 'safe parent', usually the mother, as the arbiter of whether something has happened or not seem to legitimate a service for some children but not for others. Cases with medical, physical or witness evidence are in a minority, and even these do not always warrant further action. If there is no disclosure from the child, no admission from the alleged perpetrator and a mother who is assessed as supportive, then the case will almost certainly proceed no further (Parton et al., 1997). Farmer and Owen (1995) found by the end of their study, that most of the children who had been sexually abused were living with their 'non-abusing parent', but only half of these children had received any sort of counselling and those who had not were reported to have adjusted 'markedly less well'. They found that it was frequently assumed that because the perpetrator was out of the household, the mother could protect the children and no further intervention was required. Any help was withdrawn far too quickly and the difficulties for both mothers and children worsened. Similar findings were also evident in the study by Sharland et al. (1996); however, they also found that children who were sexually abused by someone outside the immediate family were least likely to receive help or to have their needs met. The evidence from these studies and our own experience demonstrates that services for children living with non-abusing parents in the aftermath of sexual abuse are being neglected.

It is particularly noteworthy that of those who have come to MOSAIC, in only two cases have the children ever been placed on the child protection register and in all cases the children stayed with the mother. It seems that registration was rarely seriously considered and few were ever case conferenced because the child was seen as 'safe' and the mother was deemed a 'safe parent'. However, support services were rarely ever provided by a mainstream service and when they were this was not in a form or at a time the mothers said they wanted or needed it. They felt abandoned and their needs were not addressed. As one woman commented:

'As regards social services, I didn't get allocated a worker because the perpetrator wasn't there, my children were perfectly safe. I was told there was nothing they could do for me, I wouldn't be getting a worker, I wouldn't be getting anyone.'

All of the women spoke positively of the way they and their children were treated by the police when the initial investigation was taking place. It was the way they were treated subsequently which was problematic:

'My dealings with the police I found were exceptional. It was the feeling of safety, they knew what they were doing, very professional and discreet, very caring and gentle with the children and considerate of what they had been through. I admired all that, I felt safe . . . as I left the building they reassured me that I would get counselling for the children and that I would get counselling for myself, Social Services would be in touch . . . I remember ringing Social Services on day five, I hadn't cried, I sort of hung on, I felt like my finger nails were going it was that long. I rang Social Services up and said my child's disclosed abuse, we've been to the police station, when is somebody coming out to see me? I was shocked when they said to me, Oh, there's a letter about to go into the post today and we've arranged an appointment for you a week on Friday, which was something like another ten days. I just burst into tears. I thought, how can they leave it that long, it's just too long.'

This demonstrates a failure to recognise the impact on the mother of the disclosure of the sexual abuse, which is like an 'emotional earthquake' (Salter, 1998, p. 56). The mother is trying to cope with the full range of emotions at the same time—guilt, anger, hatred, hurt, isolation as well as loss. One of the issues is that she doubts and questions her own judgement and is trying to understand how and why this should happen and what she could have done differently. Invariably such people experience a variety of feelings which can reflect a range of ambivalences associated with being a mother in contemporary society. It is mothers who are given the responsibility for caring for and protecting their children and it is mothers who are held responsible if things are seen to go wrong (Hollway and Featherstone, 1997). Much of the blame for child sexual abuse, often in quite subtle and pervasive ways, is seen to reside with the mother; the abuse reflects on her as a wife/partner and woman/individual as well as a mother (Hooper and Humphreys, 1998). She is placed in an ambivalent position (at least in part), blamed for the abuse while also given the responsibility to care for the child just at the time when she is having to come to terms with her new situation and fundamental questions about her own identity and abilities. The mother is expected to protect her child from further abuse at the same time as she and others are feeling she has failed to do so.

One of the worst things the mothers in MOSAIC could be told was that they were 'coping':

'It seems as if you're coping on the surface. But you've no option but to cope, you feel you're going to crumple if you don't. I sat for two hours and I will admit, I sat down and cried. I went back for a following session and at the end of it she told me that I was clearly coping . . . and you don't want to hear that.

No, you don't want to hear that. I said we're coping because we have to. I said what about my family, my family are distressed.'

Issues related to loss are central (Walton, 1996) following the devastation of learning that your child has been sexually abused, particularly when this was by a trusted partner—identity, self-esteem and trust in others is put at severe risk. As Hooper (1992) has suggested, women's psychological development means that, more than for men, loss of attachments are experienced as a loss of self. The disruption to family relationships which the discovery of sexual abuse triggers is often intensely threatening. One of the most distressing losses felt by mothers is the loss of their 'innocent' child and the fact that there may be a loss of trust in their mothers engendered in children who have been sexually abused (as well as a sense of betrayal by the perpetrator).

However, it is not only that the mother's role is key in relation to the child who has been abused, but it is key for other members of the family, both other children and wider family and neighbours. They can be not just un-supportive but have strong views and feelings of their own which can complicate an already very difficult situation, and all the time it is the mother who is expected to support and mediate between the various parties (Hooper, 1992; Walton, 1996) including contact with the official agencies—schools, the police, social services, social security.

As one of the mothers in MOSAIC has said:

'As well as yourself you have to cope with everyone else. In my case it had been my partner who had been abusing. Where I had been in a happy relation-ship, on the day of disclosure by my daughter she told me her stepdad had been abusing her. I became a single parent that day through choice. I chose to stand by my daughter and get rid of him, there didn't seem to be any difficulty with that although it was a big shock. I had to cope with all this alone without the support from a partner because he was the abuser. I was trying to support her because she had been abused, and I was feeling a lot of responsibility for him coming into our lives in the first place, and my two sons he was their stepfather and they were very hurt, they had lost a dad—he had been their dad for five years. They had animosity towards their sister who had disclosed and it all got really confusing and there wasn't support even under my own roof. I felt totally alone.'

The losses and changes are also practical and material with the actual or potential departure of the father and his income. There may be the loss of the home because it is impossible to pay the mortgage, the loss of job because there are no babysitters or childminders available and the children may need mother to be more available. The demands upon the mother in a fraught and very difficult situation are tremendous—yet there are no ob-vious places to turn to for help or advice. It is a very isolating experience (Todd and Ellis, 1992).

A major factor in the mother's feelings of hostility and mistrust of professionals is that they do not feel they are listened to and their views and contributions valued.

> 'I needed to talk to somebody and find out how to handle all this . . . if a social worker had come and sat and listened that would have helped. Someone who could have given us suggestions of what to do.'

Unfortunately when they found someone in whom they had confidence and trust, they often did not stay on the case—there was a lack of continuity and consistency.

> 'This particular social worker was very good, she was very thorough. I felt very safe and everything was listed very clearly. I explained about a bad experience I had in a working situation, and how I'd been very let down and I didn't want to feel that this time, she really did try her best. I did appreciate she had a lot of other cases to deal with but she said if I need to phone her at all, that was okay, which I did twice, that was all right. She did get back and was very concerned but she made it clear that she wasn't assigned to the case and she did send me a letter to say she would be visiting one more time She did show concern about the counselling for my daughter and I have nothing but praise for her. She was strong, she was caring, but she didn't stay with me. The point being, we build a trusting relationship with this person but she had to go away, which I felt my daughter was miffed about and so was I.'

It is also clear that the way these issues are handled has a lasting impact not only on future relationships between the mother and professionals but also on how the mother believes and supports the child (Smith, 1994). Professional disregard for the mother's responsibility for her child can seriously undermine the mother's efforts to protect. For example, Farmer and Owen (1995) have demonstrated that mothers often discover that their child had already been interviewed without them being informed or involved, marginalising the mother from the outset and thus reinforcing the abuse of trust and secrecy of the abuse itself.

While the members of MOSAIC have not had direct experience of case conferences, the literature seems to support that mothers feel that the key decisions have already been made and that their contributions are neither listened to nor valued. Clearly the way partnership is handled in child protection (DOH/SSI, 1995) and participation is planned for and operationalised in case conferences is time consuming and requires sensitive work if it is to be productive.

It is also clear that while the central concerns of child protection are forensic, this does not mean that 'non-offending' carers are pleased with the way the criminal justice system operates. Most are angry that the process is so complex and treats them, their children and what they have to say, with such suspicion that it is difficult to get justice. This is not only concerned with the nature and delays of the judicial process, but that it can also be difficult to get help, counselling and advice while it is going on. While most want the offender prosecuted, the way it currently operates not only makes this very difficult but it can actively hinder the victim from coming to terms with the new situation.

These issues are well illustrated in a recent analysis of calls to ChildLine (MacLeod, 1997). Out of 177 calls about sexual abuse where police, social services or school had been involved, 90 callers (51%) described dissatisfaction with the outcome, either because there was to be no further action—which was very common for young children—or because there was a decision not to prosecute, or the alleged abuser was released on bail and was living nearby, or there were immense delays in getting to court, or there was little help or support. Four carers specifically said their children were refused counselling until after the court case. 'Carers were deeply frustrated if nothing had been done. This was usually because social services or police indicated that no proof existed which was deemed convincing enough to satisfy a court, or because the child had not made a clear enough statement on video. These calls conveyed a striking impression of the difficulty of achieving child protection especially when the child is young' (MacLeod, 1997, p. 24).

What mothers value from MOSAIC is that it offers a confidential, non-judgemental place where they can talk, be listened to and receive advice from other mothers who have been through similar experiences.

'Having been recommended by the police to MOSAIC I found it really helpful just to speak to someone that had been in the same position. After a long chat I went home and I felt to be back in control.'

'You don't necessarily want to talk about the abuse, you just want somewhere to feel comfortable . . . you just want to be in the company of somebody who isn't going to say stupid, tactless things. It's about feeling safe, it is for me. At times your head can just go to pieces and it can be triggered by anything, can't it? You feel in pieces and you just need to feel safe. Somewhere where you can go and you can deal with it, to sit quiet, have a cry, just to be there, to be yourself. I found I needed a lot of information, I felt so ignorant at the time, I needed to know all about them and how they worked, all about sexual abuse really because I had never come across it before.'

'You're scared, aren't you? You don't know who to turn to. If we could have an ideal what would we want? For any other mum going through that situation I would like to be able to give that mum the support, the phone line that's there all the time, professional help and advice, someone that can answer questions like where on earth do I get counselling for my kids, who do I talk to? Instead of going a long route round making half a dozen phone calls, wouldn't it be lovely if you just had one number who could give you access to information?'

However, the mothers are also very conscious that there are no equivalent services for others who need help. Non-abusing fathers and other siblings have nowhere to go and in effect the children and young people who have been abused have nothing in their own right.

THE EXPERIENCES OF CHILDREN AND YOUNG PEOPLE

Thus, in arguing that the development of family support in the area of child sexual abuse should recognise that the most significant protective factor is the child's relationship with the non-abusing parent, usually the mother, we are not suggesting that the needs and wishes of mothers are the same as children. While the feminist movement has been crucial in drawing attention to the issue of child sexual abuse there is also a danger that such approaches subsume children's needs within women's needs so that what is deemed good for women is also seen as good for children. This is clearly not adequate and is currently the subject of important debate within feminism. As Featherstone (1997, pp. 1–2) has argued:

'Faced with the recent onslaught against any alternatives to the traditional nuclear family, especially if they involve women's independence from men, the danger is that feminism will concentrate so fixedly on opposing that back-lash that we will not address the widespread anxieties about what happens to children when parental care fails.'

Not only must the views, experiences and actions of mothers, children and young people be disaggregated, it is children and young people who should be central. Unfortunately, the perspectives of children and young people are virtually absent from the recent research and current debates on family support and child protection.

Analyses of the work of ChildLine provide one of the few possibilities of understanding how children themselves make sense of their situation and what they want done about it. Reviews of ChildLine's work over the first ten years of its operation are particularly instructive in this respect (Epstein, 1996; Keep, 1996; MacLeod, 1996). There is clearly enormous fear among children about the consequences of involving the authorities when the alleged abuser is a member of the family and in some cases the public shame can be intolerable. Children wanting help without investigation have few places to go, and they have little opportunity to get counselling or mental health services for themselves as they are either sparse and limited or rationed and expensive. Referrals to ChildLine suggest that as soon as children mention that they are being sexually abused:

'whatever the quality of the evidence to support them in any proceedings, they are assumed to have made an allegation which has to be investigated. What children have to say suggests that this might be moving too fast and too definitively for them. In such a process there are only two choices: to "put up" with the abuse or accept the investigation—to put up or shut up. Children have no way of anticipating the quality and range of evidence required, so they are often armed with little more than their word in a process where their word counts for very little. This leaves children tolerating unacceptable, sometimes appalling, levels of violence and abuse.' (MacLeod, 1996, pp. 86–87).

One of the few research studies which has centrally involved children themselves in articulating what worried them and what they identified as harms and risks has been carried out by Butler and Williamson (1994, 1996). They interviewed 190 children including 46 living in the care system, 40 living in 'reconstituted' families, and 104 living with both birth parents. They were aged 6–17 years, but most were between 10 and 15 years of age, and about half the total had direct experience of social work. The worst experiences described varied greatly but could be clustered under three broad headings: family (abuse, arguments and separation); school and bullying; and violence and sexual abuse. Within the sample of young people interviewed, five disclosed the fact that they had been raped and one had been sexually abused by someone outside the family, while two had their mothers murdered by their fathers.

What Butler and Williamson argue, however, is that it is the *subjective* meaning given to events by young people which is most important and this is often at variance with what adults might expect. In the process we are forced to re-examine the nature of 'harms' which become designated as 'abuse' requiring an official adult response and the form those responses take. For example, it was clear that children certainly felt hurt by domestic violence and arguments, whether they were directly involved or not. However, it was the routine catalogue of harm suffered by children at the hands of other children that was often of greatest concern—an issue also identified by ChildLine (MacLeod and Morris, 1996)—but which is rarely taken seriously by adults.

An important finding by Butler and Williamson was that it was not always the originating problem which caused the 'worst experience' but the sequence of difficulties associated with it. A lack of information or explanation and a sense of helplessness can create more distress than the actual problem itself. While not specifically concerned about sexual abuse, such insights are invaluable for the way we think about 'family support'. Only by listening to the *meaning* imputed to such experiences by the young people concerned can those seeking to *support* them secure a measure of understanding of how these experiences are affecting them. An expanded awareness of what actually troubles children and young people may lead to a more sensitive and appropriate response to particular individuals (Butler and Williamson, 1994, p. 64).

The study also demonstrated that many young people had already lost faith in adults' capacity to help deal with their problems to the point that they had entirely given up on them. The reasons for this were commonly shared: adults lacked or were incapable of understanding; they imposed their own views; they either trivialised problems or over-reacted—sometimes over the same issue and were thus inconsistent. Crucially adults did not 'listen' and did not respect confidentiality. Interestingly many of the children did not discriminate between the lack of understanding displayed by 'adult professionals' (e.g. social workers, teachers, doctors, etc.) and by 'professional adults' (e.g. parents).

While the opportunity for children to share difficulties on their terms is critical in helping them to cope, it was also clear that many are 'cautious, reluctant and even fearful about discussing such issues with anyone, let alone adults who might potentially be able to help' (1994, p. 65). The net result was that children rarely talked about their problems.

However, children and young people in Butler and Williamson's study also identified the characteristics and qualities in professionals that they valued. They suggest that while the arguments were expressed in a variety of ways certain consistent views emerged which were remarkably similar to the traditional 'principles of social work' espoused by Biestek (1961) in terms of: good individualised listening; availability; being non-judgemental and non-directive; having a sense of humour; straight talking; and, crucially, working on the basis of trust and confidentiality.

These findings are supported by other studies which have considered who children look to for help. Such people must be trustworthy, take their problem seriously, be good at listening, not criticise or judge, and give reassurance and emotional support (Balding, 1997; Gordon and Grant, 1997). While not specifically concerned with sexual abuse, the studies are very instructive in showing where children and young people go for help.

Gordon and Grant (1997) found that children mostly (64%) turn to their friends to talk about their problems, followed by their parents. They turn mostly to mothers (26%) then to both parents together (18%), but only rarely just to fathers. They also turn to siblings and other relatives, but only 6% turn to teachers and 5% to boyfriends/girlfriends. A small minority turn to pets and popstar posters, but 8% feel they cannot talk to anybody about their feelings. Similar findings were found in the Balding (1997) study.

Gordon and Grant also discovered marked gender differences in those to whom young people are most likely to talk. Girls (84%) are nearly twice as likely to talk to their friends than boys (49%) and 34% of girls spoke to their mothers compared to 18% of boys. Boys (26%) are more likely to turn to both parents compared to girls (12%). Boys talk to both their brothers and sisters, but girls tend to talk only to their sisters. Boys (12%) are more likely not to talk to anyone about their feelings compared to girls (4%).

In the context of sexual abuse such findings reinforce our earlier comments about the importance of mothers, particularly for girls. What it also demonstrates, however, is that boys who have or are being sexually abused pose even more of a challenge and that we need to recognise the importance of friends in our strategies to develop help and support.

FUTURE DIRECTIONS

Butler and Williamson neatly pose perhaps the central question for the development of 'family support' if we are serious about putting children and young people actively at the centre of future developments:

> 'The essential question is whether the adult world wants to assist children who are suffering harm in feeling "safe" (as *children* define it) or to ensure that children appear to be "protected" (as *adults* define it).' (Butler and Williamson, 1996, p. 102; original emphasis)

Children's accounts strongly suggest that sexual abuse is not linked to social or family stress in the way that is often assumed, with physical harm and neglect and which seems to be assumed, both in *Messages from Research* (DOH, 1995) and in the way the 'refocusing of children's services' is often interpreted. Children's accounts emphasise complexity. Simply offering support to families in crisis or under stress is unlikely to *prevent* the sexual abuse of children—nor is it likely to diminish the need for robust interventions in some families and with some men, nor will it necessarily reduce the (often hidden) scale of misery experienced by children. Rather than see family support as trying to shift the focus from protection to prevention, as Mary MacLeod (1996) has argued, our concern should be alleviating suffering. She has articulated the views of the women in MOSAIC, which is central to our argument here, when she says:

> 'No-one can make the abuse not have happened when it has, but a great deal of child protection endeavour seems to emerge from a desire to do just that. But children are and can be much more than the abuse they have experienced if they receive a response organised to alleviate their suffering, and to treat them with decency and respect.' (MacLeod, 1996, pp. 90–91)

Children's accounts demonstrate that the issue of sexual abuse is much more complex than current policies and practices are able to recognise, and that invariably they are quite clear about the form any help should take. The key issue for 'family support' is to widen the possibilities and ensure that services are flexible and sensitive.

Crucially we have to recognise that the majority of children and young people relate to the adult world, particularly the professional world, with considerable caution. As Butler and Williamson argue, therefore, we have to consider seriously how the adult world of family support can connect with the experiences, worries and wishes of children, the vast majority of whom ultimately assume it is up to them to sort out their problems. They do not seek or expect action from others unless they ask for it. Broadly, it seems, they seek to *unload* problems on friends and seek advice, information and guidance from adults. While younger children are more likely to believe and hope that others will sort things out for them, even 8- and 9-year-olds feel they have to take most of the initiative on things that concerned them most.

'The dilemma for children and young people, as they see it, is that once they convey something to adults, the power to determine what should be done is— too often—taken out of their hands.' (Butler and Williamson, 1994, p. 82)

Thus not only do children need to be empowered they, literally, need to be given more control about what they use, when, how and with whom—hence the particular attraction of telephone help lines, for example ChildLine. Children require choices and adults can act as key catalysts to help them make choices but also ensure that things happen as a result. What is clear is that children do not simply want to be asked about their worries and concerns but also involved in the formulation of any 'action' as a result. This involves refusing compliance and saying 'no' to what may be on offer. Many of these issues run directly parallel with what the mothers in MOSAIC have said.

It also strongly suggests that it is impossible to combine the responsibilities for child protection and family support as is suggested by the Department of Health and in the 'refocusing' debates following *Messages from Research*. While the possibility of establishing clear forensic evidence of child sexual abuse is rare (Parton *et al.*, 1997), it seems that the need to try to do so is dominant in a manner that compromises the way family support can be provided and the way it is experienced. Forensic concerns dominate to the exclusion of meeting the needs of mothers and children. It seems that once a referral is made warranting investigation mothers lose control over what happens to their children, to themselves and to the wider family (Dempster, 1993). As a result they find themselves in a very difficult contradictory situation—marginalised and disempowered from key decision making yet given prime responsibility for the future protection and welfare of their children.

There is clearly a need for more therapeutic, counselling and advice services for children, adult survivors and non-offending parents to call upon together and separately, but in a way which they can approach and use in their own right. We have to recognise that at present statutory agencies have failed to provide and develop the range and type of support and counselling services required in the area of child sexual abuse (Gray *et al.*, 1997). Where they have developed, these have primarily been at the initiative of those in the community particularly derived from the experiences of adult survivors and non-offending parents of which MOSAIC is an excellent example. Statutory services should recognise that it is such groups that will continue to provide the majority of services and should act to resource and support their expansion. However, there are few examples of services *explicitly* and *exclusively* concerned with the needs of children and young people themselves. This is a priority. As a result the role of statutory services and professionals would change. Not only does this imply that professionals should be granted more discretion in what they do and the way they do it, but that they should be much more accountable to the children, adult survivors and non-offending parents themselves rather than narrowly defined procedures and organisational accountability. As Wattam (1997b) has suggested, the elective behaviour of telephone helpline use suggests that children would value something like an anonymous drop-in point for help, advice and counselling, irrespective of allegation or report. Similarly, the voices of survivors suggest there is a need for an ongoing programme of support which young people could dip into as and when an issue becomes relevant for them (Wattam and Woodward, 1996). Such programmes would by necessity recognise that children could continue to call upon such services once they enter adulthood and is concerned less with allegations or events and more on what users say they need.

It is clear that children and non-offending parents, usually mothers, need help with the emotional and practical consequences of sexual abuse whether they live together or apart. Clearly the current situation where both are either quickly dumped or sucked into the forensic gaze of the child protection system completely fails to recognise this. The study by Gomes-Schwartz *et al.* (1990) of child sexual abuse found that only 9% of families needed no further support after a 12-session crisis intervention period, and concluded that the classic crisis intervention model was applicable only to a limited range of cases. What we are arguing is that family support-type services are required *after* child sexual abuse has come to light, rather than before, as is implied in the preventive stress-based model. Self-help groups and voluntary organisations are likely to play the key role but clearly need a much stronger funding base which recognises the sensitivity of the work and the need for confidentiality. MOSAIC operates on the basis of providing a non-judgemental, confidential support and advice service where mothers can talk, be listened to and feel safe. It runs independently of the mainstream child protection and family support agencies. Because mothers are so central to supporting and helping children who have disclosed sexual abuse there is clearly a need for more and better funded similar services. However, this is not just something needed by adult survivors and mothers but non-offending fathers and other children, young people and family members affected by the impact of child sexual abuse. Crucially, however, a parallel service is required by the children and young people who have or are suffering sexual abuse.

What this implies is the development of what Keith Pringle (1998) has called the development of 'a third way', which is based on neither child protection nor family support in the way the recent debates on the 'refocusing of children's services' has developed in recent years. It is based on the recognition that most therapeutic, counselling and support services are currently provided by various community groups and that the vast majority of child sexual abuse never comes to the notice of the statutory agencies. It suggests that we must be much more systematic and co-ordinated in supporting such initiatives and that they should be central to what we do and not marginal and peripheral as at present. The role of the community is central (Smith, 1996). However, as Bill Jordan demonstrates in Chapter 10, such an approach is itself riven with difficulties because of the nature of child sexual abuse, and the nature of communities themselves.

NOTES

1. The term 'family support' which is seen as so significant in pointing to this change in emphasis, emerged in the 1980s in the Short Report (Social Services Committee, 1984) and the Review of Child Care Law (DHSS, 1985a) following a major research programme on decisions in Child Care (DHSS, 1985b) where it was argued that the natural family should be central to policy and practice and that the state should act in partnership with families keeping court interventions to a minimum so that 'we see "prevention" more positively as family support' (DHSS, 1985a, para. 2.3).
2. It has three categories: a reasonable standard of health or development; significant impairment of health or development; and disablement. It would not be acceptable for an authority to exclude any of these three—for example, by confining services to children at risk of significant harm which attracts the duty to investigate under section 47' (DoH, 1991a, para. 2.4). The term 'family support' is explicitly used in para. 2.6 of the *Guidance* when it is stated:

   'The Act envisages family support services being offered to members of a family of a child in need where the service is provided with a view to safeguarding and promoting the child's welfare (Section 17(3)). Any person who has parental responsibility for the child and any other person with whom the child is living is included so that a local authority may put together a package of services for a family which could include home help, day care provision for a family member other than the child in need (e.g. another child in the household) or a short-term, temporary placement for the child to relieve the carer.'

REFERENCES

Aldgate, J. and Tunstill, J. (1996) *Making Sense of Section 17*. London, HMSO.

Audit Commission (1994) *Seen But Not Heard: Coordinating Community Child Health and Social Services for Children in Need*. London, HMSO.

Balding, J. (1997) *Young People in 1996*. Exeter, Schools Health Education Unit, University of Exeter.

Biestek, F. (1961) *The Casework Relationship*. London, Allen & Unwin.

Butler, I. and Williamson, H. (1994) *Children Speak: Children, Trauma and Social Work*. London, NSPCC/Longman.

Butler, I. and Williamson, H. (1996) 'Safe'? Involving Children in Child Protection, in Butler, I. and Shaw, I. (eds) *A Case of Neglect? Children's Experiences and the Sociology of Childhood*. Aldershot, Avebury.

Colton, M., Drury, C. and Williams, M. (1995) *Children in Need: Family Support under the Children Act 1989*. Aldershot, Avebury.

Conte, J.R. and Berliner, L. (1988) The Impact of sexual abuse on children: empirical findings, in Walker, L. (ed.) *Handbook on Sexual Abuse of Children*. New York, Springer.

Dempster, H. (1993) The aftermath of child sexual abuse: women's perspectives, in Waterhouse, L. (ed.) *Child Abuse and Child Abusers: Protection and Prevention*. London, Jessica Kingsley.

DHSS (1985a) *Review of Child Care Law: Report to Ministers of an Interdepartmental Working Party*. London, HMSO.

DHSS (1985b) *Social Work Decisions in Child Care: Recent Research Findings and their Implications*. London, HMSO.

DoH (1991a) *The Children Act 1989 Guidance and Regulations: Volume 2, Family Support, Day Care and Educatonal Provision for Young Children*. London, HMSO.

DoH (1991b) *Working Together Under the Children Act 1989*. London, HMSO.

DoH (1994) *Children Act Report 1993*. London, HMSO.

DoH/SSI (1995) *The Challenge of Partnership in Child Protection: Practice Guide*. London, HMSO.

DoH (1995) *Child Protection: Messages from Research*. London, HMSO.

DoH (1998) *Working Together to Safeguard Children: New Government Proposals for Inter-Agency Cooperation: Consultation Paper*. Children's Services Branch, Department of Health.

Eekelaar, J. (1991) *Regulating Divorce*. Oxford, Oxford University Press.

Epstein, C. (1996) *Listening to Ten Year Olds*. London, ChildLine.

Everson, M.D., Hunter, W.M., Runyon, D.K., Edelsohn, G.A. and Coulter, M.C. (1989) Maternal support following disclosure of incest. *American Journal of Orthopsychiatry*, **59**(2): 197–207.

Farmer, E. and Owen, M. (1995) *Child Protection Practice: Private Risks and Public Remedies*. London, HMSO.

Featherstone, B. (1997) Introduction: Crisis in the Western Family, in Hollway, W. and Featherstone, B. (eds) *Mothering and Ambivalence*. London, Routledge.

Finkelhor, D. (1986) *Sexual Abuse: A Sourcebook on Child Sexual Abuse*. London, Sage.

Fox Harding, L. (1996) *Family, State and Social Policy*. Basingstoke, Macmillan.

Ghate, D. and Spencer, L. (1995) *The Prevalence of Child Sexual Abuse in Britain: A Feasibility Study for a Large Scale National Survey of the General Population*. London, HMSO.

Giller, H. (1993) *Children in Need: Definition, Management and Monitoring: A Report for the Department of Health*. London, HMSO/Social Information Systems.

Gomes-Schwartz, B., Horowitz, J.M. and Cardarelli, A.P. (1990) *Child Sexual Abuse: The Initial Effects*. London, Sage.

Gordon, J. and Grant, G. (eds) (1997) *How We Feel—An Insight into the Emotional World of Teenagers*. London, Jessica Kingsley.

Gray, S., Higgs, M. and Pringle, K. (1997) User-centred responses to child sexual abuse: the way forward *Child and Family Social Work*, 2(1): 49–57.

Hollway, W. and Featherstone, B. (eds) (1997) *Mothering and Ambivalence*. London, Routledge.

Home Office/DoH (1992) *The Memorandum of Good Practice on Interviewing Children for Criminal Proceedings*. London, HMSO.

Hooper, C.A. (1992) *Mothers Surviving Child Sexual Abuse*. London, Tavistock/Routledge.

Hooper, C.A. and Humphreys, C. (1997) What's in a name? Reflections on the term 'non-abusing parent'. *Child Abuse Review*, 6: 298–333.

Hooper, C.A. and Humphreys, C. (1998) Women whose children have been sexually abused: reflections on a debate. *British Journal of Social Work*, 28(4): 565–580.

James, A. and Prout, A. (eds) (1997) *Constructing and Reconstructing Childhood: Contemporary Issues in the Sociological Study of Childhood*, 2nd edition. London, Falmer Press.

Keep, G. (1996) *Child Witnesses—in their own words*. London, ChildLine.

Kelly, L., Regan, L. and Burton, S. (1991) *An Exploratory Study of the Prevalence of Sexual Abuse in a Sample of 16–21 Year Olds*. London, University of North London.

La Fontaine, J. (1990) *Child Sexual Abuse*. Cambridge, Polity Press.

La Fontaine, J. (1994) *The Extent and Nature of Organised and Ritual Sexual Abuse: Research Findings*. London, HMSO.

Lyon, C. (1995) Child Protection and the Civil Law, in James, A. and Wilson, K. (eds) *The Chld Protection Handbook*. London, Bailliere Tindall.

Lyon, C. and Parton, N. (1995) Children's rights and the Children Act 1989, in Franklin, B. (ed.) *The Handbook of Children's Rights: Comparative Policy and Practice*. London, Routledge.

MacLeod, M. (1997) *Child Protection: Everybody's Business*. Sutton, Community Care.

MacLeod, M. (1996) *Talking with Children about Child Abuse*. London, ChildLine.

Macleod, M. and Morris, S. (1996) *Why Me? Children talking to ChildLine about Bullying*. London, ChildLine.

Monck, E. and New, M. (1995) *Sexually Abused Children and Adolescents and Young Perpetrators of Sexual Abuse who were Treated in Voluntary Community Facilities*. London, HMSO.

Monck, E., Sharland, E., Bentovim, A., Goodall, G., Hyde, C., and Win, R. (1995) *Child Sexual Abuse: A Descriptive and Treatment Study*. London, HMSO.

Mullender, A. (1996) *Rethinking Domestic Violence: The Social Work and Probation Response*. London, Routledge.

Print, B. and Dey, C. (1992) Empowering mothers of sexually abused children—a positive framework, in Bannister, A. (ed.) *Child Sexual Abuse: From Hearing to Healing*. Harlow, Longman.

Parton, N. (1997) (ed.) *Child Protection and Family Support: Tensions, Contradictions and Possibilities*. London, Routledge.

Parton, N., Thorpe, D. and Wattam, C. (1997) *Child Protection: Risk and the Moral Order*. Basingstoke, Macmillan.

Pellegrin, A. and Wagner, W.G. (1990) Child sexual abuse: factors affecting victims' removal from home. *Child Abuse and Neglect*, 140: 53–60.

Pringle, K. (1998) *Children and Social Welfare in Europe*. Buckingham, Open University Press.

Print, B. and Dey, C. (1992) Empowering mothers of sexually abused children—a positive framework, in Bannister, A. (ed.) *From Hearing to Healing: Working With the Aftermath of Child Sexual Abuse*. London, Longman.

Queen's University Belfast, The Research Team (1990) *Child Sexual Abuse in Northern Ireland: A Research Study of Incidence*. Belfast, Greystone.

Salter, A.C. (1988) *Treating Child Sex Offenders and Victims: A Practical Guide*. London, Sage.

Secretary of State (1988) *Report of the Inquiry into Child Abuse in Cleveland*, Cmnd 412. London, HMSO.

Sharland, E., Jones, D., Aldgate, J., Seal, H. and Croucher, M. (1996) *Professional Intervention and Child Sexual Abuse*. London, HMSO.

Smith, G. (1994) Parent, partner, protector: conflicting role demands for mothers of sexually abused children, in Morrison, T., Erooga, M. and Beckett, R.C. (eds) *Sexual Offending Against Children: Assessment and Treatment of Male Abusers*. London, Routledge.

Smith, G. (1996) Reassessing protectiveness, in Batty, D. and Cullen, D. (eds) *Child Protection and the Therapeutic Option*. London, British Agencies for Adoption and Fostering.

Smith, M. and Grocke, M. (1995) *Normal Family Sexuality and Sexual Knowledge in Children*. London, Royal College of Psychiatrists/Gorkill Press.

Social Services Committee (1984) *Children in Care (Short Report)*. London, HMSO.

SSI (1996) *Children in Need: Report of an SSI National Inspection of SSD Family Support Services 1993/95*. Social Services Inspectorate, London, Department of Health.

SSI (1997) *Responding to Families in Need: Inspection of Assessment, Planning and Decision-Making in Family Support Services*. Social Services Inspectorate, London, Department of Health.

Thorburn, J., Lewis, A. and Shemmings, D. (1995) *Paternalism or Partnership? Family Involvement in the Child Protection Process*. London, HMSO.

Todd, I. and Ellis, L. (1992) Divided Loyalties *Social Work Today*, **23**(4): 14–15.

Tunstill, J. (1996) Children in need: the answer to the problem for family support. *Children and Youth Services Review*, **17**(5/6): 651–664.

Tunstill, J. (1997) Implementing the family support clauses of the 1989 Children Act: Legislative, professional and organisational obstacles, in Parton, N. (ed.) *Child Protection and Family Support: Tensions, Contradictions and Possibilities*. London, Routledge.

Van Every, J. (1991/92) Who is 'the family'? The assumptions of British social policy. *Critical Social Policy*, **33**: Winter.

Walton, P. (1996) *Partnership with Mothers in the Wake of Child Sexual Abuse*. Social Work Monograph 154. Norwich, University of East Anglia.

Wattam, C. (1997a) Is the criminalisation of child harm and injury in the interests of the child? *Children and Society*, **11**(2): 97–107.

Wattam, C. (1997b) Can filtering processes be rationalised? in Parton, N. (ed.) *Child Protection and Family Support: Tensions, Contradictions and Possibilities*. London, Routledge.

Wattam, C. and Woodward, C. (1996) And do I abuse my children? . . . No!— Learning about prevention from people who have experienced child abuse. *Childhood Matters: The Report of the National Commission of Inquiry into the Prevention of Child Abuse*. Vol. 2, Background Papers. London, HMSO.

Wyatt, G.E. and Mickey, M.R. (1987) Ameliorating the effects of child sexual abuse: an exploratory study of support by parents and others. *Journal of Interpersonal Violence*, **2**(4): 403–414.

10

CHILD SEXUAL ABUSE AND THE COMMUNITY

Bill Jordan

'Ensuring that all children within our community are safeguarded and protected from abuse is an objective to which the government is firmly committed.
We believe that the community as a whole has a responsibility for promoting
the welfare of children and preventing child abuse' (Consultation Paper, *Working Together to Safeguard Children*, Department of Health, 1998, Preface).

This quotation encapsulates the new Labour government's approach to
reform of the welfare state. It declares the government's aspirations in relation to a social outcome, and goes on to define responsibility for achieving it
as residing in 'the community'. In this chapter, I shall try to analyse the
notion of a community responsibility for child sexual abuse in the context of
the Blair government's reformulation of social citizenship.

It may seem fanciful to try to link such diverse policy reforms as social
security and the personal social services. However, I shall argue that there
are many common themes in the government's attempt to remoralise society
and regenerate the national economy. Community responsibility is an important one of these.

The Labour government is committed to reforms which will set in motion
a 'new age of welfare' through 'a change of culture among benefits claimants, employers and public servants which will break the mould of the old'
(DSS, 1998, p. 24). The welfare state is recast as a set of reciprocal relationships between active, responsible citizens, and a public power which man-
ages risks and protects those in genuine need. Citizens have obligations
towards each other and to the state, which in turn distinguishes between
those who can and should provide for themselves, and those who cannot (p.
3).

This leaves a special category of actions and people who are irresponsible,
which put the rest of the citizenry at risk, and fall as costs on the govern-

ment. The government is, if anything, more strong in its moral condemnation of such actions and such people than its Conservative predecessors. It denounces welfare free riding, fraud, and various forms of social predation unequivocally, and has presided over a continued rapid expansion of the prison population, and of the numbers excluded from benefits and schools. But its proclaimed philosophy of *inclusion* (Lister, 1998) is in tension with this hawkishness on deviance and crime. It seeks ways to reconcile its fierceness over irresponsible, welfare-dependent and dishonest behaviour with its emphasis on inclusion (rather than equality) as the ultimate means to social justice (the goal of social policy). The tension created requires a new language of solutions.

Declared policy on child abuse is an example of the way in which the Blair government tries to overcome this apparent contradiction, and 'community' is a key concept in its reformulation. The government seeks—in this matter and in many others—to justify its values and goals in terms of the morality of the family, the voluntary association and the informal, communal system of co-operation and social control. In this it appeals to 'the community' as a shared set of principles and relationships embodied in the idealised ethics of traditional working class family and neighbourhood life—a mythical reconstruction of a (majority white) Victorian England that corresponds to Margaret Thatcher's corner shop morality of the Victorian *petit bourgeoisie*.

In such a community, children are protected from abuse by the values embedded in a culture of self-help, self-discipline and co-operation, and by the vigilance of responsible parents, relatives and neighbours. There are spontaneous and indigenous systems of mutual support and social control which safeguard against both irresponsible neglect and predatory harm. The government's expert systems are merely there to reinforce these bulwarks against abuse, by assessing particular risks, and taking remedial action. 'The community' thus recognises its obligations towards children, and acts upon them, without much prompting from the public power, and co-operates gratefully with its representatives (however representative these may actually be) in cases which all recognise as threatening the common good.

This concept of community is one that survivors recognise. More often, however, this has been because children have turned to community members for help and have not been heard. Their expectations have been that those nearest to them will do something but this does not happen when there is no shared agreement on recognising sexual abuse and no consensus on what should be done about it. For example, a respondent to the National Commission noted,

> 'Community responsibility, who can help? Many of the "abused" say that they have repeatedly reported their distress to family, neighbours, teachers . . . and nobody listened.' (Wattam and Woodward, 1996, p. 75)

Letter writers to the Commission were clear that comr
more to help children experiencing sexual abuse. Many
just about seeing possible signs of child abuse but also ab
taking a collective responsibility, for example,

> 'What's it to do with me? All adults should be encouraged to take respon-
> sibility for the welfare of abused children as they would for their physical
> safety and also to support the efforts of all those who are trying to deal with the
> problem.' (*ibid.*)

> 'Schemes like neighbourhood watch where parents look out for all children at
> parks (not just their own) reporting anyone hanging about, or even a warden to
> keep an eye out for paedophiles.' (*ibid.*)

There is, however, a danger in whole-heartedly embracing a community
politics. This has less to do with the wishes of victims for greater protection
and support from neighbourhoods and more to do with the way in which
the notion of community has been applied. 'Community' can mean many
things, and it is important that the voices of victims and survivors do not get
lost in debates which are far removed from them and are designed to serve
other ends.

In the new Labour government's reformist rhetoric, 'the community' is
seen as a remedy for the atomism and selfishness of Thatcherite individualism (Marquand, 1998). It counteracts the rational egoism of the market,
through the social cement of communal norms and controls. Vulnerable
individuals, like children and frail elderly people, are protected, and wrongdoers sanctioned, by a system of morality and organisation which is essentially social, demonstrating exactly those elements in human behaviour and
structure whose existence Margaret Thatcher denied in her famous individ-
ualist aphorism.

The first part of this chapter will explore the problems and pitfalls of a
politics which derives its principles for the deployment of the public power
from such a system of morality, and which mobilises public sentiments in
support of them. Using the example of child sexual abuse, I shall show how
mixing together the artificial and abstract concepts and institutions of the
child protection system and the blood-and-guts codes of the real-life community may be a very risky process. Fanned by the media's appetite for
sensation and scandal, the 'community's' responses to such mobilisation are
unpredictable and potentially destabilising, leading to a reactive form of
policy response, which can be expensive, and may threaten more fundamental values of liberal democracy.

I shall argue that 'the community' which the new Labour government
constructs is in reality very different from the imagined working-class uto-
pia of the past age. It is one constructed by a new form of authoritarian

ᴏlitics, that derives its legitimacy from its claims to protect the public against various kinds of threat from within. This paternalistic, conservative, state-led communitarianism (Driver and Martell, 1997) deals in stereotypes and myths that summon up the ghosts of witchcraft, diabolism and heresy, and mobilise the little-mourned forces of scapegoating, shaming, the pillory and the stocks. As the century draws to a close, it is ironic that the new Labour government should feel safe to release those forces which, in the name of racism, God and folk-dancing, so devastated the inter-war world.

In the meanwhile, there are groups of people who offer help and support for children who have suffered sexual abuse, and who constitute a network of skilled and responsible activists, outside the professional, public services (Gray et al., 1997; Pringle, 1998). This network illustrates the differences between the new Labour government's concept of 'community', and an alternative approach that listens to, hears and validates the experiences of children. In the second half of the chapter I shall set out a critique of the present child protection system, and of the government's notion of 'community responsibility', in terms of an alternative model based on mobilisation and empowerment of such a network.

THE WELFARE STATE AND THE COMMUNITY

In this section, I shall set out the distinctions between liberal political institutions and communal codes on which the first part of my analysis rests. I shall argue that the former have, since the seventeenth century, been superimposed on the latter, but always exist in some kind of dialectic with them. Hence the state's systems for welfare provision and social control, such as the child protection system, are necessarily accommodations with the informal order of everyday life, and necessarily draw on its code of interaction for their legitimacy and day-to-day effectiveness. What is distinctive about the new Labour government initiative in social policy is its eagerness to rearticulate this relationship, by explicitly drawing on certain traditional values, and mobilising certain moral sentiments, as instruments for its reformulation of the roles of the state and its citizens.

It is beyond the scope of this chapter to review the whole development of child protection systems as a specific example of the regulation of civil society by the state. The outlines of such an analysis have been drawn by others (Donzelot, 1983; Parton, 1991; Parton et al., 1997). My point is simply that child protection systems must be understood in this context, as a (fairly recent) instance of the imposition of rational-legal authority upon hitherto unregulated aspects of social interactions. This process of extension and redefinition is, of course, continuous, and the refinement of regulation is never final. The pace of change is accelerated during periods, such as the present, when the contours of 'the social' are being altered, in response to new forces in society.

In liberal polities such as the United Kingdom, all such developments have taken place within the discourses and institutional structures of a regulatory framework that gave high priority to individual freedom and market relationships. Unlike the more paternalistic, tutelary and protective regimes of Continental Europe, the British tradition of governance constructed its citizens as competent actors in a competitive economic and political environment (Jordan, 1996, ch. 3). This approach assumes that the crucial principle for maximising the welfare of citizens is that of voluntary exchange between autonomous individuals, and that this applies as much to interactions in civil society as to those of the formal economy. Hence all must be given the maximum degree of civil liberty, both to make voluntary arrangements over their day-to-day lives, and to contract with each other for their material needs. Indeed, the only proper basis for a good society is a system of maximally unfettered interactions between critically self-responsible individuals, who exercise moral control over their lives. Hence all systems of regulation, including the welfare collectivist post-war social services, are required to justify themselves according to these standards. Beveridge did precisely this in his exposition of the principles of social insurance and full employment (Beveridge, 1942, 1944). The state, in turn, must minimise coercion, and confine it to these spheres in which it least damages individual freedom, and most promotes the common good.

To this end, all regulation—and especially that in the social sphere—is framed in terms of basic civil, political and economic rights, which protect individual citizens against excessive or arbitrary coercion by the public power. These rights are set against the state's legal authority, and the latter is constantly tested in the courts. Rights are abstractions from these aspects of human personality and activity seen as crucial for the free flourishing of human capacities (Freeden, 1991). They are established through the political pressure of free associations within civil society, from the politicised bourgeoisie of the 1830s who pressed for the Great Reform Act, to the new social movements of the 1970s onwards.

An example of this is the current pressure to legalise homosexual acts between 16 and 18 year olds and others. On the one hand, actions which were previously interpreted as crimes are now being reinterpreted in terms of rights to equality of treatment between young people with heterosexual and homosexual orientations. On the other hand, the government is drafting (or at least seriously studying) legislation under which it would be a (new) offence for those entrusted with the education or care of young people of this age to have sexual relations with them. In other words, young men would gain the right to the physical expression of homosexual inclinations, but a new category of older offenders would be created. It remains to be seen how seriously the latter's offences would be regarded, and how this category would be aligned with the media stereotype of 'paedophiles', which has come to exert a strong influence on government policy and public sentiment. This example illustrates the fairly complex processes through which both rights and violations of rights are abstracted from the messy world of everyday social relations, and presented as issues for resolution in courts.

In the everyday world, social interactions are regulated by an informal code of conduct which I shall, for the sake of brevity, refer to as the *blood-and-guts* code. By this I mean the processes by which mutual recognition, exchanges of meaning, and the sense of social order are sustained in informal interactions (Hilbert, 1991; Jordan *et al.*, 1994, ch. 2). This everyday order is ultimately accountable to the formal, institutional order of the polity and the economy (Rawls, 1989), but it constitutes a distinctive reality of its own, through which ordinary life is lived and liveable. Social work is performed in part in the regulatory system of the public power (courts, social services departments, interagency meetings) and partly within this everyday, informal order. For example it identifies those issues in the latter which need to be referred to the formal system for adjudication, by responding to requests for investigation by the wider public. Child sexual abuse is one such issue.

Whereas in a liberal polity the rational-legal code deals in individual rights and state powers, the blood-and-guts code deals in family, friendship and communal ties of love, loyalty, trust, co-operation and sacrifice. It also deals in hatred, betrayal, revenge, rape and violence. The blood-and-guts code knows little or nothing of rights, legal powers or the protections of professional ethics. It knows only of the emotions, of the obligations of kinship and shared territory, and the sometimes brutal ways in which these are enforced. It is the oldest code on earth, and has survived the imposition of every official system of regulation, from market economics to state communism. Every political regime must come to terms with it; each must be wary of its unpredictable power.

Traditionally liberalism is *very* wary of the blood-and-guts code, and polities with a strongly liberal system of governance, like the UK, have resisted populist politics that mobilises it to achieve its ends. This is because the abstract rights that sustain both markets and a civil society based on voluntary associations are fragile and artificial constructions that are highly vulnerable to the earthy realities of the everyday world. How can the inherently thin and insubstantial notions of personal and property rights survive against the pressing claims of sex, power and religious authority? How can the meagre constructions of international law sustain themselves against the pumping, thumping rhythms of race and soil? Only by a meticulous separation between the public worlds of political authority and economic organisation, and the private worlds of blood and guts, together with an elaborate bridging system of social regulation between the two. Liberalism is such a separation and such a system of regulation, that constantly refers with horror to the twin evils of the twentieth century, the total formal regulation of civil society that was state communism, and the political mobilisation of blood-and-guts enthusiasm that was fascism.

One of the things that is new about New Labour is its reversal of this distaste for the popular moral order. This change takes two forms. On the one hand, there is the appeal to communal values on traditionally expert, technical and administrative issues of social policy like social security and social care. Here it makes a radical break with Thatcherism. Margaret Thatcher tried to reconstruct citizens as *market* actors, and to privatise aspects of the public infrastructure, including parts of the welfare state. But her emphasis was on reconstructing *both* service users *and* public-sector staff as cost-conscious, competent actors in a competitive economic environment, where there was no such thing as a free lunch. Tony Blair's active citizens are similarly required to take more personal responsibility for their welfare, but they are held accountable as much to a morality of mutual concern and neighbourhood discipline as to the realities of supply and demand and the disciplines of the market. Furthermore he constantly invokes the norms and values of the blood-and-guts code to justify his policies, and to mobilise the public against wrongdoing and wrongdoers.

On the other hand, the new Labour government's ministers seem to have little fear of overstimulating public sentiments on a number of sensitive issues. Whereas an interparty consensus has traditionally protected the criminal justice system against such populist politics (out of anxiety over vigilantism, lynch mobs and the mobilisation of authoritarian opinion more generally), Labour now seems to court such responses. The popular press is their chosen vehicle for communicating their social policy goals, even when this risks endangering that support of their traditional allies among social services professionals and other staff. These features of Blairism will be analysed in the next section.

ABSTRACT LEGAL AND BLOOD-AND-GUTS REGULATION

Let me start this section by clarifying what I consider to be the established relationship between liberal political institutions and the blood-and-guts code. This is one in which the liberal political order defines itself in terms of aspects of that code, and hence is in some sense parasitic on it; yet also limits and relegates it to a residual role, outside the public sphere of state regulation. In other words, liberalism invokes the blood-and-guts code to define and legitimate itself, but confines it to a private sphere that is insulated from the formal order of polity and economy.

For instance, the Beveridge welfare state explicitly used the rhetoric of patriarchy in its justification of the male breadwinner model of 'full employment', the family wage, and employment-related social insurance. Women were 'equal partners' in social security, but their role was mainly to be as unpaid domestic workers and providers of child and family care. This served both to legitimate the regulation of a male-dominated formal labour market, and to demarcate the boundary between the public world of employment and social insurance from the private world of the household. Similarly, although Thatcherism in many ways opened up a more 'flexible' and deregulated labour market to married women, and insisted that the economics of competition was better for women's opportunities than the politics of organised male privilege, it was strong on the ethics of family responsibility and voluntary provision for welfare needs, treated as a private sphere for altruism and the narrower mutualities of affection, sympathy and charity.

What is distinctive about new Labour rhetoric on social welfare and citizenship is its insistence that the values of the moral and familial sphere apply to the public order of the state's relations with its citizens. Hence the ideas that rights imply obligations, that welfare beneficiaries owe reciprocal duties to the public power, that it is fair for the state to require work contributions from claimants, and that the community has responsibilities for protecting itself against deviance and crime, are all derived from the application of aspects of the blood-and-guts code to public-sphere interactions. They all reintroduce preliberal, premodern elements into state–citizen relations.

Liberalism can be understood as the attempt to define, through systems of personal and property rights, a domain in which individuals can respond to market signals for 'voluntary' exchange, and opportunities for collective (political) action consistent with optimising such exchange. As such, it seeks to drive out of the public sphere all the traditional notions of personal obligation and authority (including religious and monarchical as well as aristocratic and military authority) which threaten the freedom to make contracts purely for the sake of economic advantage. It was because of this purging of the commercial economy of its feudal residues that Adam Smith could claim that consumers were free to follow their preferences, and employees their interests, rather than being forced to submit to their duties; and that Marx and Engels could praise capitalism for rescuing humanity from the 'idiocy of rural life' (Jordan, 1998, chs 2 and 3).

This implies that the public sphere is regulated by a set of institutions (money, property, contracts, legal rights, rules, courts) which abstract from wider social relations in a way that eliminates exactly those blood-and-guts elements that characterise the interactions of the private sphere (emotions, ties, faiths, superstitions, grudges). But the language of Blairism—morality, obligation, reciprocity, contribution, responsibility—brings many of these back into the public domain.

The most obvious example is the notion that claimants of welfare benefits should be willing to work as a reciprocal obligation that corresponds to their right to public assistance. Liberal rights are typically unconditional safeguards against state coercion, and the only obligations they imply are to keep the law and pay taxes. Labour contributions are characteristic of feudalism (the corvée) and state socialism (Lenin and Trotsky agreed that all citizens owed work obligations to the state). Reciprocal labour contributions are, of course, the very stuff of interactions in the family and the hand-to-mouth voluntary organisation, where the informal economy of co-operation relies on everyone doing his or her fair share. Labour markets begin where reciprocity ends, work can be given a wage, and workers can calculate their preferences and interests, and make contracts. Conversely, the blood-and-guts code of love, obligation, duty and sacrifice has survived precisely where money and contract are inappropriate means of dividing tasks and co-ordinating efforts (Jordan, 1998, chs. 2 and 3).

What I am criticising about the new Labour government is not its determination to update the social services' relation to the informal order, or its efforts to redefine social justice in terms of inclusion, but the particular version of 'the community' that it promotes, and the particular public sentiments that it mobilises. Tony Blair and his ministers are right to insist that the institutions of the Beveridge welfare state no longer sustain a viable system of social support, and that this is partly because they no longer fit the way that people live their everyday lives, or understand their worlds. This does imply the need for a new morality of welfare, and a new mobilisation of the informal, the unrecognised and the largely invisible forces of community. The trouble lies in *how* the government is choosing to do these things. Specifically, new Labour's approach:

- appeals to an imagined past 'community' of family responsibility and neighbourhood solidarity which no longer exists (if it ever did);
- insists on the imposition of a homogeneous public morality, residing in the cultural practices of this imagined 'community', rather than drawing on and strengthening the actual multicultural resources of existing networks of support for survivors of child sexual abuse, and other groups of vulnerable people in need;
- adopts a 'top down' model of remoralisation, in which politicians and officials attempt to enforce the obligations of this public morality, rather than widening and deepening the pool of public virtues already deployed in the everyday world, which enabled vulnerable and excluded people to survive the Thatcher years;
- mobilises public sentiments of fear, loathing and lust for revenge, against a small number of identified 'paedophiles', rather than raising awareness of the nature and prevalence of child sexual abuse in just those social

institutions—families, neighbourhoods, schools, churches, voluntary associations—to whose morality it appeals.

In other words, the new Labour government appeals to, imposes, enforces and mobilises exactly those aspects of the blood-and-guts code which have led to the secrecy and hypocrisy surrounding child sexual abuse, making it *more* difficult for children to get support and validation, and for professionals to form meaningful links with networks for such support. If the current inadequacies of the social services stem from the distance between the abstract, official, formal, legal system for regulating the actual sexual experiences of children and their cultural context in the everyday world, then the government's approach is likely to be counterproductive in many ways.

The blood-and-guts code of everyday life is, by definition, both the source of all grass-roots, accessible and child-centred protections for children's emerging sexuality, and the greatest dangers of abuse and exploitation that children face. The goal of social policy in this field should be to strengthen the former and minimise the latter. 'The community' to which the government appeals is largely empty of awareness and willingness to take responsibility. As one survivor noted,

> 'The community must stop turning a blind eye to the actions of others towards their children. Unfortunately, it is difficult to reproach a person you know is abusing a child or children without bringing trouble upon yourself, but we must be more decisive and inform the social services.' (Wattam and Woodward, 1996)

Instead, it responds to media frenzy, projecting its fears onto 'paedophiles' in occasional outbursts of moral panic. This last has been amply demonstrated in the early months of 1998, when crowds besieging various police stations forced the government to offer semi-secure accommodation to the released prisoners Robert Oliver and Sidney Cooke, convicted of the manslaughter and sexual abuse of Jason Swift.

AN ALTERNATIVE MODEL OF THE RESPONSIBLE COMMUNITY

There is an emerging critique of services for preventing and protecting those children at risk of sexual abuse which echoes this more general doubt about the government's version of communitarianism. In brief summary, it argues:

1. Child sexual abuse is far more extensive than existing referrals to social services departments indicate. Surveys of adults which reveal large

numbers of survivors, and calls to child helplines, both indicate that most instances of child sexual abuse are not identified by statutory services.

2. Most instances of child sexual abuse occur in families, and the overwhelming majority of perpetrators are men, acting alone. This combination of family setting and male bias strongly suggests that it is linked with the power relations of the household, either as a means of domination, or reflecting domination.

3. The official child protection system is, at best, a very blunt instrument in issues of child sexual abuse, which constitutes a special case in the broader field of child abuse. Both quantitative and qualitative evidence suggests that statutory services (and professional agencies more generally) offer little therapeutic help or social support to survivors of child sexual abuse, and are ineffective in protecting children from it.

4. These shortcomings are unlikely to be overcome by shifting policy and practice away from statutory investigation towards a 'family support' model, under the influence of European approaches. The idea of 'working alongside families' in a negotiated way is now criticised as ineffective in relation to child sexual abuse in just those European countries which are taken as models by the Department of Health and policy analysts (Pringle, 1998).

5. Surveys reveal that survivors of child sexual abuse do find help and support from networks of self-help groups and survivor-led services. They show that survivors have a strong preference for such approaches, and particularly for receiving help from those who identify themselves as survivors. 'In my case the community didn't know—sworn to secrecy. We need a network, as AA have, to help each other because we are the specialists, certainly in this field' (Wattam and Woodward, 1996). 'Victims are the most professional people when it comes to understanding child abuse (*ibid.*); 'You need more groups and a lot more co-operation with the professionals and people who have got over abuse and are now helping more abused people; because they have been in the same position and they know how the abused person is really feeling' (*ibid.*).

6. Hence statutory child protection and professional therapeutic systems should be reorganised in a way that recognises the key role of user-led organisations, and puts them in the front line of prevention and protection in this field.

This critique insists that child sexual abuse is more difficult to identify than physical abuse, and that its prevention and the protection of children who are sexually abused require a different strategy and organisation of services from physical abuse (Pringle, 1998). Large-scale surveys of the general populations of the USA and UK suggest that 1 in 5, or even 1 in 3, may experience some form of sexual abuse (Finkelhor *et al.*, 1996; Kelly *et al.*,

1991), and that even if sexual abuse that does not involve violence is excluded, 1 in 5 girls and 1 in 14 boys are sexually abused (Fisher, 1994, p. 4). When compared with the numbers of cases of child abuse identified—3.54 per 1,000 population under 18, of which 17% are sexual abuse (Hallett, 1995, pp. 33–37)—this suggests that the overwhelming majority of sexual abuse is not detected (Wattam, 1997). It also indicates that the growing orthodoxy on child protection services in the UK—that they identify most serious abuse but fail to give an adequate level of service to families of children in need—is wide of the mark in relation to sexual abuse.

Furthermore, survey evidence points to the inadequacy of the therapeutic services and support provided through statutory services in England and Wales, either for children who have been abused or for their non-abusive parents (Gray *et al.*, 1996, 1997). But it also indicates that there are many, largely underfunded or unfunded, groups and self-help organisations for both children and parents. These are mostly very small, independent and survivor-focused, as well as being organised and led by survivors of child sexual abuse (Gray *et al.*, 1997, p. 51). In other words, if the statutory agencies responsible for investigating and intervening in sexual abuse seem unable to attract the numbers of telephone calls or other referrals from children suffering sexual abuse that go to ChildLine (for example), this probably reflects the inappropriateness of their investigative procedures into these issues, and the low priority they give to therapeutic and support services in identified cases. This is borne out by the strong preference shown by adult survivors for the help available through the network of survivor-oriented and survivor-led groups and organisations (Gray *et al.*, p. 53). The authors of this study argue that one reason for this is that statutory services are organised around bureaucratic and professional control over survivors and non-abusive parents, whereas 'our survey suggests that small survivor-focused and self-help services do tend to place the survivor in considerable control over the therapeutic process and offer more flexibility in terms of provision' (*ibid.*, p. 53).

Thus the critique levelled at the present system, and at the reforms of it being canvassed by the government and its official researchers (DoH, 1995), is that statutory services are failing sexually abused children and do not recognise their needs, but that the potential for a more relevant and effective service for prevention and support has developed through voluntary groups. Hence these critics propose that community-based networks of survivor-focused and/or survivor-led groups should take the leading role in this field, and that statutory services should realign their strategy and practice to enable and support such groups and organisations, and to provide a backup of formal procedures and court sanctions (Pringle, 1998, pp. 176–178). They argue that '. . . in terms of energy, commitment and understanding, the key figures in this approach must be adult survivors, non-abusing parents of child survivors, and their allies in both communities and professional agencies' (*ibid.*, p. 177). The central thrust of this approach would be a circle of adults within the community who could insulate the child from potential and actual perpetrators (Smith, 1994, p. 79).

In other words, this model accepts that child sexual abuse should be the 'responsibility of the community', as the new Labour government insists, but it presents a very different view of the relevant community, and of the way it can prevent sexual abuse and protect children. The network of survivor-oriented and survivor-led groups and organisations is a product of recognising, listening and responding to people with experiences of such abuse, and mobilising their energies, in partnership with concerned others. The proposed model is founded on a radically empowering response to the growth of such a network, and an anti-oppressive form of practice, which addresses the power relations and cultural manifestations of patriarchy and sexual domination in traditional social relations (including the traditional working-class community). Such a network, in partnership with a reoriented statutory authority, could aim to raise awareness and re-educate communities, rather than pretend that their cultural resources already contain the necessary elements for protecting children from sexual abuse (Smith, 1996, pp. 80–81).

CONCLUSIONS

This chapter seeks to draw attention to the risky nature of the new Labour government's attempts to appeal to a mythical community as a bulwark against social problems, and to mobilise public sentiment against wrongdoers. In the case of child sexual abuse, this obscures the fact that sexual abuse is part of the blood-and-guts code through which fathers, teachers, priests, carers and others, almost all men, sustained their dominance in households and neighbourhoods, and in the hidden informal practices of official child care and educational agencies. It also mobilises mass action in authoritarian indignation, or from sheer passions of hate and revenge, against a very small group of individuals who have committed appalling offences, while allowing 'the community' in its broadest sense to project their guilt and wilful ignorance onto these convenient scapegoats. In this process, it incidentally leads to very large sums of money having to be spent on protecting these perpetrators from the very mass forces that the government has mobilised. It is estimated that the police protection given to Robert Oliver and Sidney Cooke may have cost as much as £1.5 million (*The Guardian*, 14 March 1998).

In essence, the new Labour government's notion of 'community responsibility' on this issue and all others is rooted in an uncritical adoption of traditional morality and social organisation, built around the virtues of the economically independent family, with its ethic of hard work and male authority. It is true that the working-class communities to which the government nostalgically appeals were imbued with solidarities and heroic sacrifices of many kinds, and demonstrated virtues which are conspicuous by their absence in post-Thatcher Britain. But their blood-and-guts code for informal social interactions was ultimately based on violence and sexual domination, of which child sexual abuse was a hidden but prevalent element, as survey evidence of adult survivors, and qualitative accounts of family, neighbourhood and institutional life of that era graphically reveal. While the cultures of both the traditional working-class neighbourhood and the bourgeois suburbs were highly intolerant of, and punitive towards, public manifestations of 'perverted' sexual orientations, they concealed practices of sexual abuse of children that belied the pieties of the public code.

Thus the specific form of communitarianism embraced by the new Labour government rests on backward-looking moral authoritarian principles, and looks to the traditional informal social control systems of such communities to impose discipline and curb the excesses of materialistic economic individualism and self-indulgent consumption. Its notion of the responsible community is derived from individuals' duties towards their families, and citizens' obligations towards an enforcement orientated state. It picks up just those elements in the blood-and-guts code which operate through bigotry, stigma and violence, and fans the flames of popular passions by referring to deviance in the language of the tabloid press. It is a state-led, conservative version of 'community' that reinforces majority white, populist, patriarchal and punitive morality (Driver and Martell, 1997).

By contrast, it neglects an emerging new code of informal support and mutuality among traditionally oppressed, powerless and voiceless groups, such as survivors of sexual abuse, which has the potential to take much more responsibility for such issues, if only it was recognised and endorsed by the public power, and given some resources and professional backing. In this it betrays those largely invisible and unsung heroes and (mostly) heroines of the Thatcher era, who enabled marginal and excluded communities to survive against the odds. Instead of building on these informal networks, it chooses to impose a largely irrelevant form of regulation through state agencies, in the name of a morality that is alien to the developing cultures of such groups. Such regulation acts against the potential for the development of diverse, multicultural, grass-roots communities, more suited to the issues of present-day society, and more appropriate to the diversity of children who experience sexual abuse be they black, white, disabled, non-disabled, working, middle or upper class, male or female.

This is abundantly clear from the way that the Blair government insists on the duties that citizens owe the state and which they must fulfil in order to repay taxpayers who fund benefits and services. The only recognised way of meeting obligations and paying back is formal employment, and paid work in menial services is given more recognition than informal and voluntary work in the community, even when this is highly skilled and meets pressing human needs. Lone-parent women are the main targets of the government's authoritarian formalism, and the main potential losers from the breakup of informal networks that this could cause. No wonder they demonstrated against the pressure to join the menial service economy with the slogan 'We Won't Clean Harriet's Toilet' when cuts in lone-parent benefits were announced.

Since the re-emergence of the authoritarian version of communitarianism in the 1980s, influential thinkers like Etzioni have insisted that there should be 'no more rights without responsibilities' (Etzioni, 1993, p. 4). In its enthusiasm for traditional moral values, family and citizenship obligations, the new Labour government now largely excludes *rights* talk from its vocabulary, and insists on duties-based membership. In this it threatens the whole fabric of liberal institutions, including democracy and civil liberties, as I have tried to show in the first half of this chapter. But the rights of children, and especially those at risk of abuse, should be the starting point for any reliable service for child support. Parental and community responsibility, embedded in the blood-and-guts code of majority white patriarchal authority and vengeful scapegoating, is a dangerous basis for public policy.

In the second half of this chapter, I have sketched the possibility of a very different basis for community responsibility, and the alternative moral and political underpinnings this requires. Unfortunately, British government policy gives little indication of moving in these directions at the present time. This means that the networks of informal support and therapeutic help sustained by survivors of sexual abuse are likely to have to maintain themselves for the immediate future, with the help of those few concerned practitioners who really do listen and act on what they are told.

REFERENCES

Beveridge, W. (1942) *Social Insurance and Allied Services*, London, HMSO.
Beveridge, W. (1944) *Full Employment in a Free Society*. London, Allen & Unwin.
DoH (1995) *Child Protection: Messages from Research*. London, HMSO.
DoH (1998) *Working together to Safeguard Children* (Consultation Paper). London, HMSO.
DSS (1998) *A New Contract for Welfare* (Green Paper), Cmd 3818. London, HMSO.
Donzelot, J. (1983) *The Policing of Families*. London, Hutchinson.
Driver, S. and Martell, L. (1997) New Labour's communitarianism. *Critical Social Policy*, **17**: 27–46.
Etzioni, A. (1993) *The Spirit of Community: The Reinvention of American Society*. New York, Touchstone.

Finkelhor, D. (1991) The scope of the problem, in Murray, K. and Gough, D.A. (eds) *Intervening in Child Sexual Abuse*. Edinburgh, Scottish Academic Press.

Finkelhor, D., Hoteling, G. Lewis, I. and Smith, C. (1996). Sexual abuse in a national survey of adult men and women. *Child Abuse and Neglect*, **14**: 19-28.

Fisher, D. (1994) Adult sex offenders: Who are they? Why and how do they do it?, in Morrison, T., Erooga, M. and Beckett, R.C. (eds) *Sexual Offending against Children: Assessment and Treatment of Male Abusers*. London, Routledge.

Freeden, M. (1991) *Rights*. Milton Keynes, Open University Press.

Gray, S., Higgs, M. and Pringle, K. (1996) Services for people who have been sexually abused, in Mackie, L. (ed.) *Researching Women's Health* London, Mark Allen Publishing.

Gray, S., Higgs, M. and Pringle, K. (1997) User-centred responses to child sexual abuse: the way forward. *Child and Family Social Work*, **2**(1): 49–57.

Hallett, C. (1995) Child abuse: an academic overview, in Kingston, I. and Penhole, B. (eds) *Family Violence and the Caring Professions*. London, Macmillan.

Hilbert, R.A. (1991) *The Classical Roots of Ethnomethodology: Durkheim, Weber and Garfinkel*. Chapel Hill, University of North Carolina Press.

Jordan, B. (1996) *A Theory of Poverty and Social Exclusion*. Cambridge, Polity.

Jordan, B. (1998) *The New Politics of Welfare: Social Justice in a Global Context* London, Sage.

Jordan, B., Redley, M. and James, S. (1994) *Putting the Family First* London, UCL Press.

Kelly, L., Regan, L. and Burton, S. (1991) *An Exploratory Study of the Prevalence of Sexual Abuse in a Sample of 16–21 year-olds*. London, Polytechnic of North London.

Lister, R. (1998) From equality to social inclusion: New Labour and the welfare state. *Critical Social Policy*, **18**(2): 215–225.

Marquand, D. (1998) The Blair paradox. *Prospect*, May: 19–24.

Parton, N. (1991) *Governing the Family: Child Care, Child Protection and the State*. London, Macmillan.

Parton, N., Thorpe, D. and Wattam, C. (1997) *Child Care, Risk and the Moral Order*. London, Macmillan.

Pringle, K. (1998) *Children and Social Welfare in Europe*. Buckingham, Open University Press.

Rawls, A.W. (1989) An ethnomethodological perspective on social theory, in Helm, D.T. *et al*. (eds) *The Interaction Order*. New York, Irvington, pp. 4–20.

Smith, G. (1994) Parent, partner, protector: conflicting role demands for mothers of sexually abused children, in Morrison, T., Erooga, M. and Beckett, R. (eds) *Sexually Offending against Children: Assessment and Treatment of Male Abusers*. London, Routledge.

Smith, G. (1996) Reassessing protectiveness, in Batty, D. and Cullen, D. (eds) *Child Protection: The Therapeutic Option*. London, BAAF.

Wattam, C. (1997) Can filtering processes be rationalised?, in Parton, N. (ed.) *Child Protection and Family Support*. London, Routledge, pp. 109–125.

Wattam, C. and Woodward, C. (1996) And do I abuse my children? . . . No!, in *Childhood Matters: Report of the National Commission of Inquiry into the Prevention of Child Abuse. Vol. 2: Background Papers*. London, HMSO.

11

INSTITUTIONAL ABUSE

Bernard Gallagher

INTRODUCTION

The abuse of children by adults who work with them ('institutional abuse') has been thrust to the fore of child protection concerns in recent years. This is due in large part to the seemingly unending series of investigations into child sexual abuse (CSA) in children's homes. These inquiries have revealed that some of society's most vulnerable children have been exposed not only to sexual abuse but also to physical and emotional abuse, and neglect. Often the abuse went unchecked for decades. Some cases, such as those in North Wales and Leicestershire, were organised. The treatment many 'looked after' children were subjected to could be likened to torture.

Children's homes have not been the only residential institutions in which CSA has occurred. Equally serious cases have been uncovered in independent boarding schools and residential special schools. There have also been inquiries in day schools, nurseries, Scouts, sports clubs and religious organisations. In fact, CSA has probably been reported in every type of institution for children, whether residential or non-residential, public, voluntary or private.

This wave of institutional CSA cases has been the source of considerable anxiety on the part of all sections of society. In response, policy makers and practitioners have sought to devise and implement a whole raft of measures to tackle the problem of institutional CSA. However, the scale of the response does not necessarily mean that these efforts have been in the best interests of children. In particular, there is a major question mark over the extent to which children have been listened to or heard, or have had their experiences validated.

The purpose of this chapter is to explore the extent to which the 'official' response to institutional CSA has been child-centred, as opposed to being driven by other considerations, such as agency priorities and perceptions.

The aim is not to describe the problems which are associated with the handling of CSA in general but to highlight the issues which are unique to institutional abuse. In doing this, the author draws upon not only the literature and his experience as a residential social worker but also his own research (Gallagher *et al.*, 1996; Gallagher, 1998). Although these two studies were in the area of organised abuse, many of the cases were based in institutions and consequently make a valuable contribution to this discussion.

WHICH INSTITUTIONS?

A number of different government departments have put forward measures for tackling the problem of institutional CSA. The Home Office, for example, has considered bringing forth legislation which would make it illegal for those convicted of sexual offences to work with, or to apply to work with, children (Home Office, 1996). It has proposed the setting up of a Criminal Records Agency to enable police checks for those applying to work with children to be carried out more quickly and accurately and is giving thought to extending the range of children's workers who are subject to police checks. The Department for Education and Employment has issued a number of circulars to schools offering guidance on how they should deal with child protection issues (DEE 1995a, 1995b)

By far the greatest number of initiatives, however, have originated from within the Department of Health. This includes legislation (Children Act 1989), official reports (Warner, 1992; Utting, 1991, 1997), judicial inquiries (Tribunal of Inquiry into Abuse in North Wales Children's Homes), practice guidance (DoH, 1991, 1998a) and research studies (DoH, 1998b).

This heavy concentration of measures from the Department of Health is an indication of the concern among policy makers towards the abuse of children in residential institutions, especially children's homes. In view of the innumerable 'scandals' in children's homes, it could be argued that this focus is entirely appropriate. However, this would be to negate the experience of all those children who have been the victims of sexual abuse in other types of institution, be they schools, nurseries, the Scouts or sports clubs.

Without doubt, residents of children's homes do appear to be at particular risk, and some have suffered horrendous abuse, but serious cases of CSA have been reported in virtually every type of institution for children. What the current policy response reveals is that the approach to institutional abuse is predominantly scandal-centred rather than child-centred. Consequently, while we have a battery of measures designed to tackle CSA in children's homes and some other types of residential establishment, other institutions for children remain on the periphery in terms of child protection.

This is wrong. All children should be offered equal protection from sexual abuse irrespective of the institution they attend. Children need to be protected and to be safe whether they are in a children's home, Girl Guides, a swimming club or having music lessons with a private tutor.

In the absence of any guidance from central government—and again invariably in response to 'scandals'—a number of institutions have devised their own response to the risk of CSA. The Scouting organisation, for example, has arranged for the NSPCC to provide child protection training to its staff, and some churches now ask their clergy to sign an undertaking that they have not abused children.

It may be that some of these measures are both appropriate and effective. Conversely, such ad hoc measures, particularly when they are not monitored, run the risk of having no effect (but creating a false sense of security) or worse still of having deleterious consequences.

Children deserve much better. The response to CSA needs to be thought out, considered and planned for all children's institutions, and it certainly should not be on the basis of the latest scandal. Policy makers are very inclined not only to react to events but to do so within the narrow confines of *their* responsibilities, rather than think in terms of (all) children and *their* needs.

Many institutional abusers exhibit a strong compulsion to abuse children and an ability to manipulate situations to facilitate abuse (Gallagher, 1998). As child protection measures are strengthened in one type of institution, some abusers will simply move on to less-well-regulated institutions. Thus, it is even more essential that the response to CSA looks at institutions comprehensively.

There are approximately 12 million children in Britain under the age of 16. Of these roughly 6,000, or 0.05%, are 'looked after' in children's homes. Far greater proportions of children have contact with other types of institution such as schools, nurseries, playgroups and clubs. Surely it is only right that the response to CSA should better reflect the use children make of institutions.

PREVENTION OR 'CURE'?

If child protection policy and practice in respect of children's institutions were truly child-centred then their overwhelming emphasis would be upon the prevention of abuse. All the reports, inquiries and inquests in the world mean little to a child once he or she has been abused. Regrettably, the child protection system remains resolutely a 'child-rescue service', designed to come into action only after concerns have been raised or allegations made.

Having said this, central government and local social services departments have implemented a number of measures intended to prevent CSA in children's homes. These include children having access to telephones, visits to homes by independent persons, and increasing children's involvement in the community (DoH, 1991). Policy makers and practitioners were, however, largely pressed into these measures as a result of the sheer scale of the problem in residential care.

In general, there is a pronounced inertia towards developing policy and practice in respect of the prevention of CSA in virtually all other types of institution. The reasons for this are not clear, although part of the explanation may be to do with resources and an 'official culture' which has become preoccupied with the immediacy of 'cures' to the detriment of longer-term prevention goals.

It may be that some of this inertia is due to a belief that prevention work is too 'sensitive'. It is true that prevention requires us to be proactive and take an up-front approach to CSA. This is, for some, quite alien. As has already been stated, child protection is predominantly a reactive service. On top of this, 'denial' is a potent issue in regard to CSA. Some people find it quite difficult even to think about, let alone discuss or act upon.

Crucially, it is here that institutions have some advantage in that they have not been caught up in the debate concerning the 'intrusion' of child protection into family life. In effect, institutions provide a distance, or a neutral territory, between parents/carers and their children, within which it is possible for the state to address 'sensitive' issues in an efficacious manner. School-based programmes around sex education and drug misuse are a good example of this. In the same way, then, it should be possible to engage institutions in attempts to prevent CSA.

What is clear is that the reticence towards prevention is not due to a lack of knowledge. The list of 'prevention measures' given below is just a selection of those which have been identified in official reports (Warner, 1992). Although a good deal of what is contained in this literature is based upon children's experiences in residential homes, much of it is applicable to a wide range of institutions.

- *Vetting*   All institutions for children should be subject to a vetting process prior to accepting children, and should have to meet certain, nationally recognised child protection criteria in the areas indicated below.
- *Inspection*   All institutions for children should be inspected on a regular basis to determine whether they are maintaining the minimum child protection criteria set out below.
- *Children*   Children should take part in child protection education programmes at regular intervals. Such programmes would inform them—in an age-appropriate manner—of the risk of sexual abuse and give them confidence and encouragement about reporting any concerns they might have. A specific element of such programmes would be the development

of qualities such as assertiveness and self-esteem in children which might help them avoid abusers 'entrapping' them (Gallagher, 1998).

- *Staff* Staff should be subject to rigorous recruitment and vetting processes to ensure that they are suitable persons for the post, and should be monitored in their work and given regular supervision. They should be given adequate training in child protection and made aware of both the opportunities and their responsibility to report concerns of abuse.
- *Parents/carers* Parents/carers should be educated about the risk of sexual abuse in children's institutions. In addition, they should reassure children that they can discuss anything of this nature if it is worrying them.
- *Ethos* Institutions should be run in an egalitarian way such that all children and staff feel confident that they can raise child protection concerns and expect an appropriate response. (Institutions could all have groups like school councils to provide children with formal means of expressing their views.)

An institution is, almost by definition, closed to all but its members. However, this approach needs to cease. Parents/carers and members of the community more generally should feel free to enter institutions, ask questions and, if necesssary, complain.

Measures to prevent CSA would have to be tailored to the type of institution, whether this be, for example, a children's home, a school or a youth club, but, as the above list indicates, many of the required practices have already been identified. As has been argued above, such work is unlikely to encounter parent/carer opposition. Indeed, with successive investigations in this area, parents/carers are increasingly likely to demand such programmes.

IS DETECTION 'BEYOND THE PALE'?

The attitude of the child protection system towards detection is even more ambivalent, if not hostile, than it is towards prevention. (For evidence of this, one needs to look no further than the fact that ChildLine has insufficient resources to answer thousands of the calls that are made to it.) Detection requires abuse to be actively pursued and confronted, and as such it represents a formidable challenge to child protection. As a result, the issues mentioned above in relation to 'denial', official inertia and resources are even more acute. Furthermore, any attempt to discuss detection is likely to meet with charges of over-zealousness and looking for abuse which isn't there.

It might be thought that detection would be less of an issue in institutional cases compared to familial ones, owing to the fact that institutions are generally more 'open'; the relationship between victim and abuser is weaker; and abusers have less power over children. As such, it could be expected that victims would find it easier to disclose. In practice, children's experience reveal that such differences are negligible, if they exist at all. Many institutions have been found to have been as insular as families, and abusers have been very successful in their use of entrapment techniques to abuse and silence children. Similarly, institutional abusers have found a variety of means of exerting power and control over children. Some have done this through physical force, others have used the authority given to them by their position within an organisation or the wider community, and others have used the influence they have by virtue of being involved in children's sporting or academic progress.

The experience of victims indicates that abuse within institutions may be long-running, involve multiple abusers and be quite sadistic in nature. Children may even be abused in more than one institution they attend. Even with the most effective preventative measures available some children will still be abused within institutions. Thus, there should be no doubt of the critical need to detect CSA in institutional settings.

As with prevention, there is no lack of knowledge of the practices that would increase the likelihood of detecting institutional CSA. Indeed, many of these are contained in the list provided in the previous section. For example, if the ethos of an institution is egalitarian, children will be encouraged to report any concerns they have, confident that they will be listened to and heard. With appropriate training, staff would be better able to detect signs in children which might indicate abuse. Although much of this knowledge has been obtained from the experiences of children in residential care, a great deal of it can be applied to institutions in general.

Some measures, however, have to be developed specifically with detection in mind. Children need to be provided with specific mechanisms by which they can disclose abuse, such as access to telephone lines, access to independent visitors and the community, and participation in formal discussion situations such as 'circle time' and school councils. Also, training is needed such that when children disclose abuse in very oblique ways, as they sometimes do, staff are more likely to 'hear' what it is they are saying.

It is also important to prevent the silencing of victims. In addition to abusing children, perpetrators also ensure that their victims are so intimidated that they are very reluctant to disclose their abuse. This intimidation often involves threats, for example, to remove the child, to hinder the child's progress within the institution and, particularly in closed institutions, physical violence. If abuse is to be detected then it is essential that attempts by abusers to silence children are challenged. By telling children that adults would not be able to harm them for disclosing abuse, the silencing efforts of abusers would be pre-empted and victims would be more able to disclose their abuse. (If these messages were given to children as a matter of routine, they would also act as a preventative measure, as abusers would be less likely to abuse a child if there is a good chance of that child disclosing.)

While accepting that efforts to detect abuse can be enhanced by providing children with opportunities to disclose, it must be emphasised that responsibility for detecting institutional CSA ultimately rests with adults. A primary part of this responsibility includes a willingness on their part to look for abuse; to be educated as to its signs; and to be sensitive to the 'language' children use to talk about their experiences. This applies not only to the staff of institutions, but also to parents/carers and members of the community who, because of their distance or independence, may be better placed to identify abuse.

Without doubt the detection of institutional CSA is a controversial issue and one which raises much concern, particularly around becoming preoccupied with abuse and the risk of false allegations. However, if handled appropriately, there is no reason why detection could not make a valuable contribution to child protection but avoid adverse consequences. Because institutions are less politically sensitive environments than families—as discussed in connection with prevention— this type of approach to child protection is far more feasible. More importantly, it has to be recognised that the child protection system has thought very little about the detection of abuse. It is partly as a result of this that abuse has gone on for so long in so many institutions.

REPORTING: 'DO WE HAVE TO WASH OUR DIRTY LINEN IN PUBLIC?'

One of the cases which featured in the author's research on the investigation of organised CSA involved a worker who abused a number of children in the institution in which he worked (Gallagher, 1998). Eventually, one of the children disclosed the abuse to another member of staff. This staff member then took the matter to the manager who replied: 'Do we have to wash our dirty linen in public?' Fortunately, the disclosure was reported to police and social services whose investigation ultimately led to the abuser's imprisonment. Though shocking, the reaction of the manager should not be surprising. One of the single most persistent and recurring features of institutional CSA has been the flagrant failure by the staff of institutions to report concerns or allegations of CSA to the police and social services. This behaviour has also been identified in numerous inquiries into institutional abuse

The failure of institutional staff to report concerns of CSA is probably explained by many of the same factors which account for prevention and detection not being adequately addressed within the child protection system. However, the conscious decision to ignore the plight of a child who is being abused is of a different order and, consequently, requires additional explanation.

Sometimes staff may be fearful of the consequences of taking such an action, particularly if the person to whom the allegation relates is in a more senior position (Kirkwood, 1993) Like victims, they may worry about their position within the institution; be fearful that the abuser may become hostile towards them; or fear being undermined if the allegation is, for whatever reason, not substantiated.

Many people, even though they may have significant involvement with children, simply do not understand the seriousness of CSA. Like the manager above, they may think it is in some way comparable to the problem of 'dirty linen'. Other staff, especially those in more senior positions, may have more selfish reasons for not reporting the abuse, in particular the desire to 'protect the reputation' of the institution.

The failure to report CSA is also a reflection of children's generally low position in society in terms of status and power. As a result of this, the word of children is simply not given as much weight as that of adults. Indeed, in the case referred to at the start of this section, one child had previously disclosed his abuse to another member of staff but had been chastised and warned of the consequences of making such 'malicious' claims.

Having said this, it has to be recognised that workers in institutions are susceptible to false allegations. Although it is not known how extensive such claims are in relation to, say, those in familial settings, some professional groups, such as teachers, have argued that it is a significant issue (de Gruchy, 1994). Whatever the extent of the problem, it is almost certainly much less than genuine allegations and far less again than the incidence of non-disclosure by victims.

If children do disclose to a member of staff in the institution and are subsequently disregarded, it can only have a very deleterious impact upon that child. As is well recognised, children have to summon up a great deal of courage to disclose abuse. Thus, if anyone ignores or, worse, contradicts their statement, this will add to the distress and trauma caused by the abuse. Furthermore, it is likely to make them less likely to disclose abuse in the future, thus rendering them even more at risk.

As with detection, much of the problem of non-reporting could be rectified by implementation of the measures listed under prevention. For example, staff training could and should include components on the handling and reporting of child abuse concerns, and the action to take if reports are not acted upon. Likewise, if institutions are made to develop an egalitarian and open structure, it should be easier for staff to take their concerns 'outside' should they feel the need to do so.

There are, in addition, more specific measures which need to be developed. Foremost among these are employment rights and safeguards for staff who report concerns of CSA. It is as a result of disquiet in this area that the government drafted the Public Interest Disclosure Act which is due to come into effect in 1999. This legislation has been enacted following a series of cases in which 'whistle-blowers', in child care and other fields, were victimised for reporting concerns relating to standards of care. Through this legislation, future 'whistle-blowers' will have more rights to report their concerns and more safeguards against their employers who might want to sanction them.

As well as rights, staff also need to be fully aware of their responsibilities. It is debatable whether the staff of institutions should be subject to the mandatory reporting laws of the United States, but what should be beyond doubt is their professional and moral duty to report abuse.

In the course of his research the author uncovered situations in which staff who did not sexually abuse children in the institution, actively sought to cover-up abuse perpetrated by their colleagues. In one such case, the two most senior members of staff, plus a religious worker who was attached to the residential institution, covered up a series of allegations made by children. One of their ploys was to hold a 'trial' in which the victim would have to repeat his 'charge' in the presence of the abuser. Not surprisingly, the vast majority of children retracted their disclosure at this point. At other times, the religious worker would visit the parents to undermine any disclosure their child had made to them. Eventually, the abuse was reported, investigated and the abuser imprisoned. So blatant was the covering up of the abuse by the three members of staff that the police and Crown Prosecution Service agreed they should be prosecuted for child neglect.

This case indicates that 'non-reporting' may be carried to quite extreme levels. This is often done—as in the above case—to 'protect the reputation' of the institution. At other times members of staff may wish to deflect criticisms of their practice which had the effect of facilitating the abuse. If children are to be protected from these cover-ups, then it is essential that staff are made fully aware that such actions will be pursued with the full force of the law.

INVESTIGATING FOR CHILDREN OR AGENCIES?

The investigation of institutional CSA has improved significantly over the past ten years. This is due to developments which followed on from the Cleveland inquiry (Butler-Sloss, 1988); lessons from the handling of familial cases; and, sadly, the ever-increasing numbers of institutional abuse cases. Despite this, institutional investigations still carry with them the risk of being process-centred rather than child-centred, where the concerns of agencies are ahead of the interests of the child.

While this is a risk with all child abuse cases, many institutional abuse investigations face challenges which are not present in other CSA cases. These include large numbers of victims and abusers; the need to trace and identify victims; and agencies having to investigate their own staff. As a result, investigations face a whole set of additional internal and external pressures. The internal pressures include, for example, the selection and supervision of staff; the collation of huge amounts of data; and issues of confidentiality. Much of the external pressure comes from the involvement, interest or interference of elected members, the community and the media.

Given these factors, there is an added need in institutional investigations for agencies to remind themselves that children are people and not 'objects of concern'. Also, agencies need to recognise—as the following examples illustrate—that children's experience of institutional abuse may be quite distinct from that of say familial abuse. If investigations of institutional abuse are to be child-centred, then it is important that agency workers appreciate these differences.

Owing to the great diversity of children's institutions there is much variety between them in terms of the way in which they are run. Some institutions are quite 'egalitarian' (for example, sports clubs) in that they are open to the public and staff and users are on a par with one another. At the other extreme, institutions may be quite 'authoritarian' (for example, a secure units) with staff and children part of a rigid hierarchy and with little contact with the community.

The way in which children experience abuse varies with the regime of the institution. For example, in more open institutions, such as sporting and leisure clubs, abusers have less power relative to children and are compelled to make greater use of subtle entrapment techniques (Gallagher, 1998). Entrapment involves the abuser supplying the child with inducements and drawing them into increasingly intimate physical contact. Invariably, the child feels that because he or she has 'accepted' these inducements—be they sweets, cigarettes or attention—they are to blame for the abuse. This then makes it even more difficult for them to disclose.

At the other end of the spectrum are the more closed institutions, such as children's homes and boarding schools. These are more akin to family situations in which the abuser is able to behave like an autocratic or an unaccountable parent/carer. These abusers tend to behave in a more coercive manner as they do not have to worry about overcoming any defences around the child because he or she, in effect, has none. This more coercive behaviour often involves more serious sexual and physical abuse, which may be accompanied by much intimidation and humiliation. Sometimes it is accurate to describe the abuse as torture or sadism. Children abused in this way are often especially traumatised.

It is well recognised in both practice and research that children face acute difficulties in disclosing child sexual abuse, in whichever setting it takes place. In some of the institutional abuse cases studied by the author it was apparent that children faced an additional difficulty through peer group pressure not to disclose. The children in these cases believed that to disclose abuse would amount to 'grassing'—as if they or their co-victims had done something for which they were criminally culpable. In some respects this is a manifestation of the common feeling among victims that they are responsible, or are to blame, for their own abuse. However, in these cases the feeling appears to be very intense, with children equating their experiences and that of their co-victims to criminal behaviour on their part—hence the reference to 'grassing'.

Other children, who do not appear to experience this pressure so keenly, may be prepared to make a partial disclosure. They are not prepared to disclose their own abuse but indicate that other children have been abused, although they do this very circumspectly. They might, for example, state in their interview: 'I have not been abused but I think you should speak to my friend John.' When the interviewer speaks to John, he or she meets with a similar response and is referred to a third child, and so on. It is akin to 'disclosure by proxy' (Gallagher, 1998). Agency workers need to be aware of these possible dynamics among victims if they are to facilitate disclosure.

A feature of institutional abuse which has been identified in the author's own research and which has been commented upon in other reports (Brannan et al., 1993) is the creation by the abuser of a hierarchy among the victims. The main purpose of this structure is to assist the abuser in controlling the children. At the apex of this structure is one child (or a few children) who, in effect, acts as a 'lieutenant' for the abuser. His role might be distribute the inducements, help control all the other victims and even to recruit additional children into the 'ring'. This child receives a disproportionate amount of the inducements. Beneath this child there may be a group of middle-ranking children who assist the 'top-dog' (Jones, 1994) with his various tasks but who do not enjoy the same privilege, status or power. At the bottom of this hierarchy are the remaining children who are the least powerful either because of their age, size or because they are vulnerable in some other way.

For the children at the bottom of this hierarchy, their experience of abuse may be particularly severe as they may be abused not only by the adult(s) but also by other children. The therapeutic needs of these children may be particularly acute. For the children who have been assisting the abuser, agencies may be faced with a dilemma because, in addition to being victims, they may be criminally culpable for the abuse of children themselves. Agencies may have to address the needs of these children in terms of both victims and 'young abusers'.

Probably the clearest distinguishing mark of institutional abuse is the number of children who get caught up in an investigation. Even if a large number of children have not been found to have been abused— though they often are—agencies will often have drawn a large number of children into the investigation. For example, the major investigations into abuse in children's homes in Cheshire, Merseyside and North Wales have each traced thousands of former residents.

When 'numbers' form such a key aspect of a case there is a danger that the individual victim or child will be lost sight of. This risk is even greater when one takes into account all the other issues which the scale of an investigation can give rise to, such as resourcing, information management and media interest. It is for this reason that agencies involved in institutional abuse cases must ensure that the interests of the child are not superseded by those of the agency.

CONCLUSION: 'RE-FOCUSING' OR MULTI-FOCUSING?

The publication of *Messages from Research* (DoH, 1995) initiated a debate as to whether agencies involved in child protection, particularly social services, should re-focus their efforts, concentrating less upon 'investigation' and more upon 'family support'. Implicit in these discussions was the notion that the main concern of child protection was familial abuse.

As this chapter has sought to make clear, however, institutional CSA is very much an issue towards which the child protection system needs to turn itself. It is important to emphasise that this is not an either/or situation. Child protection tends to be impeded by discussions as to whether we should focus upon familial abuse or stranger abuse; physical abuse or sexual abuse; abuse by men or abuse by women. Child protection has been found wanting in many areas: it is not that the focus should be less in certain areas but that a whole series of areas, including institutional abuse, need greater attention from the child protection system.

With increasing awareness of child abuse it becomes evident that children can be abused in an extremely wide range of settings and situations. Indeed, the debate should be in terms not of 'environments' but children: children should be protected wherever they are, or whoever they are with, be this families, the community or institutions.

By the same token, there is not just one aspect of institutional abuse which needs to be focused upon. Prevention, detection, reporting, investigation and even definition are all aspects of institutional abuse which need to be thought about and improved in respect of making child protection in this area more child-centred. Again, it is a multi-focused approach that is required.

The need to address child protection issues within institutions is all the more pressing given the increasing range of institutions children attend and the amount of time they spend in them. Single parents, for example, are being 'encouraged' by government to take up paid employment, making use of forms of child care such as after-school clubs and childminding. Nurseries now take children from the age of 3 years rather than 4, and large numbers of children now attend organised activities in the community.

This chapter strongly advocates that child protection should be a far more conspicuous aspect in the setting up, operation and philosophy of children's institutions. However, this new focus need not and should not be introduced in isolation. There are, unfortunately, a number of areas in which some children's institutions fall seriously short.

The first among these are standards of physical safety. As a number of tragedies have shown, institutions—or those providing services to them—have been grossly negligent in terms of ensuring the safety of children. Similarly, many institutions appear either unable or unwilling to ensure that children do not receive or propagate prejudice whether on the basis of gender, race, disability, sexual orientation or religious beliefs. As a number of suicides—particularly among schoolchildren—have indicated, bullying, whether physical or emotional is another aspect of children's welfare which needs to be urgently addressed within institutions. Institutions should also have to meet certain minimum standards in the quality of the particular work they are involved in.

What is needed is a radical change in our attitudes to children's institutions. Institutions should not be seen as autonomous entities, somehow divorced and unconnected with the rest of society. Collectively, institutions fulfil a massive and fundamental role in the lives of children, and consequently the future of society. So important is this role, that it is essential that all aspects of children's welfare—safety, equal opportunities, emotional well-being, development and protection—are guaranteed to the highest standards possible.

Institutions can provide a great deal to children whether this is in the form of care, education, sporting and artistic achievement, leisure interests or ameliorating the effects of disadvantage. Therefore, no one would wish, in principle, to inhibit institutions in the work they do. However, many institutions have failed children in terms of protection, and their other responsibilities. A great deal needs to be done before children's institutions are truly child-centred.

REFERENCES

Brannan, C., Jones, J.R. and Murch, O.D. (1993) *Castle Hill Report; Practice Guide*. Shrewsbury, Shropshire County Council.
Butler-Sloss, E. (1988) *Report of the Inquiry into Child Abuse in Cleveland 1987*. London, HMSO.

de Gruchy (1994) Belief in the balance, *The Guardian*, 13 July.

DEE (1995a) *Protecting Children from Abuse: The Role of the Education Service* (Circular 10/95). Darlington, Department for Education and Employment.

DEE (1995b) *Misconduct of Teachers and Workers with Children and Young Persons* (Circular 11/95). *Darlington*, Department for Education and Employment.

DoH (1991) *The Children Act Guidance and Regulation, Vol. 4. Residential Care.* London, HMSO.

DoH (1995) *Child Protection: Messages from Research.* London, HMSO.

DoH (1998a) *Quality protects: Objectives for Social Services for Children.* London, The Stationery Office.

DoH (1998b) *Children Living Away from Home: Messages from Research.* Chichester, Wiley.

Gallagher, B. (1998) *Grappling with Smoke. Investigating and Managing Organised Child Sexual Abuse: A Good Practice Guide.* London, NSPCC.

Gallagher, B., Hughes, B. and Parker, H. (1996) The nature and extent of known cases of organised abuse in England and Wales, in Bibby, P. (ed.) *Organised Abuse—The Current Debate.* Aldershot, Arena/Ashgate.

Home Office (1996) *Sentencing and Supervision of Sex Offenders (Command 3304)* London, The Stationery Office.

Jones, J.R. (1994) *Organised/Multiple Abuse within Institutions: A Causal Analysis Highlighting Issues of Prevention and Detection Utilising Perspectives from Victims of the Castle Hill Regime.* Unpublished MA dissertation, The University of Birmingham.

Kirkwood, A. (1993) *The Leicestershire Inquiry 1992. The Report of the Inquiry into Aspects of the Management of Children's Homes in Leicestershire between 1973 and 1986.* Leicester, Leicestershire County Council.

Utting, W. (1991) *Children in the Public Care: A Review of Residential Care.* London, HMSO.

Utting, W. (1997) *People Like Us. The Report of the Review of the Safeguards for Children Living Away from Home.* London, The Stationery Office.

Warner, N. (1992) *Choosing with Care. The Report of the Committee of the Inquiry into the Selection, Development and Management of Staff in Children's Homes.* London, HMSO.

12

WORKING WITH ABUSERS TO PROTECT CHILDREN

Marcus Erooga and Helen Masson

INTRODUCTION

The regulation of sexual relationships between adults and children through folklore, informal sanctions, religious laws and criminal legislation has been a feature of societies for centuries (Kilpatrick, 1992) with attitudes changing over time about the acceptability of various forms of sexual contact. Attitudes toward the children and adults involved in such contact have varied similarly. However, the recognition of child sexual abuse on which this publication is based is a relatively modern phenomenon, with increased consensus about adult (primarily male) responsibility for such contact and its abusive nature, although ambivalence towards those who are victimised is still more persistent and pervasive than a 'modern' society might want to acknowledge.

What has become a major feature of the latter half of the 1990s is the focusing of attention on those who abuse in a fashion which seems to exemplify the description of a moral panic (Cohen, 1973) and a concomitant role for 'paedophiles' as folk devils (see, for example, media coverage of the cases of Robert Oliver and Sid Cooke, convicted sex offenders who were released in 1998 after serving long prison sentences). Unfortunately such a reaction renders such abusers as less than citizens, without civil liberties, and views them as homogeneously unmotivated to change their attitudes, beliefs and behaviour. This chapter is written in the belief that those who sexually abuse are as varied as any other population with problematic behaviours, and that working with them in order to effect change is a worthwhile activity with the potential to reduce the likelihood of re-offending and, hence, increase the safety of children in society.

Work with the child victims of sexual abuse was being developed, re-searched and written about some considerable time before work with adult sexual abusers emerged as a discrete area of work. As the prevalence of sexual abuse in the United Kingdom became clearer during the 1980s there was a rise in the number of such cases being dealt with by those agencies, social services departments, the NSPCC and health professionals, who have a primary task in child protection. The problem for these agencies rapidly became one of finding a way off the treadmill of dealing with the con-sequences of child sexual abuse without dealing with the immediate cause, those men who had already abused children and who would probably do so again if their offending behaviour was not addressed. For agencies with a focus on the alleged abuser, such as the probation, prison, police and psy-chological services, the problem became the provision of effective interven-tions with singularly persistent and damaging behaviour. Initially drawing on work from North America, and subsequently developing work specifi-cally in the United Kingdom context, professionals have gradually de-veloped the current assessment approaches and treatment interventions which this chapter will overview.

Of particular significance in this arena has been the development of NOTA, the National Organisation for the Treatment of Abusers. This multi-disciplinary professional body developed from the support and training needs of practitioners in this area of work and has played a leading role in the development of services for sexually aggressive behaviour, contributing to policy and practice debates, producing publications and organising train-ing events. Its good practice guidance (NOTA, 1993) states that the aims of the organisation and its members are to: 'protect and benefit the victims of sexual assault by promoting the development of a comprehensive, multi-agency response to those engaging in sexually abusive behaviour'.

It is hoped that by understanding the beliefs, attitudes and behaviour of those who abuse, and by working with them, it is possible to reduce offend-ing and thereby prevent future victimisation. Through work with abusers there has also been an effort by the professional community to hear the voice of children more clearly—to make sense of what children tell us about their experiences of abuse, to help children make sense of what has happened to them and to help them tell their story when they may be struggling to do so or are fearful of the responses of those listening.

UNDERSTANDING ABUSERS: HOW MANY ARE THERE AND WHO ARE THEY?

Current statistics and research literature focus predominantly on child sex-ual abuse perpetrated by adult males, who comprise the vast majority of those reported for sexual offences and this section will focus mainly on such abusers. However, a smaller but still significant proportion of sexual offences are committed by children and young people themselves and by adult females, and so a brief overview will also be provided on these populations with suggestions for further reading.

How many abusers are there? Incidence and prevalence

To know the extent of potential risk to children in the community it is necessary to have information relating to both incidence—the frequency of occurrence of new offences and prevalence—the proportion of the population who have been the victims of offences. Both are notoriously difficult to establish.

In relation to offending, a recent summary from the Home Office (Marshall, 1997) based on conviction rates estimates that 0.7% of men in the general United Kingdom population born between 1953 and 1973 had a conviction for a sexual offence against a child by the age of 40. Given the high attrition rates on convictions for sexual offences this is likely to be a considerable under estimate of the actual incidence of sexual abuse. In a North American study published in 1991, Weinrott and Saylor elicited self-reports from offenders in secure treatment of their offence history. Sixty-seven men with a total of 136 recorded child victims disclosed over 8,000 offences against an actual total of 959 children. In addition, their self-reported offending was against a far wider range of victims (intra-familial and stranger abuse) than had previously been known—a finding replicated by the self-reports of 567 sex offenders elicited by Abel et al. (1987), who also estimated the probability of arrest for a sexual offence involving contact as 3%.

Information regarding victimisation is similarly problematic. Russell (1984) estimated that less than 10% of all sexual assaults are reported to the police and less than 1% resulted in the arrest, conviction and imprisonment of the offender. In 1995 a study commissioned by the NSPCC of 1,032 adults aged 18–45 years found that 16% recalled sexual abuse before the age of 16, 11% of incidents involving physical contact; 58% of the respondents had not told anyone about the incidents at the time (Creighton and Russell, 1995).

We must conclude that we have no reliable way to establish the true extent of sexual risk to children, although it is clear that it is a significant problem. It therefore seems more productive to focus our energies on understanding who sexual abusers are and on the dynamics of sexual offending, both in order to protect children more effectively and to reduce recidivism in identified offenders.

Who abuses?

Given the high profile media coverage of extreme cases of child sexual abuse, it is all too easy to assume that abusers will be easily identifiable, and that their differences from 'ordinary people' will be obvious. However, we must accept the overt normality of most abusers, and indeed evidence of the numerous convictions of high-achieving 'pillars of the community' serves as a salutary reminder that people we may least expect may be sexually abusing children. One lesson is that we must listen carefully to children's concerns and stories and not dismiss them on the basis of our 'certainty' that particular individuals could not possibly be capable of abusing them.

Adult male sexual abusers

Fisher (1994) provides a useful overview of research into adult male sexual abusers. She notes (with reference to Wolf, 1984) that 'it is a general finding of surveys of sex offender populations that variables such as level of intelligence, age, ethnicity, education and psychiatric status do not differ significantly from the rates in the general populations from which the samples are drawn' (p. 7).

Despite similarity with non-offender populations on these basic demographic variables, men who sexually abuse children do evidence other interesting characteristics. In particular, what seem to be significantly different are the high rates of convicted child abusers who have been themselves sexually abused as children as compared with non-offender populations (see, for example, Abel et al., 1987). Rates vary up to 80% depending on the studies cited, although this equally means that at least 20% of convicted abusers have not been so victimised. Studies also indicate that although a small number of abusers are responsible for many offences, the majority have abused relatively small numbers of children. However, contrary to earlier thinking, a key finding from the research by Abel et al. (1987) is that abusers also have the potential for, and some are likely to demonstrate, a variety of deviant behaviours across a range of victims (male and female, pre- and post-pubescent, inside and outside families). Those making assessments of risk, therefore, have to attend to this possibility.

To focus in more detail on the characteristics of men who commit sexual offences against children, what emerges from these studies is a picture of men exhibiting a number of relationship and other problems often originating from childhood. While most of the data are derived from studies of those convicted and in treatment programmes and may therefore suffer from bias, Wolf (1984) based his Multi-Factor Model of Deviant Sexuality on a sizeable sample of some 1,200 offenders. He found that feelings of isolation within the family as a child, described by the offender as a feeling a lack of closeness with parents and siblings, were reported by 47%. Family members questioned about this same quality typically described similar feelings, although at a much higher rate. Also found were histories of violence in the family of origin, both with the offender as victim, 30% of the time, and as witnesses to physical violence, 36% of the time; 27% reported being victims of sexual abuse and 24% were victims of psychological abuse; 17% recalled, as children, witnessing inter-family sexual abuse with some other family member as the victim (Wolf and Conte, 1984). One might suggest that if, as children, they had been listened to and their needs for good enough parenting met, then they might not have developed into adult sex offenders.

In their evaluation of seven treatment programmes for sex offenders, comprising 59 men, Beckett *et al.* (1994, p. 5) report similarly that those in treatment were:

'typically emotionally isolated individuals, lacking in self-confidence, under-assertive, poor at appreciating the perspective of others, and ill-equipped to deal with emotional distress. They characteristically denied or minimised the full extent of their sexual offending and problems. A significant proportion were found to have: little empathy for their victims; strong emotional attachments to children; and a range of distorted attitudes and beliefs, where they portrayed children as able to consent to, and not be harmed by, sexual contact with adults. . . . The men with the most problems in the above areas tended to be the most serious offenders.'

However, other important factors contribute to their offending which we will address under the question of why they do it and allude to when discussing female sexual abusers.

The predominantly white ethnicity of most samples reflects a more widespread problem. The evidence is that black sex offenders against adults are over-represented in the United Kingdom prison population and that this over-representation becomes greater in the longer sentence groups. Cowburn (1996) examines these facts in the context of white constructions of black sexuality, arguing that racist stereotypes about the predatory and dangerous nature of black male sexuality have 'pervaded western clinical, police and judicial responses to sexual crimes for many years' (p. 126). Such racism also results in black sex offenders being less likely to be given the opportunity to attend treatment facilities and their willingness and ability to make use of what are overwhelmingly white-dominated services may anyway be inhibited.

Other studies concentrate on sex offenders with a learning difficulty, Bowden (1994) and McKenzie *et al.* (1997) providing useful introductions to the additional complicating factors of working with such offenders, particularly in a context of societal prejudice towards those with such difficulties and the general lack of attention paid to issues of their sexuality.

Adult female sexual abusers

Adult female sexual abusers account for only a tiny proportion of recorded sexual offences. Criminal Statistics for England and Wales (Home Office, 1997) indicate that between approximately 50 and 100 females were cautioned for sexual offences in each of 1995 and 1996 (as compared with approximately 2,200 men in each year), with similar numbers of women found guilty in Court of a sexual offence as compared with approximately 4,500 men per year.

Finkelhor (1986) has argued that rates for women who sexually abuse children have been underestimated in the past, suggesting that the true figure for women who sexually abuse children is 5% for girl victims and 20% for boy victims. Some writers (see, for example, Lawson, 1993 and Krug, 1989) offer several reasons for possible under-reporting of female sexual offending such as mother–son incest. These include differing societal perceptions of maternal behaviour and presumptions about maternal innate goodness and asexuality as compared with the motivations and sexual interests of fathers; assumptions that boy victims are not really harmed by their abuse and/or may be too shamed to disclose abuse; and overextension of feminist explanations that male dominance, differential socialisation and sexual explanation are the sole causes of child sexual abuse. Other writers, however, have expressed concern that a search for equivalence in male and female offending rates (which has *not* been established) has the negative effect of detracting from the need to acknowledge fundamental issues of male power in society (see, for example, MacLeod and Saraga, 1988 and Forbes, 1992).

Concerning the characteristics of women who sexually abuse children, Freel (1992 pp. 8-9) comments:

> . . . there is general agreement on certain issues—that they are more likely to have been sexually abused as children; that they have had a traumatic childhood; that they are more likely to co-offend with men; (and) that they are likely to use alcohol or drugs . . . There is (also) evidence that female abusers are more likely to be the mothers or close relatives of the victim . . .

However, as Adshead *et al.* (1994) suggest in their article, this is a relatively unresearched area worthy of further study (see also Saradjian, 1996).

Young people who sexually abuse

Estimates of the proportion of child sexual abuse committed by children and young people vary from about one-quarter to one-third of all sexual offences (National Children's Home, 1992). Clearly this means that a sizeable minority of sexual offenders are very young. Statistics are not always clear as to whether such offenders are male or female although, as with adult sexual offenders, research and literature indicate that they are predominantly male. Estimates often do not distinguish between children and adolescents of different ages, most offenders being described in their middle teenage years. In this section we will focus on adolescents who abuse. For information about younger sexually aggressive children the reader is referred to Johnson (1988), Lane with Lobanov-Rostovsky (1997) and Elliott and Butler (1994).

Early thinking, as reported in the National Children's Home report (NCH, 1992) and repeated in the central government guidance *Working Together* (DoH 1991), was that, unlike other juvenile delinquents who typically grow out their offending, young sexual abusers will continuing in their abusive behaviour unless treated, preferably under some kind of legal mandate. More recent findings, largely based on North American studies, suggest, however, that the majority of such adolescents do not progress into being adult abusers (Beckett, 1997, personal communication). In a climate of scarce resources, an imperative must be to try to identify the factors which contribute to long-term sexual offending in order to target those youngsters most at risk of pursuing such a career.

However, based on the studies that have been completed to date, O'Callaghan and Print (1994) offer a useful overview of the current state of knowledge in relation to adolescent male sexual abusers. The victims of such youngsters are usually younger by a number of years; they comprise both male and female children and are usually known to the abuser as a sibling or through a babysitting relationship, although in cases of rape the abusers are less likely to know their victims.

Where attempts have been made to compare young male sexual abusers with the wider delinquent population, studies seem to indicate that there are few differences between adolescent sexual offenders and other young males engaged in criminal behaviour. In common with most young people in trouble, young male sexual abusers seem to have a number of social skills deficits, often being socially isolated, with anger management problems and high levels of social anxiety. They are often doing poorly at school both in terms of behaviour and educational attainment and, like adult male sexual offenders, relatively high proportions of them (between 25 and 60%, depending on the study) report having been victims of sexual abuse themselves. A number of studies not surprisingly, therefore, also suggest that the families of such youngsters may have a number of difficulties in terms of their stability and intra-familial dynamics (Ryan and Lane, 1997). Most young adolescent male sexual abusers in treatment are white, but this finding may well, as with black adult sex offenders (Cowburn, 1996), reflect the racism inherent in criminal justice and other systems which result in young black offenders being dealt with more punitively and having less access to treatment facilities.

In one of the few studies of young female abusers (Johnson, 1989) it was found that all of the sample of the 13 girl abusers had been subjected to prior sexual victimisation of a serious nature, often with close relatives, and had usually received little support and validation from other family members when they had disclosed their abuse. In their overview of female youth who sexually abuse, Lane and Lobanov-Rostovsky (Ryan and Lane, 1997) also comment on the very disturbed backgrounds of the young female abusers with whom they have worked, noting victimisation issues, problematic parental relationships, family separation, problems at school and with peers in particular. However, they also comment:

'Many of the developmental experiences are similar to those identified in the history of male youth, although they may be experienced differently by female youth based on gender, socialisation and role expectations' (p. 348).

They suggest that young female sexual abusers may well benefit from the same kinds of treatment approaches as young male sexual abusers, although they comment that issues of autonomy and the consequences of female socialisation experiences may well be useful additional foci.

In relation to all the groups discussed above it is clear that treatment may at some point have to attend to the abuser's own experiences of having been abused and victimised, particularly in the case of young abusers. However, as already stated, the paramount concern in the treatment and management of (adult) offenders is community safety and the need to protect potential victims, rather than simply the benefit of the offender (Prison Reform Trust, 1992; HMIP, 1998).

UNDERSTANDING ABUSERS: WHY DO THEY DO IT?

Feminist perspectives on sexual aggression

As will have become apparent, sexual offending is largely perpetrated by males and any explanation of such offending has to be considered within a context of much larger, unreported rates of 'normal' male sexual aggression against females. Kelly et al. (Prison Reform Trust, 1992) argue that research on convicted offenders and theories of behaviour emerging from a clinical focus have tended to maintain the dominance of the medical/ pathology perspective in relation to particular individuals rather than (also) addressing social constructions of masculinity and prevalent societal attitudes and beliefs which condone or justify sexual violence against female adults and children. While acknowledging the importance of acting on this much broader perspective, our analysis will focus on the most promising, existing theories and models of treatment for addressing sexually abusive behaviour.

Understanding sexually abusive behaviour

During the early 1980s models were developed in North America which have remained extremely influential in the United Kingdom in understanding sexually abusive behaviour. They can only be explored here briefly and the interested reader is recommended to review the original texts to gain fuller benefit from them.

Four preconditions model

In the introduction to his model, David Finkelhor (1984) indicates that there was a need for a comprehensive theory which addressed the range of knowledge about sexual abusers without being specific to a particular school of thought. He proposes a model which . . . brings together knowledge about offenders, victims and families . . . is at a level of generality capable of accommodating many different types of sexual abuse from father–daughter incest to compulsive and fixated molesting . . . (and which) incorporates explanations at both the psychological and sociological level. This model he called the *Four Preconditions of Sexual Abuse*, which is expressed diagrammatically in Figure 12.1.

In summary, the model suggests four preconditions which must be met before sexual abuse can occur.

1. The potential offender needs to have some *motivation* to abuse a child sexually. This may be because the child meets some important emotional need and/or sexual contact with the child is sexually gratifying and/or other sources of sexual gratification are not available or are less satisfying.
2. The potential offender needs to overcome any *internal inhibitions* against acting on that motivation. This, commonly, is by way of 'cognitive distortions', self-serving distortions of attitude and belief, whereby children become seen as in some way consenting to or responsible for their own abuse. This is best illustrated by way of a list compiled by Abel *et al.* (1984) of the seven most commonly held distortions:

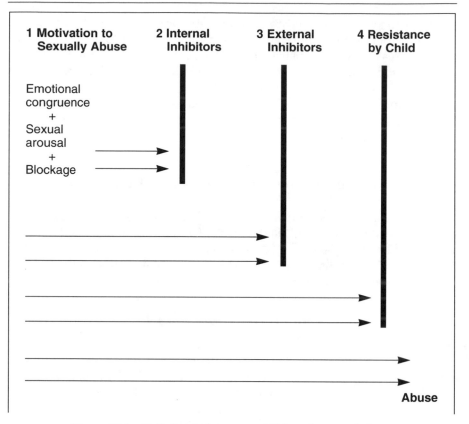

Figure 12.1 Finkelhor's four preconditions for sexual abuse

- A child who does not physically resist really wants sex.
- Having sex with a child is a good way to teach a child about sex.
- Children don't tell about sex with an adult because they really enjoy it.
- Some time in the future our society will realise that sex with children is really all right.
- An adult who feels a child's genitals is not really being sexual with the child so no harm is really being done.
- When a child asks about sex it means that the child wants to see the adult's sex organs or have sex with the adult.
- A relationship with a child is enhanced by having sex with him or her.

3. The potential offender needs to overcome *external impediments* to committing sexual abuse—most importantly the supervision the child receives from others. Those interested in pursuing further the issue of non-abusing carers and their significance as deterrents to abuse are commended to (a) Gerrilyn Smith's 'Parent, partner, protector' chapter

(Smith, 1994), which includes an adaptation of the Four Preconditions Model and (b) the authors' own description of running groupwork programmes for mothers of sexually abused children (Masson and Erooga, 1990);
4. The potential offender needs to overcome or undermine a *child's possible resistance* to the abuse. Finkelhor emphasises that this is not an issue to be regarded simplistically but may relate to a complex set of factors involving personality traits which inhibit the abuser targeting a particular child as well as more straightforward resistance to the abuse itself— resistance which may be highly ingenious, determined and fierce (Kitzinger, 1997).

What can be seen, therefore, is that there are a number of potential barriers to abuse, the first two relating to the offender and the third and fourth relating to factors external to the offender. The model offers a way of beginning to understand something of the dynamics of the abuser as well as the abuse, and will be reconsidered below in conjunction with one of the other influential models, Steven Wolf's 'Cycle of Abuse' (Figure 12.2).

Compulsive Behaviour Cycles of Sexual Abuse

Prior to the development of models of compulsive sexual offending in the early 1980s a common view of such behaviour, among others, was of inexplicable uncontrolled urges. Practice experience with adults and with adolescents, however, has led to the development of the concept of sexual abuse cycles involving dysfunctional responses to problematic situations or interactions. In these models responses are based on distorted perceptions relating to power and control which then become sexualised. Such models are now regarded as generally applicable irrespective of age or intellectual or developmental functioning.

The sexual abuse cycle for adults (see Figure 12.2) itself part of a more extensive model to explain the development and maintenance of sexually deviant orientations (Wolf, 1984), represents cognitive and behavioural progressions prior to, during and after an abusive incident. It is represented cyclically because of the repetitive compulsive nature of the behaviour sequence and indicates that previous offence incidents often parallel and reinforce the subsequent offence pattern.

In this model the abuser has past experiences and personality characteristics which lead to an emotional predisposition to resorting to sexual fantasy about sexual contact with children as a dysfunctional coping mechanism. Fantasy is then reinforced across time by masturbation, which in turn has a disinhibiting effect on the potential abuser. 'Grooming' the environment and the child refers to a similar process to that outlined by Finkelhor, that of

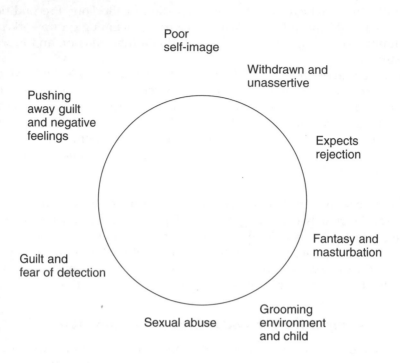

Figure 12.2   Steven Wolf's 'Cycle of Abuse'

enabling opportunities to abuse to arise and gaining sufficient emotional control or physical access to the child both to enable the abuse and minimise the chances of subsequent disclosure. In some cases this may not be a consciously thought out strategy so much as a series of decisions or actions which lead to a situation where an abuser can act 'impulsively', thereby reassuring himself that he does not have a problem, but is merely acting 'uncharacteristically' on impulse. Following the abuse itself there may be a period of remorse, guilt or fear as the abuser reflects on the implications of what he has done, but across time is likely to overcome or reframe his fear or guilt by further use of distorted thinking, and so the cycle can continue.

At the point of reframing or overcoming his fear or guilt, the offender is quite likely to believe that he can control any future impulse, thereby minimising the seriousness of his problem. There is thus a cumulative, corrosive effect on feelings of self-efficacy when he does re-offend, with a consequent effect on self-esteem.

An important issue at the point of intervention is that the exposure of the behaviour, which is likely to precede professional involvement, will possibly increase any sense of guilt or remorse. The therapist may therefore encounter a highly sincere level of remorse and certainty that further offending is not going to happen, which is unlikely to be matched in reality by the individual's ability to maintain consistent control of his behaviour.

The adult offender's cycle is strikingly similar to that developed independently in relation to work with adolescents by Lane and Zamora (1982, 1984) and subsequently evolved further by Lane (1997). The main difference between the adult and adolescent cycles appears to be that the adult may have greater internal inhibitions to offending and may therefore experience greater amounts of guilt or remorse about the offending than adolescents.

When considering models with which to understand abusive behaviour it may be helpful to consider the Wolf's cycle and Finkelhor's preconditions models as complementary, offering different perspectives with which to understand similar phenomena. Thus, if the first precondition, *motivation to abuse a child sexually*, is viewed in conjunction with the first section of the cycle, a broader perspective on possible motivations is offered. Similarly overcoming any *internal inhibitions* can be viewed in conjunction with Wolf's notion of the function and effect of fantasy and masturbation, overcoming *external impediments as related to grooming the environment* and overcoming or undermining a *child's possible resistance* to the abuse as similar to the notion of 'grooming' the child. Of course Finkelhor focuses on antecedents to abuse while Wolf helpfully goes on to indicate the cyclical nature of the behaviour, but by considering both in conjunction (see Figure 12.3) it is possible to derive the broadest understanding of the individual offender's functioning. As with any model, however, it is important to maintain awareness that they are tools to begin to understand patterns of behaviour and should not be applied mechanistically to individuals.

FRAMEWORKS FOR INTERVENTION: BEFORE TREATING ABUSERS

Although space precludes a detailed discussion, it must be emphasised that interventions with people who have sexually abused children should be addressed within a total package of management, care and control (HMIP, 1998). As the Report of the National Commission of Inquiry into the Prevention of Child Abuse (1996) advocates, one aspect of preventing child abuse is the regulation, treatment and follow-up of offenders. The Commission and others (see, for example, Kelly *et al.* in Prison Reform Trust, 1992), in seeking the views of child and adult survivors on policies in relation to sex offenders have received clear messages that they want perpetrators of such abuse to be

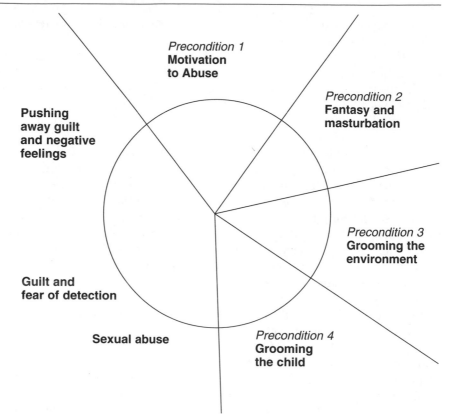

Figure 12.3   Finkelhor model and modified Wolf cycle combined

monitored, rehabilitated *and* punished (as a fundamental part of the process of obtaining justice to redress the pain and anguish they have suffered). Thus, in relation to sex offenders a full investigation of the alleged abuse has to be undertaken with a paramount concern for children's safety and best interests as an overarching guide. Decisions about possible criminal proceedings against the alleged offender have to be considered and made in the context of victims' wishes as well as other considerations such as the likelihood of a successful prosecution. Assessment of an abuser's attitudes and behaviour and the risk he presents are all part of this process and will help to inform any treatment and follow-up plan that is then developed. Such plans have now also to attend to the requirements for registration and follow up under the Sex Offenders Act 1997.

Developing comprehensive packages of policy, procedures and treatment facilities involve co-operation and partnership between the various professionals and agencies involved, from Area Child Protection Committee level down. Morrison (1994a) argues for a framework of collaboration which includes:

- recognition of the need to collaborate;
- a mandate for collaboration;
- collaborative structures and leadership;
- a shared philosophy of intervention;
- agreed policies and procedures;
- training for staff;
- provision for victims, non-abusing carers and abusers;
- supervision for staff and staff care.

Establishing such an infrastructure would create arrangements for working together which are stronger than the feelings aroused by the sexual abuse of children and would combat mirroring processes and processes of identification with the immediate client (Reder *et al.*, 1993) which can impede multidisciplinary working. Ironically, evidence seems to suggest that many paedophile networks typically work more effectively than professional networks which surely should be an incentive to more focused and successful collaboration?

PRINCIPLES AND METHODS OF TREATMENT

As Morrison outlines (1994b), practice cannot be value-free in this field; rather, an explicit value base is needed and he suggests the following, based on work by American psychologist Anna Salter (1988):

1. Sexual assault is always unacceptable and should be investigated as a crime.
2. Sexual assault is damaging to the victim.
3. Sexual assault results from an intention on the part of the offender to seek both sexual and emotional gratification from the victim.
4. Sexual assault represents an abuse of power.
5. The overarching aim of intervention is to protect victims and potential victims.
6. Intervention must be based on the offender taking full responsibility for the feelings, thoughts and behaviour that support his offending. Male sexual arousal is controllable.
7. Where it is in the victim's interests, sex offenders should be prosecuted.
8. The goal of intervention is to ensure that sex offenders can control their behaviour so that they do not re-offend or sexually abuse others.
9. The management of offenders requires a co-ordinated response involving criminal justice and child protection agencies.

10. In the longer term the prevention of sexual offences needs to address the gender role expectations of males in our society.

Intervention components with sex offenders

Most intervention approaches used by British treatment providers are cognitive-behavioural in approach (Barker and Morgan, 1993; Procter and Flaxington, 1995) and for detailed descriptions of United Kingdom cognitive-behavioural approaches to assessment, individual and group treatment the reader is referred to *Sexual Offending Against Children: Assessment and Treatment of Male Offenders* (Morrison *et al.*, 1994). The discussion which follows relates primarily to adult males and readers interested in interventions with female offenders or young people are referred to Saradjian (1996) and Erooga and Masson (1999) respectively.

The Thematic Inspection of Probation Service work with Sex Offenders (HMIP, 1998) suggests that treatment should apply *'What Works'* principles to work with sex offenders (see, for example, McGuire, 1995). Thus treatment should be concentrated on those individuals at highest risk of re-offending; be targeted at the features of the offender directly related to their offending; be matched to the learning styles of the client, which, for most, will comprise participatory and non-didactic methods; be community based where appropriate; draw on cognitive-behavioural principles and resources, including an emphasis on relapse prevention and must feature programme integrity – monitoring and evaluating the match between objectives, methods of delivery (including resources and staff training) and outcomes.

There are common components of an intervention plan in individual and group settings, a brief outline of which may provide some flavour of the activities involved. Often at an early stage there will be a focus on the *Sexual Assault Cycle,* including the abuser's own pattern of sexual arousal. Changing patterns of sexual arousal may require specific behavioural interventions as part of a wider focused treatment programme (Maletzky and McGovern, 1990; Erooga, 1993). Work on the cycle is designed to enable the abuser to gain an understanding of his individual pattern of abuse—for example, identifying what he was doing, thinking and feeling at each stage of his cycle, identifying attitudinal and situational triggers to his cycle, and subsequently beginning to identify strategies to deal with triggers and disrupt the cycle. A key component will be developing an understanding and awareness of *Cognitive Distortions.* This will entail coming to understand the concept of 'distorted thinking', what purpose that thinking is serving by beginning to identify examples of current distortions. Subsequently, restructuring of distortions will be possible by appropriate challenge and use of learning from other sections of the programme.

Victim Awareness is intended to develop an awareness of why children cannot give true consent, children's likely experience of abuse, and understanding its damaging effects on victims. This serves both to increase any internal inhibitors and to reduce cognitive distortions. In order to achieve victim awareness it may be necessary to work on enhancing the abuser's awareness of his own feelings and emotional functioning, as such self-awareness is a key tool for victim empathy. The importance of this sequence is highlighted in the STEP Report (Beckett *et al.*, 1994).

Finally, though possibly not in terms of the order of interventions, is the process of developing *Relapse Prevention* plans with identified triggers, danger situations and strategies to avoid risk situations, lapses into risk behaviour or relapse into re-offending.

A key aspect of work with offenders is its potential for use in work with child victims. If multidisciplinary structures are in place to avoid workers mirroring the potential conflict of interest between offenders and their victims, then the adults' work can be used constructively in a number of ways. At its simplest this may involve dialogue between those working with abusers and those working with their victims to inform the work with child victims in order to relieve them of worries and concerns and to validate their experiences. With motivated offenders in treatment it may be possible to use carefully controlled offender–victim communications, commonly by letter, to re-emphasise the victims' non-responsibility for their abuse and address any particular issues that may be of particular concern or significance (Bera *et al.*, 1990).

Groupwork versus individual work

While groupwork can be seen to have many positive functions in work with sexual offenders (Clark and Erooga, 1994), with men who were themselves abused as children it is often necessary to work on their victimisation issues separately from any group experience. Adult perpetrators who were sexually victimised as children have often minimised, reinterpreted and suppressed those experiences in the process of becoming abusers. These experiences need to be addressed without, however, detracting from the focus on their more recent abusive behaviour, the priority being to reduce the likelihood of re-offending.

EVALUATION AND RECIDIVISM

Having reviewed a range of issues relating to work with those who sexually abuse, the question remains: Does it serve any useful purpose? While recidivism is a poor indicator of effectiveness it does give some indication of effect. The most current United Kingdom measure of treatment effectiveness is the Sex Offender Treatment Evaluation Project (STEP), a three-part initiative initiated by the Home Office in the early 1990s to consider what is effective in community-based treatment for adult male sex offenders in the United Kingdom.

Phase One was a review of research into programme efficacy in Europe and North America and a 1991 survey of work undertaken by the 55 Probation Services in England and Wales. The review found that cognitive-behavioural approaches were considered most effective, enabled offenders to change their attitudes to victims and offending and provided sufficient behavioural controls to avoid further offending (Barker and Morgan, 1993). *Phase Two* was undertaken during 1992/93 to provide empirically-based research into the efficacy of a sample of treatment programmes (Beckett *et al.*, 1994). *Phase Three* is a consideration of conviction rates at two, five and ten years after completion of treatment, with the two-year follow-up published in 1997 (Hedder and Sugg, 1997). While acknowledging the limitations of reconvictions as an indicator of offending and the likelihood that five years is a more satisfactory minimum follow-up period, it found that 8% (11 of 133 offenders) who had been included in community programmes had been reconvicted for any offence. Six of the 11 were for a further sexual offence while five were for non-sexual and non-violent offences. All but one of the sexual reconvictions were for a similar or less serious offence, and all of those reconvicted had at least one previous conviction. By comparison, 191 sex offenders placed on probation in 1990 had reconviction rates nearly twice (9%) the rate of the treated sample.

Because of the difference in re-offending rates the study goes on to consider the correlation between reconviction and attitudinal change before and after treatment. None of the 24 offenders considered in *Phase Two* to have responded well to treatment were reconvicted, including nine who were assessed as highly deviant before treatment. They conclude that '. . . for a two-year period at least, changes in (assessed) deviancy do have some correspondence with changes in offending behaviour'. An optimistic beginning.

A further tangible benefit to children of work with offenders has been the information provided about child protection strategies. Both in literature (Conte and Wolf, 1989) and in practice the knowledge gained from theorising about the motivations and patterns of behaviours of offenders has informed thinking about how best to protect children and communities.

Finally, and possibly most tragically, it is by hearing from offenders themselves about what they are capable of that we have come to believe more fully the nature and extent of the sexual abuse of children. Victims have been attempting to disclose their abuse for many years; it is relatively recently that the adult community has been able to hear them. Studies of incidence as cited above have also helped to increase our thresholds to believe those disclosures.

CONCLUSION

At the close of the millennium we seemed to have achieved something of a dichotomy. On the one hand, treatment approaches have moved from simple confrontation to an understanding of the dynamics of motivation which have enabled treatment efficacy to be continually improving. On the other hand, public demonisation of 'paedophiles' is such that innocent men, mistaken for sex offenders, have been attacked on the streets. While this vilification may meet a range of societal needs it does nothing to prevent children being abused.

Children's interests may be better served if society can develop sufficient maturity to recognise the sexual abuse of children for the problem it actually is, not the one we fear it to be. If we can recognise that it is not sex offenders *per se* but their behaviour which is the problem, then we may continue the move forward. As Anna Salter expresses it, the task for workers is to 'extend respect to people as human beings, to empathise with their pain and to believe in their capacity to do better, while not colluding with their sexual abuse an inch' (Salter, 1988).

Workers at least need societal recognition that their activities are worthwhile. More fundamental, however, is the need to develop a 'primary prevention' approach (Ryan, 1997) of altering our attitudes to male socialisation and responding to inappropriate behaviour in boys, sexual, physical and emotional, so that others are not regarded as objects for their gratification. If these can begin to be achieved, then children's voices will finally begin to be heard.

REFERENCES

Abel, G., Becker, J. and Cunningham-Rathner, J. (1984) Complications, consent and cognitions in sex between children and adults. *International Journal of Law and Psychiatry*, 7: 89–103.

Abel, G., Becker, J., Cunningham-Rathner, J. and Rouleau, J. (1987) Self reported sex crimes of 561 non-incarcerated paraphiliacs *Journal of Interpersonal Violence*, 2(6): 3–25.

Adshead, G., Howett, M. and Mason, F. (1994) Women who sexually abuse children: The undiscovered country. *The Journal of Sexual Aggression*, 1(1): 45–56.

Barker, M. and Morgan, R. (1993) Sex Offenders: *A Framework for the Evaluation of Community Based Treatment*. London, Home Office.

Beckett, R., Beech, A., Fisher, D. and Fordham, A.S. (1994) *Community-Based Treatment for Sex Offenders: An Evaluation of Seven Treatment Programmes*. London, Home Office Publications Unit.

Bera, W., Hindman, J., Hutchens, L., McGuire, D. and Yokley, J. (1990) *The Use of Victim Offender Communication in the Treatment of Sexual Abuse: Three Intervention Models.* Vermont, Safer Society Press.

Bowden, K. (1994) No control of penis or brain? Key questions in the assessment of sex offenders with a learning difficulty. *The Journal of Sexual Aggression*, 1(1): 57–63.

Clark, P. and Erooga, M. (1994) Groupwork with men who sexually abuse children, in Morrison, T., Erooga, M. and Beckett, R. (eds) *Sexual Offending Against Children: Assessment and Treatment of Male Abusers.* London, Routledge.

Cohen, S. (1973) *Folk Devils and Moral Panics: The Creation of Mods and Rockers* London, Paladin.

Conte, J. and Wolf, S. (1989) What can sex offenders tell us about protecting children? *Child Abuse and Neglect*, 13(2): 293–301.

Cowburn, M. (1996) The black male sex offender in prison: images and issues. *The Journal of Sexual Aggression*, 2(2): 122–142.

Creighton, S. and Russell, N. (1995) *Voices from Childhood: A Survey of Childhood Experiences and Attitudes to Child Rearing among Adults in the United Kingdom.* London, NSPCC.

DoH (1991) *Working Together Under the Children Act 1989. A Guide to Arrangements for Interagency Co-operation for the Protection of Children from Abuse.* London, HMSO.

Elliott, C. and Butler, L. (1994) The stop and think group: changing sexually aggressive behaviour in young children. *The Journal of Sexual Aggression*, 1(1): 15–28.

Erooga, M. (1993) Observations of behavioural treatment of sexual offenders in the USA. *NotaNews*, 6: 28–35.

Erooga, M. and Masson, H. (1999) *Children and Young People who Sexually Abuse Others: Challenges and Responses.* London, Routledge.

Finkelhor, D. (1984) *Child Sexual Abuse: New Theory and Research.* New York, Free Press.

Finkelhor, D. (1986) A Sourcebook on Child Sexual Abuse. Beverly Hills, Sage.

Fisher, D. (1994) Adult sex offenders: Who are they? Why and how do they do it?, in Morrison, T., Erooga, M. and Beckett, R. (eds) *Sexual Offending Against Children: Assessment and Treatment of Male Abusers.* London, Routledge.

Forbes, J. (1992) Female sexual abusers: the contemporary search for equivalence *Practice*, 6: 102–111.

Freel, M. (1992) *Women who Sexually Abuse Children.* Social Work Monograph, University of East Anglia, Norwich.

Hedder, C. and Sugg, D. (1997) Does treating sex offenders reduce reoffending? *Home Office Research and Statistics Directorate Research Findings, No. 45* London, Home Office.

HMIP (1998) *Exercising constant vigilance: The Role of the Probation Service in Protecting the Public from Sex Offenders.* London, Home Office, HM Inspectorate of Probation.

Home Office (1997) *Criminal Statistics England and Wales 1996.* London, Government Statistical Service.

Johnson, T.C. (1988) Child perpetrators—children who molest other children: preliminary findings. *Child Abuse and Neglect*, 12: 219-229.

Johnson, T.C. (1989) Female child perpetrators: children who molest other children. *Child Abuse and Neglect*, 13: 571–585.

Kilpatrick, A. (1992) *Long Range Effects of Child and Adolescent Sexual Experiences. Myths, Mores and Menaces.* Lawrence Erlbaum Associates.

Kitzinger, J. (1997) Who are you kidding? Children, power and the struggle against sexual abuse, in James, J. and Prout, A. (eds) *Constructing and Reconstructing Childhood*, 2nd edition. London, Falmer Press.

Krug, R.S. (1989) Adult male report of childhood sexual abuse by mother: case descriptions, motivations and long-term consequences. *Child Abuse and Neglect*, **13**: 111–119.

Lane, S. (1997) The sexual abuse cycle, in Ryan, G. and Lane, S. (eds) *Juvenile Sexual Offending. Causes, Consequences and Corrections*, 2nd edition. Lexington, Lexington Books.

Lane, S. with Lobanov-Rostovsky, C. (1997) Special populations: children, females, the developmentally disabled, and violent youth, in Ryan, G. and Lane, S. (eds) *Juvenile Sexual Offending. Causes, Consequences and Corrections*, 2nd edition. Lexington, Lexington Books.

Lane, S. and Zamora, P. (1982 and 1984) cited in Lane, S. The sexual abuse cycle, in Ryan, G.and Lane, S. (eds) *Juvenile Sexual Offending. Causes, Consequences and Corrections*, 2nd edition. Lexington, Lexington Books.

Lawson, C. (1993) Mother–son sexual abuse: rare or underreported? A critique of research. *Child Abuse and Neglect*, **17**: 261–269.

Maletzky, R. and McGovern, K. (1990) *Treating the Sexual Offender* Beverly Hills, Sage.

Marshall, P. (1997) The prevalence of convictions for sexual offending. *Research Findings, No. 55*. London, Home Office.

Masson, H. and Erooga, M. (1990) The forgotten parent: groupwork with mothers of sexually abused children. *Groupwork*, 3(2): 144–156.

McGuire, J. (ed.) (1995) *What Works Reducing Offending?* Chichester, Wiley.

McKenzie, K., Chisolm, D. and Miller, L. (1997) Up the slippery slope: groupwork with sex offenders with a learning disability. *The Journal of Sexual Aggression*, 3(1): 35–52.

MacLeod, M. and Saraga, E. (1988) Challenging the orthodoxy: towards a feminist theory and practice, in *Feminist Review*, **28**: 16–55.

Morrison, T. (1994a) Learning together to manage sexual abuse: rhetoric or reality? *The Journal of Sexual Aggression*, 1(1): 29-44.

Morrison, T. (1994b) Context, constraints and considerations for practice, in Morrison, T., Erooga, M. and Beckett, R. (eds) *Sexual Offending Against Children: Assessment and Treatment of Male Abusers*. London, Routledge.

Morrison, T., Erooga, M. and Beckett, R. (eds) (1994) *Sexual Offending Against Children: Assessment and Treatment of Male Abusers*. London, Routledge.

NCH (1992) *The Report of the Committee of Inquiry into Children and Young People who Sexually Abuse other Children*. London, National Children's Home.

NOTA (1993) *Good Practice in the Multi-agency Management of Sex Offenders who assault Children. NOTA Briefing Paper*. Sponsored by the NSPCC, London.

O'Callaghan, D. and Print, B. (1994) Adolescent sexual abusers; research, assessment and treatment, in Morrison, T., Erooga, M. and Beckett, R. (eds) *Sexual Offending Against Children: Assessment and Treatment of Male Abusers*. London, Routledge.

Prison Reform Trust (1992) *Beyond Containment: The Penal Response to Sex Offending*. London, Prison Reform Trust.

Procter, E. and Flaxington, F. (1995) *Community-Based Interventions with Sex Offenders Organised by the Probation Service: A Survey of Current Practice*. Association of Chief Officers of Probation.

Report of the National Commission of Inquiry into the Prevention of Child Abuse (1996) *Childhood Matters*, Vol. 1 and 2. London, The Stationery Office.

Reder, P., Duncan, S. and Gray, M. (1993) *Beyond Blame. Child Abuse Tragedies Revisited*. London, Routledge.

Russell, D. (1984) The prevalence and seriousness of incestuous abuse: stepfathers vs. biological fathers. *Child Abuse and Neglect*, **8**: 15–22.

Ryan, G. (1997) Perpetration prevention: primary and secondary, in Ryan, G. and Lane, S. (eds) *Juvenile Sexual Offending. Causes, Consequences and Corrections*, 2nd edition. San Francisco, Jossey-Bass.

Ryan, G. and Lane, S. (1997) *Juvenile Sexual Offending. Causes, Consequences and Corrections*, 2nd edition. San Francisco, Jossey-Bass.

Salter, A.C. (1988) *Treating Child Sex Offenders and Victims*. Newbury Park, Sage.

Saradjian, J. (1996) *Women Who Sexually Abuse Children*. Chichester, Wiley.

Smith, G. (1994) Parent, partner, protector: conflicting role demands for mothers of sexually abused children, in Morrison, T., Erooga, M. and Beckett, R. (eds) *Sexual Offending Against Children: Assessment and Treatment of Male Abusers*. London, Routledge.

Weinrott, M.R. and Saylor, M. (1991) Self-report of crimes committed by sex offenders, in *Journal of Interpersonal Violence*, 6(3): 286–300.

Wolf, S. (1984) *A Multifactor Model of Deviant Sexuality*. Paper presented at Third International Conference on Victimology, Lisbon.

Wolf, S. and Conte, J. (1984) *Characteristics of Sexual Offenders in a Community Treatment Programme*. Unpublished, cited in Wolf (1984).

INDEX

Index compiled by Sylvia Potter

Related titles of interest..

Children, Child Abuse and Child Protection
VIOLENCE AGAINST CHILDREN STUDY GROUP
0471 986410   200pp   June 1999   Paperback

Joining New Families
A Study of Adoption and Fostering in Middle Childhood
DAVID QUINTON, ALAN RUSHTON, CHERILYN DANCE and
DEBORAH MAYES
Wiley Series in Child Care & Protection
0471 97837X   282pp   November 1998   Paperback

Interviewing Children
A Guide for Child Care and Forensic Practitioners
MICHELLE ALDRIDGE and JOANNE WOOD
Wiley Series in Child Care & Protection
0471 970522   248pp   October 1998   Hardback
0471 982075   248pp   October 1998   Paperback

Making Research Work
Research Policy and Practice in Child Care
DOROTA INWANIEC and JOHN PINKERTON
0471 97952X   302pp   September 1998   Paperback

Making Sense of the Children Act
3rd Edition
NICHOLAS ALLEN
0471 978310   298pp   April 1998   Paperback

Preventing Family Violence
KEVIN BROWNE and MARTIN HERBERT
0471 927716   402pp   1997   Hardback
0471 941409   402pp   1997   Paperback

WILEY